*Reconceptualizing
the Peasantry*

CRITICAL ESSAYS IN ANTHROPOLOGY

Series Editors **John Comaroff,** *University of Chicago*
                    Pierre Bourdieu, *Collège de France*
                    Maurice Bloch, *London School of Economics*

Reconceptualizing the Peasantry: Anthropology in Global Perspective,
Michael Kearney

Language and Communicative Practices, William F. Hanks

FORTHCOMING

Discourse, Knowledge, and Culture, John D. Kelly

Imaginary Subjects, Illusory Sovereignties: States, Nations, Cultures, Derek Sayer

Mind in Society, Society in Mind: A Critical Anthropology of Cognition,
Dorothy C. Holland and Claudia Strauss

La Ponkalavera Güera © 1984 by Juana Alicia

Reconceptualizing the Peasantry

Anthropology in Global Perspective

Michael Kearney
University of California–Riverside

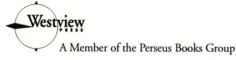
A Member of the Perseus Books Group

For my mother,
Ellen Kearney

Critical Essays in Anthropology

Copyright © 1996 by Westview Press, A Member of the Perseus Books Group

Published in 1996 in the United States of America by Westview Press, 5500 Central Avenue, Boulder, Colorado 80301-2877, and in the United Kingdom by Westview Press, 12 Hid's Copse Road, Cumnor Hill, Oxford OX2 9JJ

Library of Congress Cataloging-in-Publication Data
Kearney, Michael.
  Reconceptualizing the peasantry : anthropology in global
perspective / Michael Kearney.
      p. cm. — (Critical essays in anthropology)
  Includes bibliographical references and index.
  ISBN 0-8133-0987-5 (cloth). — ISBN 0-8133-0988-3 (pbk.)
    1. Ethnology—Philosophy.   2. Ethnology—History.   3. Peasantry.
I. Title.   II. Series.
GN345.K43   1996
305.8'001—dc20   96-12426
                                                                          CIP

The paper used in this publication meets the requirements of the American National Standard for Permanence of Paper for Printed Library Materials Z39.48-1984.

PERSEUS
POD
ON DEMAND   10   9   8

Contents

Figures

Preface

When I was invited by the editors of the series Critical Essays in Anthropology to undertake this project, I initially thought that it would entail little more than a summation of the state of peasant studies in anthropology that would serve as a platform from which to nudge the concept out of the discipline and into history. I saw 'the peasant' as a concept whose time had come and gone. But then a greater challenge presented itself: If the peasant concept indeed no longer accords with contemporary identities and ethnography, then what replaces it?

In presenting an answer to that question I have benefited from the assistance, inspiration, and listening of many colleagues and friends. For close and critical readings and discussions of a recent version of the manuscript I am grateful to John Comaroff, George Marcus, Bill Mitchell, Jay O'Brien, Bill Roseberry, Jonathan Turner, Angus Wright, and Carole Nagengast. In addition to providing fundamental intellectual support, Carole Nagengast moved this project to closure by her frequent encouragements to "just get it done."

And thanks also, for reading and discussing parts of or entire copies of earlier versions, to Gene Anderson, Federico Besserer, Howard Campbell, Ron Chilcote, Matt Gutmann, Dottie Holland, Jean Lave, Michael Peter Smith, and Gayatri Spivak. And thanks also to Paul Willis for convincing me that *polybian* is not a horrendous neologism.

In writing this book I also benefited from being able to talk out my ideas with Bonnie Bade, Les Field, Paul Gelles, Josef Lapid, Daniel Mato, Juan Vicente Palerm, Dave Runsten, Nina Glick Schiller, Rob Smith, Rodolfo Stavenhagen, Connie Sutton, Stefano Varese, Carlos Vélez Ibáñez, and Carole Zabin. And among students who have contributed to various stages of this project are Diana Carr, Michael Hogan, Andrew Mouat, and Ramona Pérez.

This book is also very much the result of almost daily contact with members and leaders of the Frente Indígena Oaxaqueña Binacional and the Organización Regional Oaxaqueña, with whom I have the privilege of working in numerous contexts in Mexico and in the Californias, and most especially with Arturo Pimentel and with Gaspar Rivera who in typically post-peasant fashion confounds identities such as informant-collaborator and student-teacher.

I am also indebted to innumerable other Mixtec and Zapotec friends who have given me the opportunity to discover and explore some of the ideas that are presented in this book. Also, this book would be less than it is were it not for the stimulation and knowledge that I constantly receive from my comrades in the *Latin American Perspectives* collective.

The staff at Westview Press has been a joy to work with. Dean Birkenkamp and Kellie Masterson, who were nominally my editors, are indeed valuable colleagues. Cheryl Carnahan's copyediting of the final version was superb, and I am indebted to Scott Horst for keeping production on the fast track.

Much of the research and preparation has been supported by the U.C.-Riverside Academic Senate Research Committee and UC MEXUS. I have also benefited from opportunities to present parts of this project in fora supported by the Wenner-Gren Foundation, the School for American Research, The New York Academy of Science, the Mexican National Council for Culture and the Arts, the University of Zurich, and the Center for Ideas and Society at U.C.-Riverside.

Finally I am grateful to Juana Alicia for permission to reprint her *La Ponkalavera Güera* on the cover. I first saw La Ponkalavera when this book was taking shape, and I was struck with how she represents its basic themes. First of all the image has a direct connection with Mexico and California. La Ponklavera is a Mexican *calavera* from San Francisco. Calaveras are the dead who rise up from their graves once a year on the Day of the Dead to come back and visit their relatives and friends. The peasant concept is rather like a calavera—dead, but not buried, and living on in skeletal form. Calaveras are typically depicted as *campesinos*, as peasants. La Ponkalavera has traces of a peasant background, but just as she is no ordinary punk, she is also not much of a peasant. Her skateboard is a cosmopolitan artifact, hardly appropriate for the unpaved streets and trails of a peasant community. And unlike most dead peasants, she is a transnational skateboarder who has come back to life to cross boundaries and blur categories and identities into more complex forms.

Michael Kearney

Introduction

This book is based on the proposition that the category *peasant,* whatever validity it may once have had, has been outdistanced by contemporary history. Within anthropology and within peasant studies generally, '*the* peasant' was constructed from residual images of preindustrial European and colonial rural society. Informed by romantic sensibilities and modern nationalist imaginations, these images are anachronisms, but nevertheless they remain robust anachronisms even at the end of the twentieth century. As such, they are appropriate targets for a house-cleaning that clears space for alternative theoretical views.

What are these postpeasant perspectives? In the most general sense they move from a narrow circumscription of what are held to be peasants per se to, first, a re-examination of rural society in general and then to a consideration of the problematic distinction between rural and urban.

Evaluation of the peasant concept in anthropology—its inception, growth, and demise—is inseparable from an evaluation of the broader intellectual context of social anthropology in which it is found. Although this book is not a comprehensive assessment of social anthropology, it does sketch the general features of different phases of the discipline's history, each of which predisposed anthropology to construct its objects of study in distinct, characteristic ways. Moreover, this outline of social anthropology's history is an effort to extend anthropology's holistic purview to encompass the discipline itself. Whereas most intellectual histories establish ideas within the context of their own genealogies and the intellectual pedigrees of their authors, this historical sketch seeks to extend the framing context to recent global history. What is called for in a fully anthropological history of anthropology is not just a situating of ideas within the context of the discipline but also a situating of the discipline within the global context.

In brief, then, the thesis is that as the world changes, rather distinct periods can be discerned, each of which conditions anthropology to construct itself and its subjects in ways distinctive of each such moment. This being so, a fully anthropological assessment of an anthropological category such as the peasant requires reference to this broader historical context. Such a fully anthropological history of the discipline has yet to be written, but this present effort points in that direction and suggests that the present shape of the global context is predisposing anthropologists toward such a comprehensive reflexivity.

In my estimation the single most incisive statement of the political economy and ideology of 'peasants' is Eric Wolf's (1966) book of that title. This small book, whose size belies its comprehensive review and synthesis of the ethnography and theory of peasant society, provides an important benchmark for subsequent reference. Thus, if we take Wolf's book as state of the art in 1966, we can assess what developments have occurred in the intervening thirty years along the road to the dissolution of the category.[1]

In *Peasant Wars of the Twentieth Century,* Wolf (1969:xiv) portrays peasants as populations that are existentially involved in and making autonomous decisions about cultivation. The initial formulation of this definition is his landmark "Types of Latin American Peasantry," which establishes three basic criteria of peasants as a social type: (1) primary involvement in agricultural production, (2) "effective control of land," and (3) a primary orientation toward subsistence rather than reinvestment (1955:453–454).[2] Invoking these and other criteria, numerous anthropologists reify a social category that more often than not has no singular objective ethnographic or class basis. For in reality, the great majority of the world's so-called peasants reproduce themselves within complex economic and social relationships of which autonomous cultivation of a nonfarmer type is relatively unimportant—and increasingly so. Indeed, a glance at rural peoples reveals a plethora of forms not only in the material constitution of their relationships but also in their self-perceived identities and consciousness. Such manifold identities are most evident in 'peasant migrant workers' or 'land-owning proletarians' and other such contradictory categories, which call into question any theory that reifies the peasantry. Nevertheless, it is within this multiplicity, this broad and dynamic spectrum, that 'the peasantry' is bracketed and given a privileged identity as the theoretical and historical center of gravity in the countryside.[3]

In 1966 Wolf wrote that *feudal* is "a term fraught with so many implications that it had better be avoided" (1966:50). Neither then nor in subsequent writing has Wolf revealed a comparable concern with the usefulness of 'peasant.' I, however, will argue that 'peasant,' like 'feudal,' also belongs to discourses that are being superseded and that the emergent discourses articulate a consciousness of history, society, and self that is not well conveyed by 'peasant.'[4]

In my approach to rural society, the central issues are structure and history. Inexorable forces of social differentiation constantly churn local rural populations but seldom transform them qualitatively. Such transitions, when they do occur in the modern era, appear to be linked to and dependent on the fate of the nation-state within which any local population is located. This necessitates that any genuinely anthropological approach to rural communities must theoretically situate them within global contexts and must attend to the history of the nation-state and its position within global society. As Wolf has shown in *Europe and the People Without History* (1982), rural types (such as tribal peoples, pastoralists, fishermen, and so on) were often as not brought into being historically—along with slaves, proletarians, and peasants—by diverse mercantile relationships and other processes of subsumption. It is these usually transitory and interpenetrating categories that anthropology has objectified ethnographically and assigned primordial ontologies. This propensity toward reification invites a shifting of attention from the presumed objects of peasant literature to the literature that objectifies them.

Accordingly, in this book I elaborate a critique of representation itself. In this subproject I regard ethnography as literature while simultaneously elaborating an alternative form of representation of the other. A basic proposition here is that the production and consumption of conventional ethnography are largely, in Frederic Jameson's terms, "strategies of containment" (Jameson 1981; Horne 1989). I suggest that we are in a position to apply such a critique to ways in which 'the peasant' is constantly reinvented. For such a critique to be anthropologically reflexive it must situate the production and consumption of representations of the peasantry within the relationships that join the anthropological self to the 'peasant' other it presumes to represent. In other words, it is not sufficient to situate only 'the peasantry' within a global setting; the conventions—the texts—whereby it is represented must also be so contextualized.

Only with such anthropological reflexivity can we ask and answer such questions as why peasant studies within conventional anthropology continue to dwell on issues of peasant rationality, decisionmaking, personality, and economic differentiation. To note, for example, that theoretically these studies are situated within developmentalist visions of the 'peasant community' and that such research is consistent with the methodological individualism that informs it only elaborates variations on the original question. I hope to develop a more comprehensive, incisive critique that opens the way for alternative views. Likewise, a similar critique must also be mounted of radical peasantology. Classic Marxist studies of 'the peasantry,' as compared to neoclassical and cultural anthropological approaches, have attended to the social issues of class and history but with class defined categorically such that until recently the Marxist anthropologist had to adopt either a peasant (e.g., Maoist) or a proletarian (e.g., Leninist) line of one kind or another. This peasant-proletarian debate has now been largely superseded, but much intellectual housecleaning is still needed to prepare for postpeasant studies.

Some people may point to the presence of contemporary peasants, and I would agree that some pockets of them might remain in Latin America, Asia, and elsewhere. But the point of this book is that peasants are mostly gone and that global conditions do not favor the perpetuation of those who remain. My examples are drawn mainly from Mexico, long the site of peasant studies in anthropology. Today an adequate ethography of seemingly rural Mexican communities must situate them within transnational and global contexts that effectively dissolve old intellectual oppositions such as rural-urban, modern-traditional, and peasant-nonpeasant. As the argument goes, if current conditions do not support peasants as a type in Mexico, then perhaps we should also reevaluate their status elsewhere. But more than this, the ethnography of contemporary Mexico suggests that we must also reconceptualize the concepts with which we define identities and communities.

The Death of Dualism

At its inception anthropology was distinct from the other Western social sciences in that it was predicated on the *difference* between the Western anthropological self and the alien ethnographic other epitomized by 'the primitive.' This difference was constructed on several bases, one of which was the geographic separation between self and other such that the self was in 'the West' and the other was located in 'non-Western' areas. The other bases of difference were sociocultural and temporal: 'Primitive' others were different kinds of peoples because they had technologies and ways of life that were comparable to previous phases in the social evolutionary past of Western society that had 'advanced' beyond these 'simpler' forms to become *modern.* Implicit in the definition of the modern is this contrast with the primitive that it has transcended. Just as the modern represents a structural opposition to the primitive, so is it also a historical antithesis that exits at the end point of history, far removed from the distant past of human beginnings.

This oppositional difference between modern and primitive was the axis upon which anthropology was initially constructed and practiced. No wonder, then, that the disappearance of the primitive implied a crisis for anthropology insofar as it was a kind of natural history based on field research. But the crisis was averted by the discovery of another type—'the peasant.' The peasant, as we will see, has been a problematic type for anthropology, problematic not only in a theoretical sense but also with respect to the constitution of the discipline itself.

The initial anthropological construction of an oppositional and evolutionary difference between 'modern' and 'primitive' was itself the practice of a distinctly modern sensibility and worldview. This style of thought tends to make the continuous discrete and to cast difference into binary oppositions. In this sense such thought is manifest in digital programming and logical positivism, which are both thus structurally consistent with empiricist epistemology, based as it is on a categorical distinction between self and other. The more general argument here is that this style of binary but nondialectical thought is predicated upon and leads to social practices that perpetuate social differentiation, both locally and globally.

Chapter 2 lays out the basic thesis, which is that 'the peasant' is associated with a major development in the history of anthropology—a crisis of sorts—of which the peasant is both symptom and cause. The argument is that the basic structure of classic anthropology was put into place in the late nineteenth and early twentieth centuries. This structure is a dualist worldview comparable to that of classic worldviews, hence its name. But it differs from them in that it is reconstructed within the context of young nation-states, colonialism, and imperialism, and assumes forms, such as social evolutionism and positivism, that explain and justify devaluation of non-Western others. An early classic phase culminates in Frazerian anthropology, whereas late classic anthropology is associated with the Malinowskian revolution. Whereas the former, typified by Frazer's encyclopedic *The Golden Bough,* eclectically assembled bits of ethnographic data from around the world in efforts to reconstruct the broad outline of human social evolution, Malinowski pioneered the study of entire communities in which cultural traits could be examined in their living social context. Already in the late classic phase this dualism has started to unravel, occasioned in large part by the Malinowskian revolution (see, e.g., Jarvie 1964).

Subsequent world events associated with World War II and its aftermath coincide with the emergence of modern anthropology, which is distinguishable from classic anthropology by a more pronounced decay of its dualist structure and also by the appearance of a new prototypic ethnographic other—'the peasant'—which was subsequently essentialized in ways comparable to the way in which 'the primitive' was previously constructed out of its difference with 'the modern.' But 'the peasant' brought with it into anthropology implications for the structure of the discipline that were not implied by 'the primitive.' For unlike the categorical absoluteness of the primitive, which is the primary conceptual antipode of the modern, the peasant is located on the margin—geographic, historical, classificatory—between them. Because it is marginal it is conceptually ambiguous, and because of this ambiguity the peasant is the most problematic social type within the social typology of anthropology.

The peasant opens new horizons for modern anthropology but as a type is powerfully disruptive of its classic structure, threatening its epistemological and political bases. Anthropology responds to the opportunities and threats presented by the peasant with strategies of containment. The first and most basic of these strategies is indeed the invention of '*the* peasant,' which occurs within the structure of modern anthropology. The invention of the peasant is thus an attempt not only to contain troublesome new types of others that have come into the purview of anthropology at mid-century but also to preserve the basic structure of classic anthropology in a historic period that is inexorably dissolving it.

Turning attention from primitives to peasants saved anthropology as a field-based discipline, but it was an imperfect solution to the degree that the peasant is—categorically—an imperfect social type for modern sensibilities, which think in terms of discontinuous, absolute categories such as subject and object, self and other. Because the peasant relocates anthropological practice and thought to the margins of the modern and the primitive, its appearance within anthropology contributes to the deconstruction of the primary oppositional metaphysical categories out of which anthropology invented not only its others but also itself. Further intentional critical work such as this book is but the conscious articulation of this general historical trend.

The peasant as an anthropological type is still robust, as is indicated by the continued frequent references to it in the literature. The main thesis of Chapter 3 is, however, that ever since its invention the peasant as an anthropological category has become evermore out of alignment with 'reality' and thus has become a disruptive category. Therefore, anthropology, which has staked so much of its future on this type, must continue to contain the peasant, and to do so certain strategies of containment are mobilized by both right-wing and left-wing anthropologies, strategies that coincide with the postwar foreign policies for the 'containment of communism.' Both the anthropological peasant and the strategies for its containment were invented during the Cold War, which was a historic moment that elevated the dualistic "us-versus-them" structure of the classic worldview to levels of hysteria that appear within the context of the nation-state. It was within these specific cultural dynamics of the Cold War nation-state that anthropological essentialization of the peasant occurred, thus enabling its containment in time and space.

But containment is necessary only because counter forces are at work. Chapter 4 therefore further explores global tendencies that have been promoting the deconstruction of the temporal and spatial dualisms that underlie the essentialization of 'the peasant' in the modernist mode. The preliminary conscious awareness of these trends, contrary to the modernizationist interpretation of history, has its own sociology and ideological loadings, which can be summed up as romantic reactions. Although these currents also reified social types, they were nevertheless important phases in the reconceptualization of the peasantry.

Whereas Chapters 1 through 4 deal with the peasant as an anthropological category, Chapter 5 examines global conditions that are shaping postpeasant identities and anthropological representations of them. Chapter 6 then turns from the categories of anthropology to the sociology and consciousness of ethnographic subjects, to those peoples designated as 'peasants.' To carry forward the analysis of how anthropology has essentialized the peasant I turn here to a rethinking of the most debated and controversial issue in peasant studies—namely, social differentiation—and recast it in light of the emergent multipolar social field discussed in Chapter 5 by introducing the concept of 'internal differentiation,' as compared with the more common notion of external differentiation whereby 'individuals' are differentiated into classes and class fractions. The theory of internal differentiation is not offered as an alternative to external differentiation, as is the case with most postmodernist critics of Marxist theory and most analysts of new social movements, but as an addition to it. This reconceptualization thus presents an analysis of class as more complexly structured than is the case with dualist models that posit unitary class strata and identities.

Such a view should not be seen as wrong (indeed, in many nineteenth-century situations it was an adequate representation of class structure) but instead as a first approximation of the link between relations of production and consciousness. Thus, rather than rejecting class analysis, it should be taken for what it is—

the still most powerful theoretical perspective for understanding the differentiation of identities in complex societies.

The basic argument advanced here is that postpeasant theory and research must turn from an obsessive concern with the external differentiation of 'types of peasants' (which are but reified objects) to the internal differentiation of subjects. The shift from an anthropology of peasants as unitary objects to peasants as complex subjects marks a maturation of peasant studies whereby the very idea of peasant is transcended such that its continued invocation serves only to constrain the anthropology of communities formerly known as rural and peasant. However, such a full realization of class theory entails its application in association with that equally basic concept of its author, namely, the theory of value, but a theory of value that also benefits from contemporary understanding of the differential distribution of value in the formation of complex identities and relationships that is the theme of Chapter 7.

If the appearance within anthropology of *the* peasant marked the end of its classic phase, then its departure—an event this book encourages—signals the end of anthropology's short-lived modern phase. Chapter 8 deals with the shape of a postpeasant anthropology. The basic thesis is that such an anthropology will be increasingly situated in marginal zones comparable to the zone the peasant once occupied and that in this historic shift what was marginal will become central. I envision an anthropology so decentered as concerned with problems that are not constructed upon the armature of modern versus primitive/peasant. Just as the modern will have disappeared with the primitive, so will anthropology as a modern sensibility become transformed into a sensibility that is consistent with a world in which there are neither peasants nor a teleology of immanent modernization, of *development*.

Images of peasants and of programs for their development as conceived in the 1960s and 1970s were similar to those with which feminist theory of the 1970s theorized gender and routes to sexual equality. Both peasants and women were envisioned as marked forms that had to be assimilated into the unmarked. In the one case peasants would have to be incorporated into modern developed society; in the other women would enjoy the same rights and identities men had previously monopolized only when they became organized with sufficient political power and will to claim them. In both cases the solution to underdevelopment and inequality was the extension of the forms and values of modern liberal society to those who were not yet the full beneficiaries of that society.

In retrospect, contemporary critical feminist theory has seen this strategy of obtaining sexual equality as an unwitting acceptance and reification of an underlying dualist structuring of gender inequality.[5] This line of reasoning implies that the route to women's liberation lies not in becoming the equal of men in a social and cultural universe that has been constructed largely on dualist categories that are the bases of inequality but instead by challenging the presumed ontology of this inequality. In other words, attempts to assimilate to identities that have been constructed on structures that are the bases of inequality serve not so much to liberate as they do to reinforce the structuring of that inequality. This situation suggested that progressive movement might best be gained by displacing analysis to this level, which had been unexamined by earlier feminist theory. In such a nondualist world, possibilities thus open for multiple legitimate forms of difference, such as women of color and varieties of lesbianism, in addition to the conventional norms of male and female (see, e.g., Barrett and Phillips 1992). In a similar way I envision the emergence of multiple identities from the category *peasant,* which has been imposed on and assumed by subaltern peoples in ways not dissimilar to the way in which norms of 'female' have defined what it is to be woman within structured relations of sexual inequality.

Whereas the peasant was constructed within and consistent with the dualist structuring of the nation-state, the now-emerging postpeasant subject often has a transnational identity. This transnationalism is most readily apparent in the high and growing rates of transnational migration of poor rural people whereby they deconstruct the spatial and occupational dualisms that structure images of 'the peasant.' But transnational migration, although a major one, is but one of many contemporary global processes eroding the power of the nation-state to inform identities.

Chapter 8 examines the expressions of several of these transnational trends in consciousness and their corresponding social and political forms, forms that are emerging as conceptual vehicles for the reconceptualization of rural types formerly known as 'peasants.' Briefly, whereas the peasant was essentialized as having a primordial connection with land, a condition that made the agrarian issue the fundamental peasant concern, postpeasant rural politics is increasingly elaborated in terms of human rights, ecopolitics, and ethnicity. Human rights conceived as universal, ecopolitics conceived as global, and ethnicity conceived as inherently transnational are thus consistent with the postpeasant, who has moved from periphery to center, from past to present, and from object to subject and who in doing so has largely dissolved the distinctions between these oppositions. Among the new facets of postpeasant identities, I single out one for consideration—the *indígena.* This type is highly disruptive not only of the category *peasant* but of political authority in general.

The Context of This Book

With respect to the interaction of biography and the historical moment within which I write, five conditions have strongly shaped my sensibilities toward and perceptions of the peasant question. First, I have had fieldwork experiences in Mexico and Poland, two nations that are important in the history of peasant studies.[6] The first great 'peasant revolution' of the twentieth century occurred in Mexico, whereas it was in Poland that serfdom was reestablished in the fifteenth century and persisted into the nineteenth century; its traces still affect agrarian politics in the post-glasnost era. Today Poland—along with Rumania, Bulgaria, and Yugoslavia—is by most measures still one of the most strongly peasant nations of Europe. And in both Mexico and Poland, 'rural' communities demonstrate a demographic and what appears to be a cultural persistence few observers foresaw a decade ago. The degree to which these social and cultural traits are indeed peasant is a central theme of this book.

Another condition that shapes my writing is my work in both Mexico and California with highly migratory Mixtec- and Zapotec-speaking peoples from the state of Oaxaca. The ethnography of contemporary Mixtecs and Zapotecs well illustrates a basic theme of this book—the formation of persons and communities that do not conform to the classic categories of rural society, being neither peasant nor proletarian, neither farmer nor petty merchant, and neither rural nor urban. I speak here of such *types* both as anthropological categories—typologies—and as social types, as, for example, kinds of communities and identities. The central goal of this book is to establish a point of view from which we can observe the tension between these two kinds of categories—the historically given and the anthropological apprehension of these communities. By "historically given" I do not mean to imply some concrete empirical reality accessible purely by scientific means, for historical realities are, like the anthropological categories, also the products of local human practice carried out with varying degrees of consciousness of how such practice is affected by more global conditions. I thus write as an anthropologist attempting to apprehend such peasant realities, even as I reassess the vocabulary anthropology has given us to do this task.

To carry out such critical work, it has been necessary to displace my writing to a different point of view that is on the margin between the other two, such that I am in a position to comment *on* them rather than *from* them. This strategy of escaping the influence of the local is, of course, an ideal that constantly recedes as we move toward it, but it is nevertheless a necessary ideal for the kind of bifocality entailed by any critique of anthropology that itself presumes to critique the other, such as, in this case, 'the peasant.' I am thus, as it has become fashionable to say, writing from the margin, which gives me a vantage point on both the shape of anthropological categories and the communities they seek to represent. But I am also writing from a margin in a more literal sense, and this leads to the third circumstance informing my work.

For some time I have been residing and working in the greater U.S.-Mexican border area, surely one of the most fascinating marginal areas of the world precisely because it is evolving from its current marked status to a primary unmarked region and type such that what was marginal or peripheral becomes typical and what was 'normal' is reduced to a secondary, minority status. This border area is a complex region that lies between the so-called First and Third Worlds, partaking of both and yet in other ways resembling neither. It is also a region that encompasses 'peasant' and 'nonpeasant,' 'indigenous' and 'nonindigenous,' 'modern' and 'traditional,' 'First' and 'Third World.' I indicate these categories with single quotation marks to signal their problematic status, which becomes all the more apparent here in this border region (see Kearney 1991; Kearney and Nagengast 1989; Nagengast and Kearney 1990).

California is noted for being on the leading edge of social and cultural change in the United States. But when we extend our purview to the Californias, our attention is directed to an international region whose seeming ambiguity is representative of global trends. Tijuana, once the butt of jokes and stereotyped as a town of bars and brothels, is now the second-largest city on the Pacific Coast of North America, second only to Nuestra Señora Reina de Los Angeles, with which it is becoming evermore culturally and economically stitched together as both cities become integrated into a transnational megalopolis. Tijuana's phenomenal growth is driven largely by immigration of low-income rural people from mainland Mexico and Central America. Mixtecs and Zapotecs from Oaxaca have formed colonies in Tijuana and elsewhere throughout the greater binational border area. Consequently, fieldwork among them takes me from seemingly prototypical, indigenous, highland Mesoamerican communities—which are the cradle of so much anthropological thinking and writing about 'the peasantry'—to the shantytowns of border cities, to the orchards, fields, and inner cities of California, and to other niches into which indigenous Oaxacan migrants and immigrants have established themselves while for the most part also maintaining their seemingly peasant way of life in the mountains of southern Mexico.

The tens of thousands of rural-origin Mixtecs and Zapotecs in urban areas of Mexico and the United States are at a first approximation another instance of "cities of peasants" (Roberts 1978; cf. Mangin 1970 and Simic 1973). But given the strong linkages between these urban residents and their rural communities and the complex identities that result, the logic of this typing could be turned around to refer with equal appropriateness to 'urbanites in the countryside.' And at the same time neither of these characterizations does justice to the multiform experiences and complex differentiation that exist in Mixtec and Zapotec migrant communities. As I discuss later, especially in Chapter 8, such complex persons and communities require innovative metaphors to represent their multiform identities.

I also write from another margin, which is itself within the greater border area. This is the 'development' that in the past five years has overrun the formerly rural area of southern California in which Carole Nagengast and I live, as hundreds of acres of chaparral and orange groves have been replaced by thousands of slick and flimsy suburban look-alike houses and mini-malls. 'The peasant question' is embedded within a number of prior intersecting discourses, one of which is the dualist opposition between "the country and the city," which, as Raymond Williams (1973) has so effectively shown, is a major conceptual axis structuring much of Western literature. In California the inexorable spread of so-called suburban development obliterates rural environments at ever increasing rates, such that it seems to be only a matter of time until almost all of the "country" is gone. But in a logic that is now apparent, this suburbanization is somewhat of a contradiction in terms, for not only does it obliterate countryside, but it is also transforming cities into new kinds of social spaces that bear less and less resemblance to the bounded metropolitan areas and sociologies depicted in modern sociology and urban anthropology. I discuss these transformations in urban ecologies in Chapter 5.

The main point to note here is that the decomposition of the distinction between country and city is proceeding not as a replication of the city in the country but instead as a historical process that is also transforming the city, such that different social spaces are emerging on the margins of city and countryside that subsume the older spaces into them, transforming both of them in this suburbanization's own image. This double transformation is less a process of suburbanization than what Gottdeiner (forthcoming) refers to as "deconcentration"—partaking of both rural and urban and yet being neither. This disintegration of the distinction between country and city that is taking place in California is but one dimension in the collapse of the broader distinction between 'developed' and 'underdeveloped' nations that has been central to concepts of modern history since World War II. Greater Los Angeles now spills across the U.S. border into Mexico, dissolving in its complex integrity the distinction between First and Third Worlds. This *City of Quartz,* as Mike Davis (1990:6) calls it, now stretches from the country-club homes below Ronald Reagan's ranch near Santa Barbara south to the shanty *colonias* of the West Coast Mexican port city of Ensenada.

Middle-class bedroom communities in California are one variation of this global trend; inner-city 'urban ghettos' are another, and Latin American favelas and contemporary shantytowns in general are others. I do not mean to imply that these various instances of this more general type do not fit into the global economy and society in basically different ways. The point is rather that these new social forms are reflected in nascent forms of representation that it is my task to explore and to articulate more explicitly. Presently, some of the most prescient representations of these new social forms are found in fictional literature.[7]

Finally, I am also writing on the constantly receding border between the present and the future. Although much of this book traces the past development of the peasant concept in anthropology, it also has the practical aim of better comprehending and advancing the politics of subaltern communities and organizations like the ones I work with in Mexico and California. I thus examine the history of the peasant concept to better innovate other constructions of identity that will better serve the political needs of such communities, which have passed from being peasant communities or are in the process of doing so.

Although in this book I explore what I see as novel trends in the social and cultural identities of people who are often called peasants, I do so to better understand that most vexing perennial issue of rural political economy, namely, social and cultural differentiation, which proceeds through a corresponding differential production and consumption of economic value so that some get rich and some become poor. I unabashedly retain a strongly classic Marxist concern with economic exploitation as it occurs within specific class systems that make such exploitation possible. My strategy here is the same as that in the various scenarios just described—that is, I position myself on the margin between two modern spheres, which in this case are spheres of theory, namely, the economic and the cultural. Simply stated, I see previous approaches to peasant differentiation as either excessively economistic or too culturistic to adequately comprehend social and historical processes of such a nature. Reconceptualization of this 'complex whole,' I hold, cannot be achieved by wedding some cultural interpretations to economic analysis. Instead, a reconstitution of the economic and the cultural is called for.

Fortunately, the foundation for such a transdisciplinary approach is available in Bourdieu's (1986) work on forms of capital and their transformations, transformations that when they become apparent, as Bourdieu has made them, obviate limiting the economic to economics and the cultural to cultural/symbolic analysis. Economic capital is convertible to symbolic and cultural capital and vice versa. But what is more, the production, consumption, loss, and transformation of capitals both construct and constitute social identities in the socially ordered subject positions I know as classes and class fractions. But these class identities are constituted not only by the press of relations of production but also by the consumption of signs imbued with various forms of value. Such a subject is thus, as it were, doubly internally differentiated: first by participating in multiple relations of production and indeed even in different modes of production and second by consuming a veritable smorgasbord of cultural signs and values emanating from globally diverse sources.

By pushing the theory of capitals and their transformations per Bourdieu, I think it is possible to arrive at a general theory of value. *Capital* resonates with capitalism and is thus an adequate term for Bourdieu's sociology of capitalist society and culture. But *general value* is a term more appropriate for a general anthropology encompassing capitalist and noncapitalist social formations. My evaluation of peasant studies is that they tend to dwell too much on either economics or culture and as such are unable to move forward on the problems they have set themselves—for example, analysis of development, ritual, symbolism, resistance, and differentiation. All of these issues are at the same time economic and cultural, and their reconceptualization requires a theoretical synthesis as is enabled by the theory of generalized value, which allows us to query the unity and transformations of economic and aesthetic values and how they become inscribed as the identities of persons who produce, lose, consume, and transform them and who in doing so become constituted and, on occasions, themselves transformed.

Chapter 5 examines the decline of 'traditional' culture as it is replaced by elements of mass and popular culture in the construction of 'peasants.' But in an ironic affront to the assumptions of modernization theory, consumption of mass culture promotes difference even as in some way it homogenizes. We are thus brought back to the perennial issue of peasant differentiation but with two notable new twists. One is that to the degree that it is influenced by production and consumption of forms of general value beyond the local 'rural peasant' sphere, the scope of investigation must be extended beyond the 'peasant community' to include, for example, transnational contexts. The second innovation regarding the analysis of differentiation (Chapter 6) is to define it not just with respect either to the subject's location in the relations of production or to consumption of economic value and cultural signs but to explore the internal differentiation that results within the subject who so produces and consumes. This strategy is not a capitulation to recent pronouncements that the postmodern subject is dead but instead is an insistence on recognizing that 'peasant' subjects are more complexly constituted than imagined by theories of external differentiation per, for example, Lenin and Chayanov. Historically, internal differentiation seems to be increasing along with increased transnational production and consumption of economic and symbolic values and signs. These more complexly constituted subjects are predisposed to and, one might even say, need social organizations whose own collective forms and political objectives, ideologies, and tactics correspond to the social identities of their members and advance their political interests. The examination of human rights, ecopolitics, and ethnicity in Chapter 8 is thus built on this discussion of internal differentiation.

Earlier I called attention to new milieus of difference, only to note that I am writing from within one that profoundly conditions our understanding of 'the peasant question' and demands reconceptualization of conventional categories of peasantology. For were I to attempt to comprehend the reality within which I write in conventional terms, I would be snared in immobilizing contradictions. How, for example, in terms of the conventional categories of 'traditional' and 'modern,' of 'Mexican' and 'North American,' and indeed of 'peasant' and 'nonpeasant' are Carole Nagengast and I to comprehend the way in which the tidal wave of deconcentration that has swept over us has been effected in part by Mixtec peasant lives?

Looking down from where we live on a hill we see spread before us a sea of new roofs. And turning our gaze to the field and trees below we see where two Mixtec 'peasant' families have borrowed some land from us to live on for awhile. The arrangement is reciprocal; they put us up when we go to their town in Oaxaca. The men of these seemingly very traditional peasant people from highland Mesoamerica are away at the moment working as roofers, constructing in a very literal sense the new social space that is engulfing us. The musical tonality of Mixtec language comes up to where we, the ethnographers, stand. The children of these roofers are playing, and their wives are working at handicrafts, which they sell in the parking lots of local shopping malls. In the afternoon the men will come home in their truck with wild edible greens they have collected along the road, and they will cultivate their corn and other plants they have planted with some seeds bought in a local supermarket and with others carried from Oaxaca. And in the evening they and their families will rest in the shade of a eucalyptus, in the boughs of which some years ago another Mixtec 'peasant' tied his son's placenta after his wife gave birth to their child nearby.

Clearly, we and our visitors/neighbors—more confounded categories—share a historical moment that defies conventional anthropological categories.[8] But it is not the case that we and they are marginal but that all of us, albeit in different ways, are assuming complex and interpenetrating identities. It is to be expected that these contemporary identities and the conditions that shape them should be reflected in anthropological thought. This book is intended as such a reflection.

Notes

1. I make these comments on Wolf's *Peasants* having the benefit of more than a quarter of a century in time since its appearance. Although I call for discarding the idea of the social category it set out to explain, I do embrace the broad outlines of Wolfian historical-structural theory and method.

2. Wolf also locates peasants in a global, historical context and establishes an alternative paradigm to the prevalent synchronic anthropological studies focused on cultural content of peasant communities.

3. Indeed, the enduring persistence of this concept has been recently reaffirmed by the appearance of the second edition of Shanin's *Peasants and Peasant Societies,* which seeks to define the "qualitative particularity underlying the use of the term peasantry as a valid generalization and a theoretical concept" (1987:2).

4. When Wolf first formulated the working definition of peasants used herein, he also anticipated their decline in the twentieth century as a result of displacement by industry, trade, and large-scale agriculture, which has produced a crisis "related to the increasingly marginal role of the peasantry within the prevalent economic system" (1955:453). Part of my effort in this book is a continued exploration of this observation.

5. This situation is comparable to the dilemma faced by colonized authors attempting to resist colonial hegemony. They can oppose it by writing about it in their own words; but if by writing they reinforce European genres and forms, then perhaps they have collaborated in the reproduction of colonial culture.

6. I have worked regularly in Mexico since the mid-1960s and have gone to rural Poland with Carole Nagengast and learned most of what I know of it from her (e.g., Nagengast 1991).

7. Fictional writing in general is more sensitive to such social change than is nonfiction; see, for example, William Gibson's *Neuromancer* (1984) and *Monalisa Overdrive* (1988) and other cyberpunk writing, as well as Tama Janowitz's *A Cannibal in Manhattan* (1987) and Hanif Kureishi's *The Buddha of Suburbia* (1990). And to the degree that the present work is situated on borders between nations and anthropological categories, I am sympathetic to the blurring of forms and assertion of new identities in Gloria Anzaldúa's *Borderlands/La Frontera: The New Mestiza* (1987) and Ana Castillo's *The Mixquihuala Letters* (1986) and *So Far from God* (1993).

8. At this point I stop the constant use of single quotes to signal the categorical nature of terms for basic social types and trust that the reader will continue to give them the double readings I intend—first as artifacts of anthropological thought and then and only then as labels for presumed social types.

Chapter 1

San Jerónimo: A Peasant Community?

My first major fieldwork effort was conducted in the state of Oaxaca in southern Mexico in the 1960s in Ixtepeji, a Zapotec "town of peasant farmers" (Kearney 1972:4). This fieldwork was done in the classic mode in the sense that I dropped into Ixtepeji from outside and saw it locally, largely from the inside out, as a more or less self-contained community.[1] The structure of my initial fieldwork in the Mixtec town of San Jerónimo was, however, rather different. In the late 1970s I came to know men from the town in Riverside, California, where they were working as orange pickers. I arranged for one of these men to take me and my colleagues and former students James Stuart and Roberto Perez to San Jerónimo with him. We thus arrived in San Jerónimo in 1978 already sensitized to the importance of migration to search for cash income for its inhabitants.

When I first began to work in San Jerónimo in 1978, it appeared to be the epitome of a traditional peasant community. Spatially, San Jerónimo is remote, indeed isolated, lying at the end of a dirt road in the Mixteca region of Oaxaca in southern Mexico. The road is often impassable in the rainy season. If ethnographers were to parachute into San Jerónimo Progreso, it would be as if they had entered a prototypical 'peasant' community of highland Mesoamerica, for here the daily round is the stuff of the classic ethnography of 'peasant society.' And indeed, one could write a volume on the 'peasant' society, culture, and economy of San Jerónimo. All of the characteristics of peasant economics, society, and culture are there. All households have access to farmland that is communally owned by the town, and most households also have some de facto private land they also work. Almost all production is for auto consumption and is produced with simple technology powered by human and animal energy. In addition to self-employment, agricultural production is carried out within a complex set of social and economic relationships that include labor exchange, varieties of sharecropping, and hired labor. And in nearby towns a few large landowners absorb some labor of small holders by means of feudal-like relationships.

A rich ceremonial life in the town celebrates its collective symbols and is financed within a general set of economic relations, including bride price, that defy the logic of market production and exchange. These relations are transacted in a dialect of the Mixtec language—the language of everyday life—unique to the town. Embedded in the language is an extensive body of ethnoscience concerning botany, biology, health, human nature, and so. Faces of people from different households throughout the town have family resemblances with one another, no doubt as a result of many generations of endogamy within the community. The language, customs, and social identity thus all map onto a corresponding dense web of kinship such that it is possible to trace complex multiple kinship relationships between any two members of the community.

These, then, are certain irrefutable objective characteristics of San Jerónimo that are eminently 'peasant.' An ethnographer from the sky would have no trouble filling notebooks documenting expressions of a corresponding 'peasant culture and mentality.' Non-Western forms of thinking and knowledge guide daily life, and indeed the general 'culture' of the community is markedly distinct from the 'modern' national culture of contemporary, 'educated' urban Mexico. Thus, in sum there is ample reason to refer to San Jerónimo using the Mexican term *patria chica*, "small republic," which connotes a self-contained social, cultural, and economic universe—a conception that is echoed in Wolf's (1957) "closed corporate peasant community."[2]

Viewed locally, San Jerónimo was in all apparent respects a prototypical Mesoamerican peasant community, except that we arrived there with a growing appreciation of the importance of wage labor in its economy. The base of the diet—that is, of biological reproduction—in San Jerónimo is corn and beans. Therefore, one of the first research tasks we undertook was to assess local agricultural production to better understand the relationship between peasant farming and cash income in the overall economy of the town. Our initial findings were surprising: Only about 20 percent of the town's corn and beans, the staples of the diet, was supplied by local peasant production. The shortfall was made up by the purchase of imported corn and beans. With virtually no appreciable local sources of cash income, the only alternative to starvation for the great majority of the town's households was and still is to send migrants and immigrants out in search of cash income that can be remitted to purchase imported corn and beans. This is an old pattern. The oldest residents remember going with their parents as children to cut sugar cane in Vera Cruz on the Gulf coast. Then in the 1950s, when large agro-export operations—especially tomato production—were developed in the state of Sinaloa on Mexico's northwest coast, people from San Jerónimo began to migrate there as seasonal farmworkers, a pattern that was later extended into the San Quintín valley of Baja California and, as noted earlier, into California.[3]

In the 1970s and early 1980s, migrants from San Jerónimo were heavily involved as field hands in commercial agriculture in northern Mexico and California. Accordingly, our initial interpretations of the economy of San Jerónimo were made in terms of dependency theory (Stuart and Kearney 1981) and articulation theory (Kearney 1986a).[4] However, continued fieldwork with the community took me to an ever widening range of sites as migrants spread into increasingly diverse economic activities in Mexico and California. The formation of enclaves of people from San Jerónimo in California and in shantytowns of Mexican border cities facilitated their movement into self-employment, especially in urban informal economies, as well as their access to forms of public assistance (Bade 1993, 1994; Kearney 1986a; Mines and Kearney 1982). These multiple sources of income, in addition to wage labor and subsistence farming, began to cast doubt on the adequacy of articulation theory to model such increasing complexity of reproduction. However, at the same time it was apparent that San Jerónimo was maintained as a seemingly "traditional" community precisely because of the high degree to which migrants from the town penetrated into distant and diverse socioeconomic niches elsewhere in Mexico and in California. Transnational patterns of production and consumption were supporting a seemingly traditional society that in fact was in many ways fairly modern.

This ethnographic complexity, in which San Jerónimo was neither remaining traditional nor modernizing in the usual sense of those terms, led to consideration of the town as a transnational community (Kearney and Nagengast 1989; see Chapter 5). In the technical sense of the usual productionist criteria, the community of San Jerónimo is only about 20 percent 'peasant.' Its other 80 percent of income-generating activities is divided mostly between informal activities and wage labor. Now to the degree that the people of San Jerónimo are proletarians, they are unusual proletarians in that although they work mainly in modern corporate industries, they maintain and indeed have elaborated such seemingly traditional practices as a complex communal ceremonial cycle, the bride price, an intense communal solidarity vis-à-vis neighboring Mixtec towns and the Mexican government, and their own indigenous language. Clearly, to consider San Jerónimo as just a peasant town provides an impoverished description of its complexity. Furthermore, concentration on productionist aspects of the town's reproduction would severely slight the importance of local and global social and symbolic influences on the total reproduction of the community.

But how does San Jerónimo fit into the greater society? It is when we seriously begin to examine this question that characterizing San Jerónimo as a peasant community becomes even more questionable. As we trace the threads of this local fabric of a seemingly traditional society, economy, and culture, they take us to the edge of the community and beyond. We can follow these threads by examining the experience of typical members of what we soon come to realize is a greater San Jerónimo. I will discuss a man named Lencho Martínez, a woman named Rufina Vásquez, and two young people, a brother and sister, Eliseo and Lucrecia Mendoza.[5] The question that concerns us here is their objective identities: Are they, by formal criteria, peasants? In later chapters I take up the issue of the subjective identities of peasants, their sense of who and what they are—in a word, their social consciousness. Do they think, feel, and behave in conformity with anthropological theory of peasants? But I begin with the first question and with Lencho.

Lencho Martínez, a Peasant Man?

Two of the primary components of the definition of peasants is that they engage in self-directed subsistence agricultural production and that they exist in relations of political and economic inequality with nonpeasants, such that the economic value that originates from peasant production is transferred from the peasants to nonpeasants. Both of these criteria apply to Lencho, but in his case, as with that of the entire town, the ratio of peasant to nonpeasant production is fairly low. Furthermore, the circuits in which Lencho's peasant and nonpeasant income circulate are complex and blur the distinction between these two ideal spheres. With respect to peasant farming, Lencho works land of his own and also some his mother-in-law owns. He and his family and animals consume all they produce, which provides only about a quarter of their food needs.

In the 1970s Lencho made numerous crossings into California with other men from San Jerónimo to seek work picking oranges. At that time they were reluctant to attempt crossing from Tijuana through the gauntlet of the Border Patrol, crooked Mexican police, and robbers that prey on "illegals" in the most heavily trafficked international border crossing in the world.[6] Instead they would go east along the border past the town of Tecate and walk into the back country of San Diego, where after three or four days they would emerge from the mountains on roads where they could be picked up by labor contractors (or this anthropologist).

Now in his late forties, Lencho feels he is too old for heavy farmwork in California. Presently, he and his family have a second home in a Mixtec enclave near Ensenada in Baja California, where he works as a mason and his wife and grandchildren sell handicrafts to tourists.

He and his family split their time between their two homes. When Lencho is in San Jerónimo, in addition to farming he also builds houses for other circular migrants, who pay him mostly in dollars they have earned in California (some years ago Lencho built his own house with dollars he earned in the North). Such construction has transformed the architecture of San Jerónimo in recent years, as circular migrants have replaced their older adobe and pole and thatch houses with ones made of cement block.

Lencho occasionally needs extra cash, which he borrows from moneylender Macario Calderón. Macario, like other local moneylenders, serves in effect as a banker for the community, but he makes loans at usurious rates of interest.

Macario uses his profits to buy merchandise in the nearest city for resale in his small store in the town at greatly marked-up prices to a more or less captive clientele. He also turns a profit on corn produced in San Jerónimo by buying it cheaply and selling it dearly; he further profits by importing corn and other commodities into the town for resale to local people, who pay him with dollars earned in California. Macario and the other small businesspeople in the community have trucks and charge other residents for rides and for hauling.

Part of the definition of peasants is that they render their economic surplus to nonpeasants. But in the case of San Jerónimo, most surplus accumulated from its citizens takes the form of surplus value accumulated through wage labor at sites far from San Jerónimo. Also, as can be seen in Lencho's case, complex circuits of economic flow and accumulation exist within the greater transnational extension of San Jerónimo.[7]

Lencho is not one of the *principales*—a loose group of senior and well-respected men who form a de facto town council that guides and validates the political, economic, and ceremonial actions taken by the town officials, who are elected to municipal offices as specified by Mexican federal law. But he does have an intense interest in, and gains deep satisfaction from, participating in village politics.

Lencho's wife speaks only Mixtec, and he speaks Spanish poorly. He cannot read but usually has access to television and other electronic media. In terms of cultural tastes, while working Lencho listens to Mexican *ranchera* (country) music, but on special ceremonial occasions he most appreciates Oaxacan village brass band music. His daily food preferences are the staples and dishes of the San Jerónimo diet, although he also enjoys hamburgers and other fast foods.

Rufina Vásquez, a Peasant Woman?

Rufina was born in San Jerónimo in 1963 and did not learn to speak Spanish until she married at age fifteen and began to accompany her husband and his brothers to pick tomatoes in Sinaloa. By 1980 they were spending a lot of time with relatives in the Mixtec shantytown enclave in Colonia Obrera of Tijuana, which was a base from which they crossed the border to pick oranges in southern and central California. Her first child was born in 1981 in a county hospital in Ventura, California. After she left the hospital, her husband cut canes along the bank of the Santa Paula River and built a *nihi* (a sweat bath), in which she took a series of postpartum curings with the help of one of her *co-madres*. Following these treatments, she again accompanied her husband in the orange groves.

By the time their second child was born in 1983, they had built a house in the Mixtec colonia Nogales, Sonora. There Rufina, along with other women of San Jerónimo, sold handicrafts on the streets to tourists visiting this border city. By 1988 her husband had acquired a used van, and they began to drive to different cities in Arizona and southern California, where Rufina sold handicrafts in the parking lots of shopping centers. Within a few years, in addition to handicrafts made by Mixtec artisans, she was buying small manufactured items wholesale and reselling them in parking lots. In 1995 she moved out of the informal sector by applying for a business license and renting space in a storefront boutique run by a Japanese American woman. Her children are trilingual in Spanish, Mixtec, and English.

Rufina's father-in-law is the patriarch of her husband's family. He is a *principal* of San Jerónimo and possesses several hectares of farmable land there, considerably more than the average of about half a hectare (Stuart and Kearney 1981). Rufina's husband and his brothers and sisters will inherit this land, and each year some of them return to help their father plant, cultivate, and harvest it.

In recent years Rufina and her husband have saved enough money to build a rather substantial house in San Jerónimo. They are actively involved in the political and ceremonial life of the community and recently spent several thousand dollars as *mayordomos* (sponsors) of the town's annual festival in honor of its patron saint, San Jerónimo.

Eliseo and Lucrecia Mendoza, Peasant Youth?

Eliseo and Lucrecia are brother and sister. Eliseo was born in a Mixtec enclave in Tijuana in 1981 when his parents were taking a respite from picking oranges and other tree crops in central California. After his mother had completed her series of sweat baths, the family engaged a *coyote* (a border crossing guide) from San Jerónimo to take them back into California so they could return to orange picking. At that time they were living in a small shed behind the house of a labor contractor that they shared with sixteen other men and boys from San Jerónimo.

When Eliseo was two years old his parents were picking tomatoes in San Quintín, in Baja California, and were living in a sheet-metal cubicle in a labor camp that they shared with two other families.[8] One night an oil lamp fell on Eliseo and severely burned his legs to the point that he required reconstructive surgery, which was done four years later. Now at age fourteen he still walks with a slight limp.

Lucrecia, who is two and a half years younger than Eliseo, was born in the small town of Exeter in central California. She and Eliseo have been to schools in Exeter, Tijuana, and in San Jerónimo, but they have only been enrolled for about half of the time they should have been. They are both trilingual, but Spanish is their primary language. The Spanish they speak bears similarities to both rural Oaxacan Spanish and working-class Chicano Spanish but with a definite Mixtec accent. They speak Spanish with their parents and with non-Mixtec Mexicans and Mixtec to their grandparents. Their parents and grandparents speak Mixtec among themselves. When Lucrecia and Eliseo are speaking to each other or to Chicanos, they speak either Spanish or English, and with Anglos they speak English. They appear to have learned to speak English more rapidly and thoroughly than many young mestizo Mexican migrants in California, apparently because of the extra linguistic resources they possess as Mixtec speakers.

Their parents were *mayordomos* of the fiesta in San Jerónimo in 1994, when the family spent six months in the town. Eliseo returned to Exeter with his parents, but Lucrecia remained in San Jerónimo to help her grandparents, and there are no plans for her return. Meanwhile, she is not in school, as there is no secondary school in the village. It is ironic that Lucrecia, the only family member who is a U.S. citizen, is living in San Jerónimo, whereas Eliseo and their parents are residing in the United States as undocumented aliens. The members of the family in San Jerónimo are highly dependent on remittances from those in California and could not remain in the town without such assistance. Eliseo and his parents see San Jerónimo as a peaceful mountain haven with clean, cool air and clear water to which they can retreat from time to time for some respite from the dirty, back-breaking life of farmworkers in the sweltering San Joaquin valley of California.

Eliseo is apprehensive about his future. He does not work very well with oxen and would have trouble managing a farming household in San Jerónimo by himself. He is also very aware of his "illegal" status in California and becomes anxious when people discuss the recently passed Proposition 187, a state ballot initiative designed to exclude undocumented aliens in the state from public education and social services. He knows he faces an uncertain future in California in the current period of strong anti-immigrant sentiments.

. . .

A major question that will concern us in later chapters is the degree to which people who engage in such diverse relationships and activities are typical of so-called peasants. For example, Rufina's father and Lencho's brother, like a small percentage of other, mostly older people in San Jerónimo, have basic characteristics of classic peasants. They spend most of their time and effort working their own land independently with simple technology to produce food for their own families. But it is clear that such individuals are members of a family and a community that extends and reproduces in many other distant and diverse settings. Indeed, each of these seemingly ideal peasants is heavily subsidized by remittances from relatives working in California.

In subsequent chapters I shall inquire into the objective validity and the theoretical usefulness of the peasant concept to explain the complex identity and consciousness of persons such as Lencho, Rufina, Lucrecia, Eliseo, and their relatives in communities such as San Jerónimo. Although there may be many other rural communities in Mexico and elsewhere that have not become as transnationalized as San Jerónimo, it is likely that on close inspection they will be found to contain comparable complexity and diversity of identity that also defies simple characterization.

Notes

1. Fieldwork experience in Ixtepeji is described in Kearney (1992).

2. Note that Wolf's depiction of the closed corporate peasant community was but one type in a larger topology of rural types.

3. Wright (1990) well describes the structural and human aspects of San Jerónimo's involvement with international agribusiness.

4. See Chapter 4 for discussion of the importance of these theories in peasant studies.

5. These biographical sketches, like the names, are composites of various living persons whose identities are thus disguised.

6. On the dangers of crossing the border in this area and for a description of the living and working conditions of Mixtecs on the U.S. side, see Chavez (1992) and Kearney (1991).

7. Rodolfo Stavenhagen (1978) enumerates the basic mechanisms of such extraction and transfer of surplus.

8. For living and working conditions in labor camps and fields in San Quintín, see Kearney (1986a), Nagengast and Kearney (1990), and Wright (1990).

Chapter 2

Kinds of Others in the History of Anthropology

Critical assessment of anthropological thought about peasants requires that such work itself be treated anthropologically by relativizing it within the social and historical contexts in which it is produced. We can discern four periods in the history of anthropology: *formative, classical, modern,* and *global.* Each period has been shaped by major changes in the world political economy. Anthropology assumed its formative and classic form by accepting responsibility within the social sciences of defining 'primitive' others that lay beyond the bounds of modern society and outside of historical time. In the modern period, in the 1950s and 1960s anthropology also accepted responsibility for theorizing peasants and did so for the most part within the same dualist structuring within which it conceived the primitive.

But unlike primitives, peasants existed within contemporary history, and as a type of other they are ambiguous and thus disruptive of dualist anthropological theories. This potential for classificatory disruption was also based on their potential for political disruption within the context of the Cold War. Anthropological representation responds to these disruptive potentials with 'strategies of containment,' the primary one of which was construction of the category *peasant* in ways consistent with the dualist thinking so ingrained in anthropology, as it is in other constructed forms of human difference. To be certain, "objective" differences do exist between peoples called 'peasants' and nonpeasants. But the issue that concerns us here is the ways in which anthropological ideas of such differences, to the degree that they reflect and inform official images of 'peasants,' participated and continue to participate in the construction of such differences.

Literature about peasants is elaborated by nonpeasants whose ideas are informed by theoretical, philosophical, and political perspectives they bring to their work on the peasantry. 'The peasantry' is rather like a Rorschach test upon which are projected the dispositions of nonpeasant authors, dispositions that are shaped by the positions of the various authors in the political and intellectual fields in which they live and write.

The most comprehensive study of the anthropological literature on 'the peasants' of a single nation is Cynthia Hewitt de Alcántara's *Anthropological Perspectives on Rural Mexico* (1984). Her original goal was to elucidate the changing configurations of rural society as revealed through the empirical findings of researchers. Soon after embarking on this project, however, Hewitt de Alcántara became aware of the degree to which images of rural society were refracted through the differing paradigms that informed the research agendas and interpretations of authors. At that point she broadened her project to include a survey of these different intellectual orientations to provide a necessary control for addressing the original issue. As she says,

> Work was no longer oriented by interest in turning up comparable facts, as such, but rather by the hope of placing observations by students of the peasantry in categories which would permit comprehension of the epistemological structure within which their research had taken place. In so doing, the original goal of "seeing" real patterns of change in the Mexican countryside was not abandoned; but it was recognized that the view would always be mediated through the eyes of non-peasants, whose particular urban experience and training, in interaction with the situation confronting them upon entering rural Mexico, determined the picture encountered thereafter by all later readers of their work. (Hewitt de Alcántara 1984:xi–xii)

This problem of discerning changing rural conditions and realities from portrayals of them that are also historically contingent requires recourse to a sociology of knowledge. This in turn entails a partial displacement of attention from rural society per se to interpretations of it that are themselves social and cultural artifacts of wider sociological contexts that include not only the rural community but also the biographical and social conditions forming authors and predisposing them to adopt one particular 'paradigm' and not others. This kind of socioepistemological background check on the authors of ethnographic or other empirical works written about particular communities and regions should be considered to be a routine way of reading any work that is taken up for what it can tell the reader about the work's subject matter. Hewitt de Alcántara's study of the literature on rural Mexico is a good example of precisely this kind of necessary extra textual work that should be done by all researchers on the key literature for their areas of specialization. This corrective chore is comparable to the way laboratory scientists calibrate their instruments prior to taking measurements.[1]

In this book we enter into a somewhat different critical work than that exemplified by Hewitt de Alcántara, focusing as she does on the relationship of authors to the paradigms that guide their research. Her research strategy, inspired by Thomas Kuhn (1970), is to explore the life cycle of paradigms as they are challenged by competing ones. Such a sociology of knowledge, epitomized by Kuhn's

(1957, 1977) own studies, is a necessary but not yet fully anthropological way of reading social science literature, in that such analysis does not attempt to situate paradigms themselves within history as social and cultural artifacts.

Thus, the question that lingers is, how and in what ways are some paradigms not just alternatives to their competitors but in fact made possible by virtue of having emerged under different historical conditions? Such concern with emergent possibilities is at the center of the kind of sociology—better said, *anthropology*—of knowledge I invoke herein. These different sociologies of knowledge are not mutually exclusive but instead stand in a relationship of inclusion, running from the biographical to the global historical just noted. Clearly, the biographical is the most feasible at the regional and national levels where it is possible to control the social production of a body of literature. By the same token, the more general global purview of this book precludes such attention to local detail and lends itself better to the broader issues of how intellectual styles come and go.[2]

This more general historical anthropological approach is consistent with a central thesis of this book, which is that the category *peasant* has outlived the conditions that brought it into being. And what are these changing conditions? First, the most apparent changes—most apparent because they are the easiest to objectify—are the changing realities of rural life, realities that are refracted through the lenses of social theory. And second, social theory, itself a kind of social fact, is also undergoing transformations characteristic of this particular historic moment, a historical moment that also encompasses the rural realities anthropologists attempt to explain.

As the social sciences became institutionalized within the modern nation-states and in the process contributed to the constitution of those states, a basic division of labor was made between anthropology and the other disciplines, most notably sociology. To the latter fell the task of articulating internal diversity into national identity, and in this sense sociology is a totemic discipline of national solidarity. In sharp contrast to sociology's contributions to forging national identity, anthropology was assigned the complementary task of defining such internal solidarity by contrasting it with its antithesis, the generalized other. Thus, whereas sociology is the science of internal difference, anthropology is the science of external difference. Whereas sociology is the science of Self, anthropology is the science of Other. Given the location of anthropology within the Self, it therefore follows that anthropology is also charged with the task of defining the Relationship between Self and Other.[3] And indeed, it is the historically given geopolitical structure of this Relationship that is the armature upon which anthropology constructs difference, difference that takes the form of the opposition between the anthropological Self and the ethnographic Other. But there are various kinds of Others, of which the peasant is but one. Understanding the distinctive features of the peasant as conceptualized by anthropology thus requires some understanding of this deeper armature upon which the peasant has been constructed within a particular moment in the history of anthropology.

For our purposes here, it is useful to break late-nineteenth- and twentieth-century anthropology into four periods, each of which includes a distinctive structuring of the anthropological Self and the ethnographic Other. As mentioned previously, I shall call these periods the *formative, classical, modern,* and *global.* In each period there is a characteristic mode of conceptualizing ethnographic Others as communities and of situating them in time and space.[4] The basic thesis is that the shifts that occur between these periods—that is, in the modes of representation—correspond to major transitional moments in world history that provoke the corresponding realignments in anthropological theory and practice.

The remainder of this chapter sketches the first three of these periods and describes how each conditioned its corresponding anthropology to construct a distinctive type of Other. Whereas in the first two periods anthropology gave place of privilege to *the primitive,* in the third it constructed *the peasant* as an object of anthropological scrutiny. This overview of the conditions that call forth the peasant within anthropology positions us, in Chapter 3, to assess its future or, better said, its nonfuture. The same basic thesis that explains its origin also explains its demise: Just as the peasant comes into anthropology as a reflex of global conditions that called it forth, so does a more recent sea change in global history now make the category *peasant* anachronistic.

Formative Anthropology and the Primitive

Anthropology took form as a distinct discipline in the encounter of 'Western' societies with peoples in 'peripheral' regions. In this formative period, it fell mainly to anthropology to explain such exotic, distant others that were seen as existing at the geographic and social antipodes of the West.

Intellectually, the formative period is dominated by the social evolutionists of the late nineteenth and early twentieth centuries, epitomized, for example, by Tyler, Frazer, and especially Morgan. These were the famed armchair theorists who synthesized data collected from around the world into grand accounts of how 'civilized' societies emerged from 'primitive' antecedents. Within this grand evolutionary time perspective, the task was to reconstruct the past stages in the development of social institutions. The Others so constructed are generalized and impersonal; there are no living communities of people leading daily lives.

Classical Anthropology and the Primitive

The classical period was consolidated between the two great world wars of the twentieth century. Its distinctive literary form is the ethnographic monograph based on fieldwork in a 'primitive' society and informed in British and British-derived anthropology by functionalism, whereas its North American counterpart was Boasian cultural particularism, a kind of micro-diffusionism (cf. Stocking 1989:210–212; Torgovnick 1990).

The prime indicators of this period are the now classic British and French ethnographic texts of the discipline that were published then—for example, Malinowski's *Argonauts of the Western Pacific* (1922), Radcliffe-Brown's *The Andaman Islanders* (1922), Evans-Pritchard's *The Nuer* (1940), and Griault's *Masques Dogons* (1938). It was also during this interwar period that several classic U.S. anthropology texts—ethnographic and nonethnographic—were written: Mead's *Coming of Age in Samoa* (1928), Benedict's *Patterns of Culture* (1934), and Barton's *Ifugao Law* (1919). Although at this time few colonies existed in a formal sense, the locales within which the fieldwork for these books was done were de facto colonies of the United States. American Samoa was a U.S. dependency, and the Ifugao were a tribal people in the Philippines—one of the few cases of formal U.S. colonialism. And although they were not formally colonies or protectorates of the United States, the Indian reservations and pueblos on which Benedict's work was based can be considered "internal colonies" (see, e.g., Jackobson 1984; Martínez 1982–1983; Walton 1975).

Given the broad social and temporal sweep of anthropology, it is the preeminent comparative discipline among the social sciences and the humanities. And in its formative and classical generations anthropology structured this difference as an unambiguous distinction between the Western anthropological Self and the primitive ethnographic Other. This polar opposition was theorized as mediated in time by evolutionary 'development' and in space by the differential diffusion of 'modern' cultural traits outward toward the primitive, but it was the categorical distinction between the poles that most structured anthropological images of Self and Other. This opposition thus provided a global framework for writing and reading anthropological texts. Thus, in the classical period the anthropologist could go *out* to the antipodes and write *back* to the civilized world. Writing so structured had in effect an excluded middle, that middle being the intervening social, political, and economic links between Self and Other otherwise known as colonialism.[5] As colonialism categorically distinguished between colonizer and colonized, it also organized the production and consumption of anthropological knowledge. This social epistemological structure of anthropology reached its full flower in the interwar period of the first half of the twentieth century.

The consolidation of the classical phase of anthropology was a notable humanistic advance with respect to the way in which the primitive Other was represented in anthropological texts. Whereas Frazerian anthropology had fragmented the ethnographic community into bits and pieces that were reassembled in kaleidoscopic fashion in the grand compendium, the Malinowskian style of ethnography reconstructed these communities as places of human habitation. And what is more, living, sometimes even named and photographed individuals of these communities are brought into the texts. It is true, as Fabian (1983) shows, that these communities as constructed in the classic monographs existed outside of history, or as Stocking (1989:210) puts it, that "a powerful movement had begun within the Anglo-American tradition toward a largely synchronic anthropology" in which culture and society were "as manifest in current rather than remembered or reconstructed custom and belief." But although the ethnographies of the classical period kept the primitive out of history, they allowed him to come to the edge of real time.

In a sense, this reconstitution of community in the late classical ethnographies is a portent of the legal recognition of colonized peoples as nations that was to occur after the ensuing war, recognitions that in many cases were achieved only after wars of national liberation, opposed by conservative forces that despaired at the collapse of the imperial order. Within anthropology, such a desire to contain the ethnographic Other, to prevent it from being constituted as specific, coherent communities in real time, is expressed, for example, in Jarvie's *The Revolution in Anthropology* (1964), which laments the shift from Frazerian-type science in a natural history mode to the Malinowskian focus on single peoples, a research strategy Jarvie dismisses as nonscientific. But alas for Jarvie, by the 1960s when he was writing, the age of absolute colonial distinction was gone, and the subalterns of the world clamored for representation not just in the texts of ethnographies but also in the meeting rooms of the United Nations.[6] Jarvie's book can thus be read not only as an astute analysis of the decline of anthropology as a natural science—by a growing humanistic or interpretive anthropology on one hand and a more pragmatic applied anthropology in the service of national and corporate policy on the other—but also as indicating despair or perhaps fear at the appearance of a partially reconstituted ethnographic Other on the way to becoming a Self that is not only an impossible object of positivist science but also a troublesome political entity for the colonial project and indeed one that foretells its demise. But that comes later.

A similar construction of community, parallel to the way it occurred in British anthropology, also developed in Boasian anthropology. Although early Boasian anthropology did not attempt to synthesize all of sociocultural evolution—as did Frazer, Tyler, or Morgan—and indeed reacted against evolutionism, Boas himself never attempted to represent a living community in real time but worked only with complexes of discreet culture traits of, for example, Kwakiutl society. Nevertheless, Boas's (1940) culture historical perspective and his student Wissler's (1923) age-area diffusionism originally defined culture areas associated with identifiable groups. Thus, as in interwar British anthropology, although by a different route, specific *peoples* emerge in Boasian anthropology. In both the Anglo and the U.S. ethnographies of this period, their identities as people are reflected in monograph titles: the Trobriand, the Nuer, the Azande, the Tikopia, the Crow, and so on. Such distinct peoples were also immortalized in Benedict's *Patterns of Culture* (1934): the Kwakiutl, the Dobuans, and the Pueblo Indians.

In these monographs there is little concern with European contact and presence, aside from "cultural traits" of theirs that are "borrowed" by "the natives." As it was constructed in the classic mode, categorical anthropological difference was coterminous with the structure of colonialism, which imposed political, spatial, and temporal distinctions that differentiated the colonizer and the colonized. There is in the anthropology of this period an excluded middle that is consistent with the structure of "the colonial situation" (Balandier 1966; see also Memmi 1965). Moreover, contact and exchange, when depicted, were one-way—a flow of cultural traits outward and downward from the "advanced" to the "primitive" societies. Absent in this depiction of cross-cultural exchange is a concern with flows in the opposite direction—of land ownership, surplus value, minerals, migrant labor, and other values extracted and transferred within the structuring of the colonial situation. Indeed, ethnographic knowledge collected as raw data and transferred to the metropoles for refinement into textual cultural capital for consumption by metropolitans was a permutation of the colonial relations and their cultural reproduction.

Politically, the colonizer had a national identity and corresponding rights of citizenship and prerogatives the colonized did not possess. Spatially, the habitats of the colonizer and the colonized were typically separated by expanses of saltwater or comparable land barriers, such that the colonies were 'out there' and 'down there,' portrayed as contained within bounded communities that did not significantly participate in global society and economics. And temporally the primitive Other was a residue, a survival of a distant past stage in the social evolution of the civilized Self. Further, this Other was not seen as a force in contemporary history. Although British functionalist and North American ethnography depicted living communities in a synchronic present, their temporal gaze was directed decidedly to the past. Although these representations of 'those peoples' are progressive in identifying distinct communities, their structuring is still deeply dualist in that the communities are depicted as bounded and virtually without contact with the modern world.

Such representation was as true of Boasian-Kroeberian salvage ethnography and efforts to define distinct culture areas as it was of British anthropology, which excluded the presence of Europeans from its ethnographies. Malinowski does not mention the presence of Europeans among the Trobriands, Evans-Pritchard only mentions in passing the effects of British counterinsurgency attacks on the Nuer prior to his arrival, and Benedict does not talk about relations between indigenous peoples and Europeans.

But these British anthropologists and Boasians have a different temporal sensibility than the formative anthropologists. Rather than the grand evolutionary schema within which the 'primitive' is greatly distanced in time, these "contemporary ancestors" are drawn to the edges of history, even if they are not yet admitted into it. Although the dualism of anthropology is still firmly intact at this time, ethnographic others are starting to appear in the no man's land that is necessary to demarcate the colonial anthropological Self from the colonized ethnographic Other. Classical anthropology is thus progressive in that it does advance the movement within formative anthropology to humanize ethnographic Others and to bring them closer to the West. First, as noted earlier, it does represent living communities rather than mere "shreds and patches" of exotic cultures. True, these communities are bounded, rather like exhibits in a museum diorama, but they do have all of the homologous components of modern societies. And although it is true, as Fabian (1983) points out, that these ethnographic representations exclude peoples so depicted from contemporary history, they do draw them closer to the present. This is particularly notable in Boas's temporal sensibility, which eschews deep evolutionary time in favor of a shallower historical reconstruction of distinct peoples. Although still imperfect, these are, within the overall progressive history of anthropology, progressive movements that somewhat diminish the structuring of the colonial situation. Nevertheless, the basic disposition in classical anthropology is to represent ethnographic Others as existing in a time and a space that are discontinuous with the anthropological Self.

As defined in classic anthropology, *primitive* and *tribal* peoples were classificatory categories that were easy to imagine as bounded and discontinuous with the anthropological Self. Without some theoretical vision of linkage—for example, imperialism, colonialism, world system theory, dependency theory, articulation theory—classical anthropology had no means to imagine what might actually lie within its excluded middle. Its liberalism did much to humanize ethnographic Others, but ironically its most notable contribution to such a humanistic project— namely, cultural relativism—served to idealize images of disconnected difference. Thus, whereas Boasian liberalism made a major contribution to the humanization of victims of colonial situations, it did precious little to illuminate the global and local political-economic origins of racism and other forms of prejudice cultural relativism opposed. And as such, classical anthropology functioned to contain ethnographic Others within bounded communities within colonial situations.

The partial disintegration of the dualist structuring of the classical period brought the anthropological Self and the ethnographic Other into closer contact and opened spaces on the borders between them, spaces that were to be occupied by that ambiguous type soon to become enshrined in anthropology as the peasant, a term that both gave recognition to this troublesome new type and served to contain it. Appearing on the margin between the classical anthropological Self and its ethnographic Other, the peasant starts to upset the epistemological, temporal, and spatial structuring—in a word, the political economy—of classical anthropology.

Modern Anthropology and the Invention of the Peasant

The basic thesis of this book is that the *category peasant* has come apart at the seams. In part, this disintegration is the result of the advanced disappearance of peoples who by any objective criteria can be considered peasants. But as discussed later, this global trend was already well advanced when the category was elaborated as a basic object of anthropological theory, research, and applied intervention. Accordingly, investigation of the decline of 'the peasant' must focus not on the fate of the object of the category but on changes in the conditions that brought the category into being and that now allow it to recede from the anthropological horizon.

The other prototypical category of social anthropology, the primitive, seems to be experiencing a similar erosion of its ontology. Among the first critiques of primitive essentialism is Wolf's magisterial *Europe and the People Without History* (1982), which shows that many aboriginal communities, far from being pristine social organizations when first described by Europeans, had in fact been incorporated into and transformed by global mercantile relations. Similarly, the essentialism of one of the most iconic primitive societies, the San-speaking foragers of the Kalahari, has also been assaulted, and the ensuing debate has fueled suspicions about the integrity of 'the primitive' in general.[7] If contemporary conditions are not conducive to the viability of the master trope of classical and modern anthropology, it is not surprising that they also call into question other essentialized types such as the peasant. But before examining its demise, let us explore its rise into anthropological thought. As Roseberry (1989b:109) notes, "It was not until after World War II that anthropologists began to notice, worry about, and conceptualize fundamental differences between primitives and peasants."

The end of the classical period sketched in the previous section coincides approximately with the end of World War II and its aftermath, which coincides with the destruction of the formal structure of colonialism. No longer contained within the binary structure of the colonial situation—that of colonizer and colonized—the representation of 'the primitive' begins to erode, to open up. Also, by the mid–1900s, in no small part as a result of the war, living primitives—the prototypic Other of classical anthropology—had all but disappeared. These two conditions threatened to eliminate the social and political, and therefore the epistemological, bases upon which anthropology rested. Whereas pre-war anthropological difference was articulated on the opposition of civilized colonial Self and primitive colonized Other, the end of the war brought forth a new basis for global difference that was to shape anthropological discourse to a degree comparable to that to which the interwar colonial situation had molded it, although into a form consistent with the new international context.

Whereas the interwar global polarity that structured anthropology consisted of the tension between colonial Self and colonized Other, the major immediate post–World War II context was the East-West tension that came to be known as the Cold War. With the United States and the Soviet Union emerging as 'the winners' of World War II, future history was defined as a struggle between the 'free West,' led by the United States, and the 'Communist East.' Although of global dimensions, the Cold War was focused first in Europe, where the Western powers felt threatened by possible Soviet expansion beyond the terrain the Soviet Union had acquired and held captive in Central Europe behind what Churchill identified in 1946 as the "iron curtain." The Soviet counterpart of this suspicion was the age-old Russian fear of Western incursion. Cold War fears in the United States promoted the Truman Doctrine, which provided immediate economic aid to Greece and Turkey to stave off the 'Communist menace,' and a more general European recovery policy known as the Marshall Plan. The military counterpart of these economic and social programs was the formation in 1949 of the North Atlantic Treaty Organization. These projects were part of a more strategic policy of containment of Soviet power, but they were soon generalized to a global strategy designed to limit Communist hegemony to those areas that had already been 'lost to communism.'[8]

In the late 1940s the Cold War broadened to Asia when Chinese Communists gained control of China in 1949, and it extended to Southeast Asia in the early 1950s with the outbreak of the Korean War. Heavy U.S. military involvement in Korea was an important but unremarked stepping-stone to the subsequent emergence of peasant studies in anthropology, because it was the first major direct confrontation in the mid-twentieth century between U.S. military forces and armies of poor rural conscripts. Prior to being sent to Korea, the previous definitive formative experience of U.S. and other UN forces had been the blitzkrieg and set piece and the amphibious warfare of the European and Pacific theaters of World War II. But in the frozen wastes of North Korea the troops encountered hordes of ragged Chinese foot soldiers who attacked at the signal of tinny bugles, the first human waves often armed only with sticks as if to use up the ammunition of their opponents. The North Korean Army and, even more so, the Chinese Army, which had entered the war, came to be seen as almost endless legions of faceless warriors recruited from vast oriental hinterlands. These new foes were not yet identified as peasants, but Western cold warriors were taking account of them.

After the Korean War, which was a "hot" phase of the Cold War, East-West tensions shifted to Southeast Asia, where the Soviet Union supported insurgent guerrillas in Vietnam, Laos, and Cambodia and the United States was siding with the titular governments of these new nations. Of major political and ideological significance was the massive defeat of the elite of the French military at Dien Bien Phu, Vietnam, in 1954. Similar Cold War tensions also arose in other newly emerging nations of Africa, which were largely wars by proxy between the Eastern and Western superpowers.

The death of Stalin in 1953, subsequent openings between the United States and the Soviet Union, and a changing configuration of the political landscape in Europe all lessened the intensity of the Cold War. Its end more or less coincides with the peaceful resolution of the Cuban Missile Crisis in 1962, when the Soviet Union withdrew nuclear warheads from the island. But by then the U.S. policy of containment had been redirected to the vast new political landscape that had opened up during the Cold War and that was to become known as the Third World, composed mainly of Latin America and the dozens of new nations that emerged in the 1940s and 1950s from the rubble of the colonial world.[9] The stage was now set for the entry of the peasant. Peasants had been given bit parts before in China, Korea, and Indochina and even earlier in the Philippines and Mexico, but new scripts were being written in which they would have central roles.[10]

Global Anthropology: From Cold War to Peasant Wars

Historians of the Cold War see it as having ended in the early 1960s. This moment coincides, however, with the arrival of the first U.S. troops in Vietnam in 1961 to once again confront "little brown people," but ones who this time would defeat them militarily, as they had definitively beaten the French. Vietnam was merely the largest of numerous Third World wars fought within a global context, which Chomsky (1982, 1987) refers to as the New Cold War. Whereas the first Cold War was a direct confrontation between the superpowers, conceived and fought as a war for territories and boundaries that were to be occupied and defended, the New Cold War was this as well, but it was also a struggle for the "hearts and minds" of Third World peoples: They could "go" either capitalist or Communist.[11]

The stakes were high, as was first demonstrated by the Chinese Revolution and later by Algeria, Cuba, Guinea Bissau, Angola, and—most dramatically of all—Vietnam. The terrain of warfare had expanded considerably into ideological grounds. And the principal enemy was a rather novel type as well—the guerrilla. The Vietnam War was a turning point in U.S. military thinking away from an almost exclusive concern with strategic warfare with the Soviet Union and China to low-intensity conflict against rural populations. This thinking was informed more by the principles of guerrilla warfare written by Mao Tse-tung and Ernesto Guevara than by the strategic concepts of Clausewitz.

The appearance on the global stage of the rural guerrilla warrior who assumed a major role in history-making is inconsistent with the fundamental teleology of Western historical vision. The temporal dimension of this master narrative is dualist and linear. The most explicit expression of this structure is the Bible, which lays out a past and future history of all humanity in real time. All major eighteenth- and nineteenth-century Western philosophies of history and anthropology are permutations of the same temporal images; they range from Hegel to the philosophies of the Enlightenment to Marx, Morgan, and Spencer to other modern philosophers of progress (Bury 1920). Anthropology up to the mid-twentieth century had been occupied with the reconstruction of earlier stages of this general history and prehistory, from its earliest 'primitive' beginnings to the present. But in the 1940s and 1950s, anthropology's focus shifted from past to future points of this grand history.

To understand this shift, it is necessary to situate it within its historical context. World War II not only coincides with the end of classical anthropology; it also marks the beginnings of an era in the history of anthropology that is appropriately characterized as *modern*. Central to all discussions of 'the modern' and permutations thereof, such as modernism and modernization, is a nonclassical temporal sensibility that favors the emergent present over past time and forms. Whereas the classical anthropological sensibility placed its Other in a distant primitive (in the sense of early) time and space, the modern anthropological sensibility draws its Other near in time and space and thus upsets classical forms. As in modern art and literature generally, the creative Self becomes fascinated with innovation and emergent novelty. By the time the anthropological classics had been written, the early colonial discourse of 'civilization' versus 'primitive' was permuting into a comparable opposition between 'modern' and 'traditional.'

This new sensibility, like the old, is still informed by unilinear social evolutionism, but interest has shifted from the past to the near future as it emerges from a transitory present. Whereas nineteenth-century unilinear anthropological thinking was concerned with reconstructing the past to demonstrate superior achievements of the West compared with the rest—differences that, coincidentally, justified colonialism—modernist anthropology cast its gaze to the future course of this relationship as the 'modern' West assumed responsibility for 'helping' the 'lesser developed nations' catch up.[12] The key word in the lexicon of this modern anthropology is development. Whereas the project of classical anthropology was to reconstruct the past, developmentalism emerges in modern anthropology as the idiom with which 'the West' struggled for the future. President Truman, in his 1949 inaugural address, sanctioned this sensibility as the official view of history.

> With one conceptual stroke, he created a vision in which all peoples of the globe were moving inexorably along the same track—toward industrial development.
>
> Never mind the respective aspirations of Kikuyus and Sicilians, Filipinos and Peruvians. With Truman's pronouncement, these groups suddenly became "underdeveloped," and the road they were to follow lay clearly before the president's eyes: "Greater production is the key to prosperity and peace."
>
> Nations fell easily into place under Truman's all-encompassing definition of development, with one clearly leading the field: "The United States is pre-eminent among nations in the development of industrial and scientific techniques." The front runners, it was announced, would be generous. They would offer assistance to relieve suffering through "industrial activities" and a "higher standard of living." (Sachs 1990:52)

'Development' thus emerges at mid-century as the distinctly modern criterion for defining difference. There are two generic kinds of societies: developed and underdeveloped. This developmentalism, which emerged in postwar anthropology, was thus a variant discourse of the grand evolutionary master narrative, now focused on the modern period in real, rather than historical, time.[13]

Unlike the generic primitives, which were "peoples without history," Third World peoples began, as noted earlier, to elbow and shoot their way into modern history in rather disconcerting ways in the late 1940s and in the 1950s and 1960s. This liminal, seemingly dangerous Third World that opened up was populated with innumerable ethnic and socioeconomic types, but for anthropology one special type—'the peasant'—became iconic. And thus, the hypothesis that presents itself is that the construction of 'the peasant' was a means to reduce this ambiguity, to control the flux of history and secure these 'peripheral areas' for the West. It is within the greater drama of containment of communism that 'the peasant' was elaborated as part of a general anthropological discourse peculiar to the aftermath of the Cold War. The containment of communism became in large part the containment of masses of rural peoples. And among the U.S. disciplines, the task of identifying, defining, and objectifying these vast threatening populations of this ambiguous Third World fell mainly to anthropology. Chapter 3 explores the growth of anthropological literature qua literature as a strategy of containment that is both a response and a contribution to the more generalized policies for the containment of communism in the Third World.

With the disappearance of 'the primitive,' 'the peasant' increasingly came to typify the generalized Other, but an Other seen not as primitive nor primordial but as 'underdeveloped.' This 'underdeveloped' peasantry thus became an inversion of 'the modern,' a new, objectified and contrasting Other that well served anthropology to reconstitute itself in modernist form. Whereas in classical, past-oriented social evolutionism 'the primitive' was the primary categorical Other, in the subsequent anthropological discourse 'the peasant' becomes a stereotypic Other of comparable saliency in the structure of anthropological thought and practice. This is not to say that the primitive disappears from anthropological writing; indeed, it is retained but mainly in what becomes a highly reflexive interpretive anthropology and to a lesser extent in pure scientific modes, whereas the Third World and its prototypical inhabitant, the 'peasant,' are, as we shall see, foregrounded in anthropology in the applied mode.

Thus, whereas classical anthropology was fascinated with the evolutionary past that had unfolded from 'primitive' to Western 'civilization,' anthropological images of peasant society in large part transformed this past teleology into an eschatological vision of a 'developed' future. And as conceived by liberal North American social science, this future was, of course, to be not only a nonpeasant but also a non-Communist future, as was spelled out fairly explicitly, for example, in W. W. Rostow's *The Stages of Growth: A Non-Communist Manifesto* (1960). Another expression of the same Cold War antipeasant attitudes was Crane Brinton's *The Anatomy of Revolution* (1965). In keeping with the body imagery of the title, Brinton in this book characterizes revolutions as "a kind of fever" and an "incurable cancer" (1965:16–17). If this were true of the English, American, French, and Russian revolutions, it was for Brinton an even more appropriate characterization of Third World variants, which could install a permanent "madness." "This racist and Manichaean conclusion helped qualify Brinton's book as an authentic manifesto of the cold war" (Hunt 1983:123).

The entry of the peasant into world politics was not only politically disruptive, but as a category inserted between the primitive and the civilized it also disrupts the neat binary structuring of classical anthropological thought (see Figure 2.1). The categorical ambiguity of the 'peasant' that challenged the neat dualism of classical anthropology was thus more than just an intellectual or a cognitive discomfort to the discipline, for this categorically disruptive type was also potentially politically disruptive on a global scale. In addition to the proclivity of peasants to "go Communist," peasants differed from 'primitives' in their demographic tendencies. Whereas primitives were disappearing, peasant communities were creating a 'population bomb' that threatened to outstrip the capacity of poor nations to develop. This 'explosive' demographic characteristic of peasants is a figure of speech that resonates with their potential political explosiveness. It is not surprising, therefore, that the intellectual task of containment of peasants as a category within anthropology should coincide with the political, military, demographic, and ideological containment of this subversive type by nation-states threatened by peasant "madness."

Defined as half developed and half underdeveloped, the 'peasant' is thus midway between the polar opposites of primitive and modern and is seen as irrevocably linked to the latter. For example, in Redfield's imagery, the peasants are situated at a midpoint on the folk-urban continuum where they are the recipients of the modern traits of the urban, which, as they are 'accepted,' will transform the traditional out of existence (Redfield 1941).

Whereas the grand evolutionary master narrative of classical anthropology elaborated the evolutionary past, in modernist anthropology fascination shifts to future evolution, spoken of as 'development.' And whereas "students of this era referred to natives [primitives] as 'our contemporary ancestors' and argued that the development of institutions could be worked out by a survey of present-day customs, starting with 'lowest' societies and climbing step by step to the groups 'higher' on the scale" (Hogbin 1958:15, quoted by Jarvie 1964:37), in modernist anthropology the peasant becomes the significant Other of the present and one that will be developed out of existence in the not too distant future. This sense of peasants as having a historic destiny to develop, to modernize, is reflected in the

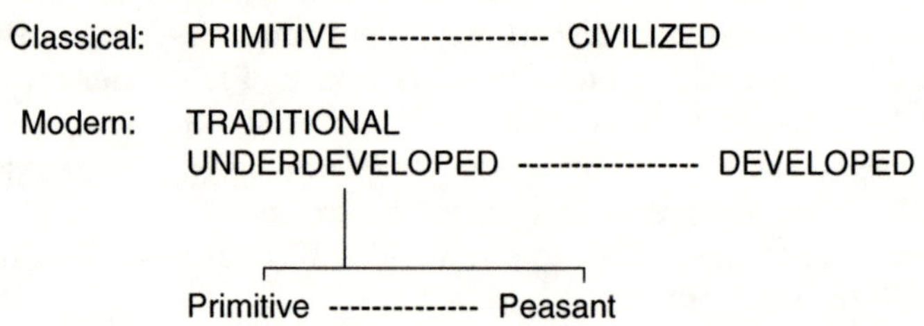

Classical: PRIMITIVE ----------------- CIVILIZED

Modern: TRADITIONAL
         UNDERDEVELOPED ---------------- DEVELOPED

              Primitive ------------- Peasant

Figure 2.1. Classical and Modern Anthropology

titles of numerous postwar monographs such as *A Village That Chose Progress* (Redfield 1950) and *The Waiting Village* (Nelson 1971).

The end of World War II and the beginning of the Cold War also coincided with a major restructuring of the global context in which 'the peasant' as an anthropological type emerged. Prior to this historical moment, rural peoples had been politically and socially situated within national spaces. In other words, the tension between rural subalterns and more powerful types was located within the context of the nation-state or within the colonies of nation-states, such that peasant problems were domestic problems. But by late mid-century, peasant issues had become transnationalized. This shift of concern with peasants from the national to the transnational is apparent, for example, in the international developmental agencies, policies, and programs that emerged in the 1950s and 1960s. Among the most notable of these are the World Bank (International Bank for Reconstruction and Development), which was founded in 1945.

Similarly, the U.S. government developed numerous projects and policies that were ostensibly designed to promote 'development.' In 1961 President Kennedy engineered the formation of the Organization of American States, and he inaugurated the Alliance for Progress less than two years after the Cuban Revolution (Levinson and de Onis 1970). The formation of the Alliance for Progress was a direct response to the success of the Cuban Revolution, which had attracted the attention and admiration of young people throughout the Third World—many of whom formed and joined Guevarist groups that fanned out into the countryside, dedicated to replicating the Cuban Revolution wherever comparable conditions were thought to exist. The Peace Corps was conceived as a countermeasure to these grassroots revolutionary groups, with its volunteers sent mainly to peasant societies. If the Peace Corps was the velvet glove of this policy of providing capitalist alternatives to Cuban- or Chinese-style revolutions, the iron fist included counterinsurgency programs designed and implemented by the Central Intelligence Agency to track down and kill grassroots revolutionaries, including Guevara himself. Such tactics were programs of institutionalized terrorism instigated and implemented as integral to U.S. foreign policy (Chomsky 1988; Herman 1982).

The Rockefeller Foundation had been financing development projects since the early 1900s, but until the end of World War II its programs were motivated primarily by the desire to increase worker productivity not only in the economic spheres in which it was operating but also in the general areas of production on whose economic health the greater economy was dependent. In the 1950s, the Rockefeller Foundation again became heavily involved in developmental programs, but now the motive was not just to promote productivity but to engineer a "Green Revolution" that would forestall a red one (Brown 1976).

It was in this transnational political context that modern peasant studies were born, financed for the most part by the vast resources of U.S. government development agencies and private foundations. In early 1960s the failure of developmentalism was becoming apparent—'the peasants' were not going away. Whereas developmentalism, in both Western and Soviet forms, was designed to eliminate 'the peasants' by developing them out of existence, postdevelopmentalism sought to stabilize them in the countryside. This latter tendency was prompted by rapid 'uncontrolled' urbanization, which became a concern in the late 1960s. The realization that peasants were not going to disappear stimulated yet greater interest in them, which was translated into various research foci in peasant studies—especially a concern with households, migration, fertility, and, as always, the insurrectional potential of peasants, from jacqueries to revolution.

With government and corporate money available to support it, by the early 1960s research on peasant societies had become a growth industry in anthropology, resulting in an increasing number of dissertations, monographs, and articles. Several milestones of this trend are the founding in the early 1970s of the *Journal of Peasant Studies* and the *Peasant Studies Newsletter*. And at about this time peasants start to appear prominently in introductory cultural anthropology textbooks. Silverman (1979:52) traces the emergence of the "geometric growth" of peasant studies by anthropologists to the mid-1950s and notes that "fostered by Western political interests in the rural inhabitants of the Third World and the corresponding availability of research funds, and with the impetus of modernization and development theory, the anthropologists were soon joined by a variety of other disciplines."

The task of development programs and of foreign policy in general was to contain this potentially disruptive type and to develop it out of existence. And given the dense institutional linkages between corporate and government funding agencies and the universities and other institutions housing research projects, it is not surprising that this same basic work of containment would also be carried out in a different modality in social science literature. There thus came together in the 1950s and 1960s a social, political, and intellectual nexus in the United States in which the peasant was reconstructed by anthropology, the discipline that history had assigned the primary responsibility for this task. This anthropological thinking about the peasantry was made of the same fabric from which both U.S. foreign policy for Third World countries and critiques of it were fashioned (see Wakin 1992).

We can summarize this discussion by noting that until World War II, the main tensions within capitalist society were the structural contradiction between labor and capital and the tension among the major capitalist nation-states. Or if this proposition is not accepted, then let us agree that these contradictions were the main tensions in discourses about capitalist society in the period that corresponds to that of classical anthropology (see Classical Anthropology and the Primitive). But by the mid-1970s this master narrative of the developed nations had been displaced by that of the Third World, located in the periphery in which 'the peasant' had upstaged the proletarian as the key critical historical actor. Proletarian revolutions had never occurred or died at birth, but the Mexican, Chinese, Cuban, Vietnamese, Algerian, Angolan, and other twentieth-century revolutions and wars of national liberation were real enough to get everyone's attention. The peasant had clamored into history, or so it seemed. Now, at the end of the period in which they appeared, it is possible to reassess their ontology and to perceive how anthropology imagined them.

The shift in the center of gravity of the global drama of the East-West confrontation from Europe to the Third World was inconsistent with the master narrative in both its capitalist and Marxist versions. Global history-making was supposed to be centered in the developed areas of the world rather than in the colonies and former colonies. Furthermore and more important, this Third World seemed to be making a lateral move into historical spaces that were neither developed nor undeveloped and that were becoming populated with social types that did not fit standard categories, being neither primitive nor modern. Other related trends also cast doubt on the inevitability of modernization, not the least of which was the postwar population explosion that was occurring among these new types. Furthermore, the master narrative of development implied the growth of Western-style democracy, but 'dictatorships' prevailed in most of this Third World.

Thus, just as *the primitive* as an anthropological category was conceived within a particular global historical configuration, so were postwar anthropological images of 'the peasant.' This redirection of the anthropological gaze to the peasant signals a major but largely unremarked moment in the history of anthropology. For in reconstructing 'the peasant,' anthropology in no small measure reconstituted itself by making the peasant the primary form of the Other in this modern period of its history. By investing heavily in 'peasant studies,' anthropology seemed to have assured its bread and butter, for apart from rural sociology—a cousin of both sociology and the agricultural sciences—the field was wide open. Furthermore, 'peasants' and 'peasant society,' as introductory texts reiterate, have been in existence since the beginnings of civilization and have been one of the most populous social types in the modern era. It is no exaggeration to say that the discipline as a fieldwork-based form of natural history was saved from obsolescence by the simultaneous discovery and invention of the peasant.

Later I further examine the social, political, and intellectual fields within which anthropology, as it were, invented the peasant. But first it is useful to understand how 'peasant' as a classificatory category differs from the various types of 'primitives'—hunters and gatherers, tribal peoples, and chiefdoms. As an anthropological construction the peasantry is comparable to these other basic social types, but yet it is structurally different by virtue of its marginal classificatory position midway between the classical polarities (see Figure 2.1). As a classificatory type it is therefore ambiguous, and its appearance thus promotes the autodeconstruction of the dualism of classical and modern anthropology, a tendency that was set in motion by the Malinowskian revolution. But the peasantry was also a disruptive type because it was more than just a third term; it was also a Third World poised historically and politically between the First and Second Worlds. In short, as a social category it is inherently subversive of dualist schemes of modernist thought, be they evolutionary (foretelling the demise of the traditional) or spatial (giving historical priority to metropoles and cities rather than to peripheral peoples).

The turn to peasant society was good for anthropology not only because it opened new peoples and geographic areas to research but also because 'peasants' have been the objects of intense debates within anthropology about their essential nature; indeed, there is less wide disagreement about any other social type—foragers, tribal societies, states, and so on. These debates are caused in part by the inherent ambiguities of 'the peasant' as a type. But the debates over peasants are also more intense because the political stakes are higher: Interpretation of the past, although of great ideological import, is less important than construction of the present and its future.

Notes

1. Instrument calibration is not a perfect analogy with the kind of corrective reading noted here. In calibration of a lens, for example, the task is to focus it correctly, but a corrective reading is, strictly speaking, more analogous to taking into account optical qualities of a lens that distort the image of its object and that cannot be corrected because they are inherent in the structure of the lens itself.

2. A major difference exists between a fully developed anthropology of knowledge of the social sciences and such an anthropology of knowledge of the natural sciences because of the basic difference in their subject matters, in that nature is potentially a neutral and final arbiter in disputes among contending human ideas seeking to represent it, but such is not the case with human sociocultural phenomena. For example, the world is either round or it is not. In contrast to this potential for a more or less empirical anchoring, objects of social scientific knowledge are typically of the same phenomenal order as the 'theories,' 'models,' or other such human constructs that presume to explain them. The primary work of natural science is to form constructs of natural phenomena, whereas that of the social sciences is also to devise constructs of constructs.

3. On Self, Other, and Relationship as universal worldview categories, see Kearney (1984).

4. This periodization of representation corresponds to Jameson's (1991) division of history into three cultural stages, namely, realism, modernism, and postmodernism. My first two periods are comparable to Jameson's first period.

5. I return to this theme of the excluded middle as basic to distinction and containment. Anthropology is in a certain state of crisis because this no-man's land is filling up with refugees, migrant workers, and other ambiguous types that crowd these marginal areas, shifting the centers of anthropological gravity from core and periphery—that is, from Self and Other—to the border areas between them (see Kearney 1991).

6. Jarvie represents the last dying gasps of early classical anthropology, and consistent with this paradigm he makes no mention of peasants as a type.

7. The key text here is Gordon (1992); see also Solway and Lee (1990), Wilmsen (1989), and Wilmsem and Denbow (1990). See also Gupta and Ferguson (1992).

8. The policy of containment was first advanced by George F. Kennan (1947) as a long-term strategy to attain either the disintegration of the Soviet Union or at least a "mellowing" of Soviet power.

9. "I have often been credited with inventing the Third World. In fact, the honour goes to the French demographer, Alfred Sauvy, who first used the term in an article in the newspaper, *L'Observateur,* on 14 August 1952, entitled 'Trois Mondes, Une Planète.' That it arose in France, and not the Third World itself, may seem paradoxical. It was a product of the Cold War, the epoch in which two superpowers tried to dominate the entire globe. The claim, by each of them, that they alone represented the interests of humanity as a whole, was, however, widely rejected by people who resisted being sucked into either 'camp'"(Worsely 1990:83).

10. The first major military-political confrontation between the United States and a 'peasant' army took place in the Philippines in the aftermath of the Spanish-American War, although the Filipino guerrillas who opposed annexation by the United States were depicted more as 'primitives' than as peasants.

11. The elusive and pervasive presence of Vietnamese guerrilla forces resulted in a restructuring of the spatiality of modern warfare, which had been a war of battlefronts and of territory lost and gained. Unable to definitely win and occupy territory, U.S. military commanders instituted "body counts" as indicators of the tides of battle. Comparable deterritorializations of space and identity are examined in Chapter 4.

12. My periodization of classical and modern anthropology differs from Manganaro's (1990) identification of "modernist" anthropology as a variant of modernist literature in general, which came into being around the turn of the century. Although theories of modernist literature situate it within global historical conditions such as colonialism that predispose modernist authors to react against, for example, realism, such sociohistorical contextualization is too coarse-grained for our concerns herein with the sociohistorical context of anthropological writing about peasants, which for the most part appeared after World War II. In contrast, the critical concern with modernist anthropological literature is conceived almost exclusively in terms of the Primitive as the ethnographic Other. For example, in Manganaro's edited volume, twenty-two entries in the index refer to 'primitives,' whereas there are none for 'peasant.' The 'primitive' is thus greatly reified as the prototypic Other of the anthropological Self, even as the 'peasant' has now become the primary de facto ethnographic Other. Thus, rather than enter the debates concerning modernist anthropology, framed as it is within a different intellectual space, I shall use *modern* to signal a more recent and contemporary moment in anthropological writing.

13. On developmentalism as a discourse, see also Escobar (1991, 1992), Esteva (1992), and Ferguson (1990). Ferguson and Escobar do not attend to the Cold War origins or the 'peasant' dimensions of developmentalism but instead seem to attribute it mainly to the perverse working of global capitalism in general.

Chapter 3

Peasants and the Antinomies of the Modern Nation-State

Modern images of the peasant have historically been constructed as part of the architecture of the nation-states with which they have been identified. To the great degree that the nation-state is structured by dualist images of time and space, so too is official thinking about the peasantry structured and congealed within these forms that inform ideas about social types.

Modernist ideas and projects provoked romantic intellectual and political reactions (Chapter 4), but until recently the basic theme concerning nations with large peasantries has been national development, a process seen as synonymous with the elimination of the peasantries of these 'developing' nations. Modernization theory and developmentalism in general are twentieth-century permutations of nineteenth-century unilinear social evolutionism. The modernist construction of the peasantry in both its bourgeois and Leninist versions came into crisis in the 1960s and 1970s. This crisis was provoked by the end of developmentalism, which provided conditions for renewed romantic sensibilities among peasantologists in the 1980s and 1990s. Both modernist and romantic peasantologies are kinds of essentialisms projected onto the 'peasants,' constructed as strategies of containment that buttress other, often more apparent forms of control and exploitation effected by the power differences so formed.

Discourses on 'the peasantry' are overwhelmingly binary and are structured on what are for the most part implicit worldview assumptions and images. These images and assumptions are variants of certain universals—Self, Other, Time, Space, Causality—of any worldview and are therefore dimensions upon which an anthropological Self constructs images of the 'peasant' Other in contrast to its Self. And as we will see, the form given to these images and assumptions constitutes a sixth kind of assumption that is about the Relationship presumed to exist between this anthropological Self and its peasant Other. These six kinds of assumptions are all logico-structurally interrelated among themselves (Kearney 1984).

My working assumption is that reconceptualization of the peasantry requires a dismantling of these binary oppositions, especially the spatial and temporal. But such reconceptualization, if it is to be anthropological, must situate itself and the subject of its project within their respective social contexts, which in this case I take to be the nation-state in the present historical moment that I characterize as transnational, postdevelopmental, and global.

The Deep Structure of the Modern Nation-State and Its Anthropology

If indeed, as this book argues, anthropological theory is at a historical juncture, understanding its new emergent dimensions requires identification of those former reigning ones that have lost saliency, which I have characterized as *modern.* This exercise may seem far afield of our main concern, but since anthropological concepts of 'the peasant' were constructed within that different intellectual environment, it is directly relevant to reconceptualization. This book is not, however, the place to elaborate a major study of the structure of modern anthropology, and so this discussion will be telegraphic. The thesis in brief is that modern anthropology is structured in a way that is actually rather archaic, the main feature of which is a dualism that is now apparent in a historic moment in which it is deconstructing, opening up the possibility of a nondualist practical anthropology.

Elsewhere I have argued that dispositions toward classificatory dualisms are predicated on culturally specific notions of the Self as discontinuous with the Other. Self and Other are the axis of any worldview, but the Relationship between them is variable (Kearney 1984:68–72, 150–152). Space is the most cognitively primitive and concrete of all the worldview universals (see Kearney 1984). The spatial opposition of rural versus urban is a physically experienced dimension that serves as a basis for the naturalization of the more abstract temporal opposition of early versus contemporary. Thus, rural is to urban as traditional is to modern.

A center that contrasts with frontiers, colonies, and hinterlands is inherent in all dualist social geographies. The peripheral spaces are invariably marked with respect to the center and are defined as deficient in that which makes the center normal, dynamic, or more powerful because it has concentrated in it that which is lacking in the periphery. This distinction is especially potent and underlies all other anthropological distinctions made between peasant and nonpeasant. Indeed, peasant essentialism is constructed in large part on such a binary opposition, construed as the difference between 'the country and the city.'

This chapter reviews anthropological theories of development that seek to define 'underdeveloped' peripheral peasant societies. I take this literature as literary genres that reflect, in highly refracted forms, not only the peasant societies they depict but also the relationships between the authorial Selves and the peasant

Others about which they write. The social structuring of this literature is not unlike that of fictional genres of colonial literature, contextualized in what Fanon called a manichean social organization: Fanon's definition of colonial society . . . is by no means exaggerated. In fact, the colonial mentality is dominated by a manichean allegory of white and black, good and evil, salvation and damnation, civilization and savagery, superiority and inferiority, intelligence and emotion, self and other, subject and object" (JanMohamed 1983:4).

In *Manichean Aesthetics* JanMohamed (1983) revealed how colonial fiction, in particular novels, reflects this oppositional structure. What I propose herein is that this general social structuring of the colonial situation has had a comparable influence on other literary genres, the case in point being writings about development and underdevelopment of colonial and neocolonial settings, as well as anthropological depictions of peasants. Furthermore, as is apparent from what I discussed earlier, such anthropological literature, like its fictional counterparts, participates in the construction of the social relations it reflects.

Thus, when I speak of modern anthropology as having essentially an archaic structure, I mean the anthropological Self is at the spatial and temporal center of its seemingly natural universe, within which the peripheries, whether countryside or colony, are inhabited by ethnographic Others. This 'modern' anthropological worldview is structured not unlike that of early Greek ideas about the relationship between the Greek city and surrounding non-Greek peoples.

> According to the Greek concept, the world is situated within a framework both temporal and spatial; its center is always normal existence, the city or country lived in, *here and now*. Farther back in time, farther back in space, the organized order of here and now disappears. In the dimension of time, there were times when humanity was ignorant of the civilized forms of existence, ignorant of fire, the gift of Prometheus, and of wheat, the gift of Triptolemus. Men lived in caves. . . . It should be added that from another point of view, this fabulous past can take on the aspects of a vanished and regretted golden age.
>
> We find the same stages in the dimension of space, where, in proportion to our distance from the organized world of society, we are led back to nonorder, to spatial chaos. In the first place there were the countries situated on the edge of the Greek world, barbarous countries with strange and paradoxical customs; then came imaginary countries with imaginary people, monsters and cannibals like the Lestrigons or the Cyclops; of course, there were also the Isles of the Blessed where, in a precise coincidence of time and space, rules Kronos, the god of the golden age; beyond that was the outermost edge of the cosmos, the Okeanos itself, besides, in a temporal sense, the origin of things. Beyond the Okeanos, outside the cosmos, there was only the world—or rather, the antiworld—of nonexistence, the realm of the dead. In the middle of these concentric circles of time and space, the normal world finds itself: the normal world, founded on the laws of Zeus, the world of human values, social norms, good and evil, joy and suffering—in short, reality. (Brelich 1966:293–301)

This archaic geography and mythohistory is consistent with its corresponding intellectualized geocentric cosmology-astronomy (Kearney 1984:124–130). As it appears in the Semitic religions, especially Christianity, this mythic time becomes historical and teleological time in the sense that creation occurred at a distinct moment, followed by a number of other events aligned on a continuum that includes contemporary human history and that will culminate in the second coming, the apocalypse, and the eventual end of history. Modern astronomy and physics have discarded this older vision of a geocentric universe and linear time, but it continues to inform most social science—just as, indeed, in our daily lives and in our ordinary speech we in effect inhabit a flat world that like other commonsensical things, such as 'peasants,' seems so natural and obvious. The social and political context that maintained this older vision of society into the modern period also nurtured the emergence of the modern nation-state.

Chapter 2 reviewed the modernist vision of history as the 'development of nations.' The first phase in this narrative was the construction of the modern Western nation-states out of the remnants of the principalities and kingdoms of the seventeenth and eighteenth centuries. In France, the primary task of consciously envisioning this new social form fell to those post-Enlightenment intellectuals, mostly of petty bourgeois extraction, known as positivists who laid the basis for the systematic study of modern society. Auguste Comte (1798–1857), who founded positivism and coined the term *sociology,* was a social reformer who sought to put empirical knowledge to use in promoting conditions in which individuals and nations could live in maximum harmony and material progress.

Comte and the other positivists were, in a word, early developmentalists, although they are usually referred to as social evolutionists. Social evolutionism and positivism constituted a coherent intellectual tradition that began to be officially institutionalized in the nineteenth century in the administrative and educational apparatus of the emergent modern state, in a dialectical relationship in which even as positivism articulated that new social form, it itself was brought to life by that form. In other words, positivism as invented by Comte was a modern version of earlier ideas of progress repackaged for consumption by a vigorous new bourgeoisie that was busy constructing the political and social forms of nineteenth-century capitalism.

In England, the counterpart of continental positivism was found in a social evolutionism and British empiricism, expressed, for example, in the works of Herbert Spencer (1820–1903), who was largely responsible for founding sociology as a discipline in England—in large part by grafting it onto the prestige of evolutionary biology. As in France, English social science was invented and institutionalized within and in the service of a young capitalist nation-state by intellectuals who manufactured a theory of society that was instrumental in the creation of the society they imagined. In France and especially in England, the vision of the modern nation-state was created out of tension with the social difference the nation-state had to devour in order to prevail.[1] And in both France and England, this process was naturalized as 'progress' (Bury 1920) and 'development' that were inherent in human society and indeed, as Spencer argued, inherent in nature. Especially in England, this social evolutionism explained the inevitability and desirability of the development of primitive forms into the modern as exemplified in metropolitan British society. And indeed, it was the grand civilizing and modernizing project of British colonialism to hasten this global trend whereby undeveloped and peripheral peoples would be remade in the image of the center.

Among other notable precursors of modernization theory were Durkheim, Maine, and Morgan, whose sociological theories were also permutations of modernist dualist thinking. They are all aptly characterized as 'official' in that their interpretations of both society and historical processes were in the positivist tradition of putting social theory at the service of the modern emergent bourgeois state. Each of their sociologies unconsciously reflects the social milieu in which they lived, just as their sociologies in turn become official definitions of the modern identity it is the task of the modern nation-state to promote.

Central to all of these sociologies is the contrasting of 'modern' persons, social relations, culture, and personalities with those of 'traditional' society, which it is the task of the nation-state to domesticate in what is concieved as an inevitable socioevolutionary process. Although he was not in the service of the state, Marx, too, built his edifice on a dualist distinction between noncapitalist and capitalist society. A basic difference between them is the predominance of use value in the former and exchange value in the latter, a distinction similar to that Polyani (1944) made between traditional economic systems based on reciprocity or redistribution versus modern economies based on exchange relations mediated by markets. These and other dual models, discussed later, are indicated in Figure 3.1.

Let us examine modern persons and their social relations as defined by these theories. A key notion here is the emergence of the individual from the traditional society. For Henry Maine (1877), who examined the transformation in law that occurred during the great transition, traditional society is governed by social relations based on the 'status' of persons as members of collective social units. But in

Author	Traditional (marked)	Modern (unmarked)
Maine	Status	Contract
Morgan	Civitas	Societas
Marx	Precapitalist	Capitalist
Tönnies	Gemeinschaft	Gesellschaft
Durkheim	Mechanical Solidarity	Organic Solidarity
Spengler	The West	(The Rest)
Park	Country	City
Wirth	Rural	Urban
Polyani	Reciprocity	Market Exchange
Redfield	Folk	Urban
McClellan	Need for Achievement Absent	Need for Achievement Present
Bachofen	Pre-logical	Logical

Figure 3.1. Modernist Models of Tradition Versus Modernity

modern society, this socialized identity gives way to law based on 'contracts' among individuals who have been liberated from the more primitive collective social forms.[2] Similar here is Morgan's (1877) distinction between *societas* and *civitas*. Twentieth-century variants of this dichotomy also abound, such as Polyani's (1944) assertion that "the great transformation" took place with the emergence of market exchange over reciprocity and redistribution.

Central here are the ways in which the state essentializes the peasant not only cognitively but also in practice and thus constitutes that which it has constructed. By means of its "technologies of power," especially its statistics (etymologically, the science of the state) the state constructs its official subjects (Cohn and Dirks 1988).[3] Legal categories are inscribed in census types and other forms of registration. These official categories also figure in debates and wars over land reform and in the categories by which land reform is implemented.

The categories of enumeration have histories; they have origins in the official documents and corresponding folk categories of the past. In Europe and Latin America, these official modern categories have antecedents in feudal rural class structure and were reflected in popular and legal language. Nagengast, for example, shows how official Polish census categories specifying rural social types were changed to construct a desired rural society and national identity: "In the very categories it devised and the constitution of those categories, the seemingly neutral and purely administrative census defined and delineated social identity" (Nagengast 1991:58; see also Hakim 1980).

The most dramatic case in history of official designation of a nominal peasantry was the Chinese government's classification in 1958 of 800 million people as a hereditary peasant caste referred to as "rural personnel," in contrast to a simultaneously created caste of around 200 million "urban personnel" (Potter and Potter 1990:296–312). "This system shapes the lives . . . of the 800 million members of the largest meaningful category in the study of social structure—the peasants of China" (Potter and Potter 1990:312). Potter and Potter note that this system of social classification is

> Based on arbitrary social and cultural definitions, rather than on rational economic considerations. There is no reason to suppose that peasant forms of organization and payment have any particular superiority over urban forms of organization and payment in facilitating agricultural production. In any case, approximately two-thirds of the income of Zengbu brigade is from local-level industrial enterprises, and only one-third from agriculture. Although the work done by peasants in these rural enterprises is similar in all essentials to the work done in urban factories by people classified as workers, the people working in such enterprises retain their social classification as peasants. (Potter and Potter 1990:299)[4]

In a like mode, Durkheim draws a contrast between the "mechanical solidarity" of tribal societies in which social units such as clans are the primary social units, each one interchangeable with the others, and the more complex and differentiated "organic solidarity" of modern society. That the former kind of solidarity is predicated on a notion of "the sacred" whereas the latter is informed by "profane" knowledge—namely, science—is consistent with positivist ideas of the modern being based on "scientific" knowledge, which comes to replace "religion." Durkheim was explicit that his sociology was itself part of this process of the formation of modern society out of the detritus of the traditional. It was, in other words, a sociology that described and made more concretely conscious a vision of the society the French bourgeoisie, as the class that most controlled the state—including education—had brought into being and was perfecting. Durkheim's sociology is aptly characterized as 'official' in that it expresses this social form it is the task of the nation-state to develop and manage even as it informs the thinking of those bureaucrats, politicians, and educators who serve to perpetuate the nation-state. And thus, the most important social function of this functionalist social theory is to naturalize the type of society it theorizes and that sustains the theorists that imagine it.

A fundamental contradiction the nation-state must resolve is to entertain and perpetuate national solidarity while also reproducing inequality among co-nationalists. In other words, once bourgeois social science and philosophy have constructed the impersonal, universal individual, their next task is to devise methods of studying and explaining individual differences—that is, inequality. This project of fusing national cultural unity with social inequality was first consolidated by the liberal philosophy and economics, which laid out the basic characteristics of "the rational individual." This creature is a choice-making, self-gratifying, maximizing actor. The genealogy of this type runs from Locke and the other social contract theorists of the state through Adam Smith and Jeremey Bentham to its most elaborate and explicit conceptualization in the neoclassic economists.

Space does not allow a review of the permutations of this basic dualist model of "individual" human differences. But most of these theories assume, in one way or another, that there are two basic kinds of thinking, one of which is more developed than the other. Here we have debates over rationality itself—who has it and who does not have it (Horton 1993). Then there are widespread assumptions in education theory about a fundamental difference between "formal" and "informal" education, with the latter a characteristic of "unschooled" individuals (Lave and Wenger 1991). And similar in structure and ideological import is McClellan's proposition that individuals and indeed entire societies can be classified into those that have a "need for achievement" versus those that do not (McClelland 1961).

In all of these dualist theories of individual differences, the marked form is defined as lacking some quality that is present in those individuals who are fully developed. Similarly, when these schemes are applied cross-culturally, the 'underdeveloped' society is defined as lacking the qualities present in those nations that have 'developed' to higher stages along the continuum in question.

The basic imagery of modernist time, like that of biblical time, is unilinear and continuous, just as spatial differences between center and periphery are gradients. But it is the task of categorical thinking to impose sharp distinctions, abrupt boundaries on these continua. The task of constructing these distinctions and boundaries is assumed by the state, and the project takes the form of nation building. Boundary work is fundamental to official social theories in the service of the nation-state. The defining feature of the modern nation-state is the either-or quality of the membership it imposes on its citizens. You either are or are not a citizen. Clearly, all types of society have definitions of members versus nonmembers, but the modern nation-state is notable among social types in imposing ideas of absolute, either-or identity on often disparate and dispersed social types within its boundaries.

This boundary work is the intellectual counterpart of those government agencies in charge of granting visas, maintaining national borders, and otherwise demarcating the identities of those who are members of the nation-state from those who are not. The basic task of this work is to naturalize distinctions that have little or no basis in nature. In antagonistic relations among modern nation-states, this is a mutually self-reinforcing process, but the construction of distinctions between the colonial or imperial nation-state and its dependencies and internal colonies has different needs and dynamics. And it is here that the socioevolutionary assumptions are invoked to explain and legitimize such relationships.

Later I examine a prototypic case (Mexico) in which this social evolutionary vision has informed images of national policies directed at the peasantry. But for the moment let us return to its development in anthropology. In anthropology the basic cognitive and ideological armature upon which the main images of 'the peasant' were constructed is the rural/early-urban/modern opposition noted earlier.[5] Later I discuss modernist variants of these images, but for the moment it is necessary to explore this underlying oppositional spatio-temporal structure. For it is here in the bedrock of worldview, rather than in the level of comparative ethnography, of surface detail, that a critical reconceptualization must be made. The basic thesis is that such critical work is now possible because contemporary history is effecting a deconstruction of this structuring that has informed images of the peasant and that, although decaying, still persists in contemporary peasantology as containment. Looking back at the general context of the Cold War, left and right variants of this deeply structured modernist view of history and the place of peasants in it are now discernible.

Right-Wing Modernism

As noted earlier, nineteenth-century social evolutionism, as inspired by liberal political philosophy and positivist social science, was part of nationalist projects led by liberal bourgeoisies who were fighting against conservatives for control of the direction of national development. In contrast, twentieth-century developmentalism, which in the 1950s and 1960s came to be known as modernization theory, was promoted in large part by capitalist states and procapitalist institutions within the context of the East-West struggle in which Communists occupied the slot previously filled by nineteenth-century conservatives.

The relocation of East-West tensions to the Third World after World War II was inconsistent with the modernist master narrative of history, which put Europe and

North America at the center of global history. But in the 1950s and 1960s it was still widely assumed that with appropriate intervention the peripheral areas could be made to conform to the general plan. The concept of *development* was already in place in postwar Europe and was adapted to what at first were called the under-developed countries. The main target of modernization theory was all that was "backward" and "traditional." Development was just a question of helping the "lesser developed" nations catch up from a historical "lag" they had experienced. The primary task of applied anthropology informed by modernization theory was to boost the potential for development inherent in all societies and realized when linked to the engine of capitalism and freedom of the individual—presuming, of course, it was not derailed by Communist subversion.

Subsequent forms of developmentalism recognized the resistance of such communities to develop and devised corresponding schemes to overcome the inertia of their traditional cultures. Some intervention in the form of developmental programs—as, for example, technical assistance, investment, or missionizing—was necessary. These interventions of developmentalism were bourgeois counterparts to the Communist concept of the necessity of a vanguard party to offset the hegemony of the dominant ideology and culture that cause the inertia of the working class. The crisis for Communist thinking was that revolutions did not occur where they were supposed to. For bourgeois thought, the counterpart intellectual crisis was that capitalist development, more often than not, did not "take off" in the Third World and therefore presumably needed intervention from the 'already developed nations.'[6]

All recent and current central theoretical debates and problems associated with the peasant are some permutation of developmentalism. Indeed, the peasant was the main target of developmentalism. The three main pillars upon which modernization theory was built were Weberian-Parsonian sociology, neoclassic economics, and Redfieldian anthropology. Here I deal mainly with the anthropological sources.[7]

Redfield's Peasants

The name most associated with the turn toward peasant studies in U.S. anthropology is Robert Redfield (1897–1958). Redfield's work is paradigmatic of modernist ideas about peasants; thus, examination of his ideas revels basic assumptions of this broader intellectual current. Indeed, his work is the single most coherent expression of modernization theory in anthropology.

Redfield's ideas about rural society and its "development" were strongly shaped by ideas associated with the urban sociologists at the University of Chicago, especially Redfield's father-in-law, Robert Park, who theorized and studied the dynamics of city life as they contrasted with rural sociology and in terms of relations between urban and rural life.[8] As Redfield himself and many others have pointed out, these ideas were prefigured in Tönnies's (1912) distinction between Gemeinschaft and Gesellschaft types of communities; the first is a small, face-to-face town or village with a minimum of social differentiation, whereas the latter is the larger, impersonal city. This dualism, which Redfield and Tönnies accepted as a natural distinction, is a permutation of the asymmetric dualist structuring of modernist spatial and temporal assumptions.

Redfield's study of the rural Mexican town Tepoztlán is generally credited as the first fieldwork-based ethnography of a peasant community written by a U.S. anthropologist (Redfield 1930; cf. Lewis 1951, and Lomnitz-Adler 1982). Redfield returned to Mexico in the 1930s to investigate how communities like Tepoztlán figure in contemporary history (Redfield and Villa Rojas 1934). All of the essential features of official dualist thinking noted here are brought together and find their most explicit and comprehensive expression in his *The Folk Culture of Yucatan* (Redfield 1941). Several years later, Redfield consolidated his thinking about non-modern communities in the delineation of "the folk society" (Redfield 1947). This ideal type is based on a distillation of the basic dualist oppositions between modern and urban and traditional and rural spelled out by Tönnies, Maine, Durkheim, Spengler, Park, Wirth, and others, as nuanced by Redfield's own fieldwork in Mexico.

The primary images informing this study and theory of modernization are spatial ones in which the modern city is contrasted with a rural periphery. History, defined as modernization, is a progressive transformation of the rural hinterlands into social and cultural forms that constitute the modern city. This transformation occurs as traits of the modern city diffuse outward into the countryside. Just as the positivists of the Enlightenment were concerned with the incorporation of difference into the culture, society, and economy of the nation, so does Redfield see this diffusion in terms of the replacement of traditional culture and social types by modern national counterparts. Thus, the spatial dualism becomes the armature for a unilinear image of time in which history is presumed to be the growth and spread of the modern nation-state into the traditional hinterland, transforming it in its own image. The periphery is 'out there' spatially and 'back there' in time. It is passive, waiting, as it were, to be discovered and awakened.

Redfield's images of peripheral areas are homologous to the images underlying the concept of *terra nullius,* which is 'discovered' and occupied by explorers in the service of states. But unlike the distant lands 'discovered' at the beginnings of the colonial period, Redfield's traditional societies are linked to modern urban centers by the outward flow of traits and forces of modernity. Redfield's (1941:xv) ideas about "this line of contrast" later became immortalized as the "folk-urban continuum" (Miner 1952). Within this array of community types, however, one was singled out and given special attention. More or less midway along this continuum, which runs from tribal society to modern urban society, lies the village of Chan Kom (Redfield and Villa Rojas 1934), which is the same type of "little community" as Tepoztlán (Redfield 1956).

The folk-urban continuum became paradigmatic for subsequent thinking about the countryside and its history as it took form in modernization theory. In this vision of history, the periphery is inexorably transformed into the same forms as the center. Peripheral peoples resist this inevitable march of progress into the countryside, mainly because of the inertia of 'traditional' culture and their ignorance of benefits to be gained from modern society, culture, and technology. 'Individuals' disposed to 'innovate' are often fettered by the communal bonds that obligate them to divert personal resources away from entrepreneurial activities. But in this teleological vision of history, the modern will eventually remake the premodern in its own image. In this historical process, Redfield identifies three major kinds of change: (1) less "organization of the customary way of life," that is, more "disorganization";[9] (2) more "individualization" of behavior; and (3) more "secularization" (Redfield 1941).

As for the resistance of peripheral peoples to the modern, Redfield says, "The people of Tusik [the indigenous 'primitive' community at the extreme folk end of the continuum] not only are more independent of the city economically but are hostile to the national government and seek to keep free of the city man and his ways" (1941:xv). This assumption underlies the prevalent conception of the role of applied anthropology as facilitating the incorporation of peripheral peoples into the orbit of the nation-state. In this regard, Redfield's theory was consistent with the Mexican nationalist project developed to acculturate indigenous peoples and incorporate them into the society and economy of the nation. In the long run, Redfield sees this transformation as a "historic process whereby two ethnically separate societies (the one Spanish and the other Indian) have moved toward the formation of a single society, composed of classes, in which the original racial and cultural differences disappear" (1941:xvi).

In 1948 Kroeber, who no doubt had read Redfield, made a deconstructive move against categorical anthropological theory, based as it is on a distinction between different kinds of 'primitive' versus 'civilized,' when he offered his often quoted definition of peasants as "part-societies and part-cultures" (1948:284). In doing so, Kroeber in effect characterized peasants as a marginal type, caught somewhere halfway between the anthropological prototypes. But this anthropological perception of marginality was subsequently suppressed as 'the peasant' was redefined as 'traditional,' the opposite of 'modern.' The potentially disruptive marginality of the peasant was thus contained by construing it as a passive category in polar contrast with the dynamic modern. The peasant thus became a prototypic Other of anthropology.

Positivists and Peasants in Mexico

A number of modern and 'modernizing' states could be examined to demonstrate the policies devised to identify and domesticate rural difference as an integral part of the nation-building project. But because of limitations of space, I shall look at one prime example. The last century and a half of official state policy for the development of Mexico provides a paradigmatic case of structural tensions and contradictions that so often underlie such projects and that rather than eliminating 'peasants' tend to recreate and perpetuate them.

Unlike the situation in England and France, where history in the early nineteenth century was on the side of the rising bourgeoisie, Mexican liberals were opposed by a large, entrenched, conservative landed gentry disposed to noncapitalist use of its land. Further anchoring Mexican society in a stagnant, backward rural economy were vast holdings of the Catholic Church, which were operated in the same quasi-feudal manner as those of the rural gentry. And extensive peasant lands were locked up in communal ownership and dedicated to subsistence production. Mexican liberals, personified by Benito Juárez, looked to the small capitalist farmers of the United States as the ideal rural type upon which to build a modern nation-state. To promote this vision and to stimulate the progressive power of capitalist relations in general, they became highly enamored of French positivism, British empiricism, and social evolutionary theory. Indeed, Mexican liberal political and intellectual leaders of this period became known as "the positivists" (Zea 1978).

For these Mexican positivists, Mexico's development depended upon unlocking the countryside to the dynamic power of capitalist market forces, the primary requisite for which was the conversion of communal and entailed lands into private property exchangeable in real estate markets. It was to this end that they enacted the reform constitution of 1857, which by fiat privatized all lands not held by the state.

In the subsequent half century, the miracle of the marketplace, amply supported by governmental positivist policymakers—dubbed *los científicos* (the scientists)—did indeed transform the rural society and land tenure of Mexico. But instead of creating a class of small and medium-sized capitalist farmers, it dispossessed the peasantry and reduced most of it to conditions of peonage, dependent on renewed and expanded feudal-like haciendas. With about 98 percent of all rural land held by 1 to 2 percent of the national population, Mexican land tenure at the beginning of the twentieth century was one of the most skewed in the world.

These, then, were the conditions in which the first major peasant revolution of the twentieth century erupted in 1910. The neoevolutionary project of the Mexican positivist liberals, which had promised to modernize Mexico's poor "backward" peasants out of existence, instead promoted their proliferation and political significance. From the 1920s through the 1950s, the Mexican state continued to use land reform to develop the countryside, although in a rather contradictory way. On the one hand, it converted millions of acres of formerly private land into collectives held by peasants who petitioned for such *ejidos,* as they came to be called. Similarly, communal tenure was restored to indigenous communities that had lost land to haciendas.

This reconstitution of a previously dispossessed peasantry was intended primarily as a stopgap measure to buy time while the second part of the state's development policy was put into place. Basically, this policy was a mid-twentieth-century variant of the nineteenth-century positivist vision of promoting a dynamic capitalist agriculture that would displace noncapitalist producers and provide an agricultural base for the national economy, which in turn would support urbanization and industrial growth. To this end the Mexican government, in association with the Rockefeller Foundation and multinational corporations, invested heavily in plant breeding and rural infrastructure—irrigation projects, electrification, agricultural extension, and the like—designed to support large-scale corporate agriculture. This strategy soon became known as the Green Revolution. The *ejidos* and communes were relatively neglected by this policy with the argument that they would become superfluous once private commercial agriculture "took off."

But by the early 1970s it was apparent that this scenario had not come about. Through the 1960s and 1970s, population in the rural subsistence sector grew at annual rates reaching 3.4 percent, at which doubling occurs in twenty years. Rather than being absorbed into commercial agriculture and the urban middle class, this rural population explosion resulted in increased rural and urban poverty. Just as the original modernization scheme of the positivists had backfired, so did that of these neopositivists (Reyes Osorio et al. 1974). Although in rural Mexico in the 1970s a number of groups were dedicated to armed revolutionary struggle, a second revolution did not occur. But nevertheless, considerable effort was expended to contain campesino agitation and armed uprisings.

In retrospect, it is apparent that Mexican national developmental plans of the 1950s through the mid-1980s were driven more by the logic of capital accumulation than by the needs of the rural poor who are lumped together as campesinos, a term of containment rather than a useful analytic category. The failure of right-wing programs to develop 'peasant' communities in this period gave renewed stimulus to left-wing theory.

Left-Wing Modernism

In the previous section I discussed mainly politically right-leaning ideas of development. A deep current of left views is based on similar worldview assumptions of unilinear evolutionism that have led to comparable ideas and policies toward peasants. Marxist theory of history is based on the same assumptions about space and time as Redfieldian theory and modernization theory in general but with some important secondary differences. For one, Marx does not talk about 'modernization' in the abstract but instead speaks of capitalist society and culture, which he sees as progressive in the short run because of its power to transform the productive capacity of human society and thus create economic conditions for general improvement in the quality of life of humanity. But to do this it must destroy precapitalist economies and their societies. Such was the history of England and Western Europe, which was replicated in other areas by means of colonialism and imperialism that would bring non-Western societies into relationships with capitalist economies.

The causes for the emergence of capitalism out of feudal society in Europe have been hotly debated by twentieth-century Marxist scholars, since an understanding of that great transition was assumed to shed light on the development of capitalism in the modern era. Peasants do not figure as prominently in the transition debate as they do in the so-called agrarian question, which is a left-wing counterpart of bourgeois rural developmentalism/modernization. The earlier prominence of 'peasants' in the agrarian question, as compared to their later appearance in modernization theory and cultural anthropology, owes to preoccupations in Marxist theory with class theory and the class identity of social types. For Marxists, peasants are a doubly ambiguous category, first with respect to their actual class status and its historical destiny—disappearance or transformation—sharing as they do aspects of proletarians, small farmers, and petty bourgeoisie types, and second with respect to the subjective political dispositions derived from their objective social identity.

Debate on the agrarian question in European Marxism opened with Marx's (1963 [1852]) *The Eighteenth Brumaire of Louis Bonaparte* and was carried forward in Kautsky's (1988 [1899]) *The Agrarian Question*. The basic issue is the nature of the peasantry and its role in history. In the nineteenth century, intellectuals and activists who saw peasants as playing a progressive role in history were a minority. They were opposed by proletarianists who saw the individual nature of peasant production as disposing them toward conservative political tendencies, in contrast to the industrial proletariat. Indeed, from this perspective, development requires the dissolution of peasant society.

Lenin's model is the prime example of such left-wing modernist analysis of the peasantry, which sees it as 'developing' itself—as it were, out of existence—by becoming differentiated into capitalist farmers and rural and urban workers. The basic structural dynamics of this model are little different from the teleology of 'the sociology of development.' Thus, for example, Lenin, in *Marxism and Revisionism: The Heritage We Renounce* (1975 [1898]) and *The Development of Capitalism in Russia* (1956 [1899]), saw the large peasantry as the key history-making rural class fraction.[10] These polemical tracts were part of intense debates on the left, and doubtlessly 'the peasant' would have appeared earlier in anthropology were it not for suppression of these basic Marxist texts. It was mainly Eric Wolf who smuggled the agrarian question into anthropology in the 1950s with a series of key articles on rural differentiation (Wolf 1955, 1956a, 1956b, 1957; Wolf and Mintz 1957) and his still popular *Sons of the Shaking Earth* (1959).

Right and Left Modernization
of the Peasantry Reconsidered

The failure of both right and left developmentalism as official strategies designed to modernize rural areas is signaled in the persistence and proliferation of peasantlike types, peasantlike in that they have superficial appearances of peasants as classically defined but in fact have multiform identities that defy any such unitary classification.[11] Indeed, the great irony of modernist programs to transform rural sociology is that even as they destroy communities and economies that by the classic definitions were indeed peasant, they also perpetuate rural types that are neither 'traditional' nor modern.

I have discussed elsewhere Latin American examples of how forms of modern capitalist agriculture simultaneously destroy peasant communities and perpetuate social identities with superficial appearances of peasants (Kearney 1980). Comparable examples also abound in Eastern European efforts to socialize agriculture. Western developmentalism emerged as an antidote to the 'spread of communism,' but ironically the Soviet model of 'development' was remarkably similar to that of Western developmentalism. Soviet developmental eschatology differed from its Western counterpart only on the issue of the end point of history.

In *Peasants,* Wolf (1966) identifies three forms of 'domain' that have traditionally organized 'the disposition of peasant surpluses': patrimonial, prebendal, and mercantile. Wolf also notes the appearance in the twentieth century of a fourth type, which he calls administrative domain.

> It shares certain features with prebendal domain, in that it is the state which claims ultimate sovereignty over the land, and the produce of the land is taxed by the state through a hierarchy of officials. Yet where prebendal domain has left agricultural production largely untouched, contenting itself with drawing upon the funds of rent produced by the peasantry, administrative domain affects agricultural production as well as the disposal of its produce. (Wolf 1966:57)

As the prime example of modern administrative domain, Wolf offers the *kolkhoz,* or state farm, of the Soviet Union. In basic structure the *kolkhoz* is comparable to capitalist agricultural corporations; the basic issue here is erosion of local control over production and disposition of product: "In the twentieth century . . . we have witnessed the rapid spread of state-owned farms which are also managed by a group of technicians furnished by the state, leaving little discretion to the individual farming unit" (Wolf 1966:57). The Soviet agrarian policymakers were hard-core proletarianists. But history followed different roads whereby small, private producers flourished on the periphery of the collectives and state farms, which have been unable to absorb them. Indeed, just as the logic of corporate capitalist agriculture requires a periphery of peasantlike types, so did Soviet developmentalism seem to require the productive efforts of small producers who are peasants only in the most superficial respects.

Modern China also offers an example of an administrative domain, per Wolf, that has promoted the creation of rural types that are peasant in name only. The study by Potter and Potter (1990) of Zengbu, a community of several villages in southern China, is a case in point.[12] During the land reform from 1951 to 1952, poor local peasants worked with the new state to dismantle the hold of the landlord-gentry on rural society. From the end of the Great Leap Forward until decollectivization in the early 1980s, the most important social unit in the villages was the production team, and in analyzing its social organization the authors characterize it as a form of bureaucratic serfdom with parallels to European feudal serfdom. Thus, although the sociology of the production team definitively broke the old partilineages that had been the dominant feature of prerevolution society, it also perpetuated basic structural features of Chinese society. This is but one example of how features of the old order are transformed into forms that are continuous with the past but yet revolutionary.

Although Potter and Potter's book is ostensibly about peasants, it is apparent from the ethnography, especially after decollectivization and the rapid growth of rural industries, that most of the citizens of Zengbu are peasants in name only and rather literally so. To extract surplus value from the countryside and prevent runaway urbanization caused by migration of country people into the cities, the state recognizes two castelike civil status groups. In one are around 200 million higher-status "urban personnel," and in the other, lower-status and less remunerated one are over 800 million "rural personnel." Membership in these categories was assigned from 1950 to 1953; it is now inherited from the mother and nearly impossible to change and "remains the most important social distinction in modern China" (Potter and Potter 1990:297).

The final chapters of their book look at the deep penetration of Hong Kong capitalism into Zengbu. But the authors note that the Communist Party has invited capital in from a position of strength acquired during the revolutionary transformation of rural China. The investors have therefore had to conform to socialist requirements that seem genuinely to benefit the workers (peasants?) in the industries they finance. The descriptions of these joint ventures suggest that sociocultural and economic forms have evolved in Zengbu that transcend any firm distinction between capitalism and communism and also between worker and peasant.

The highlighting of "peasants" in the title of Potter and Potter's book, *China's Peasants: The Anthropology of a Revolution,* is thus somewhat misleading, given that the category, which is doubtlessly the single largest officially designated group in the world—namely, the 800 million "rural personnel"—is more an artifact of China's developmental policy than a reflection of actual rural sociology. The book ends by noting that the peasants of Zengbu alternate between two cultural orientations, one a desire to attain wealth relative to neighbors and the other a desire for neighbors not to become more successful than oneself. The authors cite this latter orientation of "negative egalitarianism" as an exception to James Scott's model of a moral economy in which peasants seek to preserve an egalitarian moral order. And they note that "Scott also argues that peasants are inherently unwilling to take competitive risks, and this is equally untrue in Zengbu, where, in striving for economic success, peasants have been willing to take extraordinary entrepreneurial risks" (Potter and Potter 1990:339). But what is not addressed in this debate is the underlying issue of the ontology of 'peasants.'

This book does, however, speak indirectly to the issue of who peasants are and how the category is constructed and constituted. And although it tends to participate in the reification of a category that has largely passed from history, it also documents this grand transition. The final chapters of *China's Peasants* can be read for how the great global tension between capitalism and communism has largely been transcended, as old oppositional categories and political agendas have merged into ones that are not yet well reflected in anthropological theory. In attempting to grasp the complexity of this novel situation, the authors invoke a somewhat awkward model of the articulation of three different modes of production. But based upon the ethnography presented, an alternative interpretation might be that a new mode has emerged in China that subsumes and transcends these structuralist categories of a different era and political culture.

Although right-wing modernization often extols the virtues of small-family production units, the overall historical effect of capitalist agriculture has been to erode the autonomy of small producers.[13] Indeed, right-wing, like left-wing, modernization policy promotes not only the dissolution of small producers but also their increasing incorporation into increasingly distant and complex forms of control and surplus extraction. The recent emergence of such forms of incorporation and control, now known as "agroindustrialization," amounts to a fifth domain, which can be added to Wolf's four domains of control noted earlier (for more on agroindustrialization, see Chapter 5).

Pure peasants are defined as more or less autonomous small-scale producers who produce sufficient value for their own reproduction plus some surplus that is extracted and transferred to nonpeasant types. This classic peasant type is found most clearly in agrarian societies, such as feudal Europe, in which peasant agriculture is the primary form of agriculture. But as forms of modern agriculture begin to displace such pure peasant agriculture, they absorb displaced peasant labor even as they become dependent on it for sources of labor. Such is the case of articulated modes of production, as in the dependency of commercial agriculture on seasonal peasant labor. Thus, to the degree that such commercial agriculture, for example, displaces peasant production by appropriating formerly peasant land, so does such articulation erode the material basis for peasant identity.

In the modern period, as a result of such processes, a threshold separating such classic peasants and the peasantlike types noted previously appears to have been crossed. I take this threshold, admittedly a rather arbitrary one, to be small-scale subsistence production of less than 50 percent of the value consumed for reproduction of the producing unit, such as the family or extended family, as the case may be. The crossing of this threshold is but a point on a historical trend for a decline in reproduction by peasants by means of their own small-scale agricultural production *and* an increase in their reproduction from nonself-directed agricultural or nonagricultural production. This threshold, although perhaps mainly symbolic, signals the tendency of modern agriculture and modern economies in general to destroy peasantries. But the corollary of this law is that just as modern agriculture and society destroy peasant societies, they do not annihilate them entirely. To the contrary, they perpetuate traces of the peasantry conserved as aspects of more complex identities and communities.

Problems with Peasant Essentialism

Having outlined the macro context in which modern images of the peasant appear, we now turn our attention to the category per se. A world survey of low-income rural populations reveals a broad array of ethnographic diversity. But within this diversity one type—'the peasantry'—has been isolated by intellectuals and accorded special status within their discourses about 'the countryside.' This attitude argues, implicitly or explicitly, that there is a distinct 'peasant' ontology. The way in which the 'peasant' of post–World War II modernist anthropology was essentialized is comparable to the way in which 'the proletariat' was essentialized by an earlier leftist discourse that center staged this social type in modern history.

The point here is that students who wish to critically assess the position of *the* peasants in rural society must first come to terms with *the images* of them. Failure to do so runs the risk of pursuing a reified type, a will-o'-the-wisp that has been projected onto the countryside by urban intellectuals. Images of the essentialized peasant inform general theoretical perspectives and research, and it is in the corpus of such literature that the imagined peasant resides.

Peasant essentialisms of all but the most psychological or cultural varieties depend on two basic criteria. First is the production criterion noted earlier. Thus, for example, Wolf defined 'peasants' as rural people who are "existentially involved in cultivation and make autonomous decisions regarding the processes of cultivation" (Wolf 1969:xiv). Wolf distinguished 'peasants' from farmers in that the "major aim" of the former, unlike that of the latter, is "subsistence and social status gained within a narrow range of social relationships" (Wolf 1969:xiv). Similarly, Stavenhagen noted that

> The peasant economy can be defined quite simply as that form of farm production (and associated activities) in which the producer and his family till the land themselves, generally utilizing their own means of production (tools and instruments), with the object of directly satisfying their basic needs, although for a number of reasons they may find themselves required to sell a part of their produce on the market in order to obtain goods which they do not produce. The peasant economy occurs on small production units, nonwage labor predominates, possibilities for accumulation are limited or absent, and the principal purpose of economic activity is not to obtain or maximize profits but to guarantee a subsistence. (Stavenhagen 1978:31)[14]

The second criterion of modern peasants is that, as Wolf (1969:xiv) said, they "are subject to the dictates of a superordinate state [in contrast to primitives, who are also] rural dwellers who live outside of the confines of such a political structure." Variations of this basic definition are invoked or simply assumed in innumerable ethnographies and investigations of 'peasant' communities and their agriculture. This basic definition is also reiterated in numerous introductory cultural anthropology textbooks.[15]

The argument presented in Chapter 2 is that essentialization occurs when ambiguous categories must be contained, that is, that the 'containment of communism' necessitated the containment of ambiguous rural types within the category. Such intellectual containment is not dissimilar, and indeed is an adjunct, to the containment of dispersed, ungovernable rural populations in 'strategic hamlets.' Such a military strategy has long been employed by states to control otherwise ungovernable rural populations. Recent major examples of such on-the-ground containment are the Phoenix Program in Vietnam, the formation of rural concentration camps in Cambodia by the Khmer Rouge, and the herding of indigenous Guatemalans into fortified villages by the Guatemalan military—a variation of Spanish colonial policy for the reduction and concentration of indigenous populations into planned communities.

Essentialization occurs when the intellectual stakes are high, that is, when attention is focused on a complex field that must be cognized—objectified—because of needs the objectifying subject has to contain that which the new category represents. These are the conditions of the objectifying subject that cause it to construct kinds of social others and to enter them into official and unofficial discourses.

By his definition, Wolf also explicitly distinguishes 'peasants' from fishermen, landless laborers, and farmers. But just as the 'small peasants' shade into a 'proletariat,' so also do they merge with 'large peasants,' who in turn are often indistinguishable from farmers. The basis of such categorization that informs the problem of peasant differentiation is, as is the case with other dimensions of 'peasant' identity, dualistic. At one polar extreme is the completely landless peasant (another contradiction in terms), which as a type grades into the various degrees of "infrasubsistence" households, the members of which—insofar as they struggle to survive within the 'peasant economy'—must seek employment from those 'peasants' or other types who, having excess land, are at the other extreme of this bipolar scale defined in terms of household production and consumption. The landless peasants are de facto proletarians, save for the dispositions they often carry within to take up farming when and if such a shift becomes possible. Defined within this productionist scheme, based as it is on the contradictory notion of peasant farming, the peasant is an ambiguous type that occupies vague rural spaces in the margins between the two paramount productionist types of the modern master narrative—namely, the proletarian and the capitalist. Development schemes can be classified into those that seek to nudge the peasant, who is by definition 'underdeveloped,' into one of the other of these two basic types.

In both idealist and materialist variants of peasant essentialism there are two inherent bases of this identity. One is that it is constituted in rural areas, in 'the country,' which as a social and geographic space is assumed to exert a special influence on social identity. But clearly, other social types in addition to the peasant live and reproduce in the country, and therefore this is at most a necessary but insufficient cause of peasant identity.

The other presumed unique quality of the peasant that makes it a distinctive rural type is a special cognition of 'land' as not only a physical entity but a special primary value from which other social, cultural, or economic values are produced, such that from it 'the peasant' is able to construct his or her physical and cultural identity. 'Land,' assumed by the anthropologist to be so conceived by the peasant, is thus a basic category around which are articulated other aspects of personality, worldview, economic rationality, or social identity, depending on the particular variety of essentialism in question. 'Land' is thus assumed to have a distinctive cultural significance that derives from and also constitutes the peasant's special social identity. In other words, 'the peasant' is assumed to have a special relationship to 'the land.'

The farmer also produces value from land, but whereas the farmer produces *exchange value,* the peasant primarily produces *use value,* that is, produces for autoconsumption. This self-provisioning by means of cultivation is the rock-bottom defining characteristic that distinguishes the peasant from other rural types. The biological reproduction of the peasant is thus directly dependent on access to and control of land, which is a primary value in the peasant economy that, when combined with labor, produces the use value—the production and consumption of which define the peasant in contrast to the exchange value–producing farmer and the exchange value–consuming proletarian.

Essentialism and Containment

In identifying peasant essentialism as constituted upon a particular notion of land as value, the next step is to examine these theories of value. Anticipating what is to come, we can note here that if the dualist theory of value underlying peasant essentialism is found wanting, then one dimension of a reconceptualized peasantry needs be a different notion of value (see Chapter 7).

But peasants also exist in exchange relations with nonpeasants, such relations being ones of unequal exchange whereby part of their product must be transferred to nonpeasant types. Indeed, a distinctive feature of most anthropological conceptions of peasants is that they see peasants as existing in exchanges with nonpeasant types. Almost invariably, these relationships are seen as ones of unequal exchange in which economic surplus is transferred out of the peasant community. From such a perspective, peasant social and political consciousness is like proletarian consciousness, in that both are informed by desires to protect their respective essential values. Thus, whereas proletarian political objectives center on increasing wages and the like, those of peasants center on land reform and prices, taxes, and all other social conditions that affect their ability to produce and to retain what they produce.

The theme suggested here and elaborated in following chapters is that contemporary rural peoples designated by intellectuals, bureaucrats, and politicians as 'peasants' are invariably constituted far more complexly than is implied by this one-dimensional term. The invention of the peasant has served the cognitive needs of nonpeasant types to make sense out of this ambiguity and has also served to organize the political and military projects aimed at developing—read controlling and containing—rural populations. A primary concern herein is with intellectual contribution of anthropology to the formation of the images of 'peasants' that inform such policy.

Dualist thinking that reifies peasants and capitalism in formal terms is predisposed to envision only one 'road' for the dissolution of the peasantry and that is proletarianization. Such thinking is made uncomfortable by other routes that do not fit this scenario. It is telling that many such other routes are lumped together in the catchall category the "informal economy." In addition to being illegal by not registering with the agencies of the state that control commerce, make health inspections, compile statistics, collect taxes, and so forth, informal economic activities are categorically subversive by defying official definitions of identity. To the degree that anthropological categories of identity conform to the official categories of the state and participate in their definition and reification, such an official anthropology is also made uncomfortable by social types that so defy being regulated by official categories of the state and its forms of discipline. Such classificatory discomfort is a symptom of a cancerous erosion of the structure of dualist thinking deep within the theoretical entrails of modern theory.

The late recognition in anthropology of the extent and import of informal economic activities in 'peasant' and 'proletarian' communities, when the signs and symptoms were so evident, is no doubt the result of repression of the prognosis of such a fatal condition—fatal for dualist thinking and ideas about 'peasants' based on it. As of yet there has been no consistent effort to link thinking regarding the informal economy with theories of peasant society (see Chapter 5).

The 'peasant' serves to concretize and epitomize a large section of rural society for historical reasons that predispose such objectification. One is that rural sociology is in fact so varied and complex that ease of thinking about it demands an iconic form that simplifies the diversity. But what kind of form? The essentialized peasant is but a permutation of the previously constructed 'individual' of the modern worldview that appears in political, economic, social, and moral discourses. Deep reconceptualization of 'the peasant' thus only becomes possible in a historical moment, such as the present, when this deeper structural armature upon which it is constructed assumes a new form. Like the classic person, the modern person—the individual—is imagined as having a single basic subject position upon and around which are centered his or her social identities. In contrast, contemporary subject positions, within the socially constructed 'individual,' are dispersed and do not coincide with a single social identity.

Such coexisting identities are complex and often express contradictory voices within the presumed monovocal 'individual,' which is an official category developed by the state faced with the exigencies of governing its subjects. To govern, the state must demarcate social units—counties, shires, provinces, parishes, and so forth—within which its subjects (e.g., subjects of the king) can be addressed for purposes of censusing, taxing, recruiting, and so forth. But these seemingly monovocal "individuals" are most often complex hyphenated types, such as peasant-workers. The official construction of the individual thus contains these multiple identities within the unitary category. To the degree that anthropological thought participates in this reification of the individual and the suppression of the multiple identities within it, it is an (usually unwitting) accomplice in the state's more general policies and practices of containment. Internally differentiated subject identities are disruptive precisely because they cannot be accurately represented by typological thinking that wishes to skewer the individual on the definite article as if it were a collector's pin. I return in Chapter 5 to this theme of internal differentiation, which resists and often disrupts official categorization.

Those anthropologists who participate in the reification of the category *peasant* do so twice over: first at the categorical level of 'the peasant' per se and second at the level of the structural underpinnings of the category. Debates about 'peasants' and agrarian issues are normally elaborated at the first level, that of the categories of identity. But true reconceptualization can only occur when attention has been displaced to the other, deeper level, where lie the structures of thought and power that generate the *types* of categories that appear in consciousness at the first level, that is, in the categories of intellectuals who define peasants.

The use of social categories, for example, peasant, by anthropologists is integral to the scientific work of knowing others. But such knowing is itself a social act occurring within the structure of difference that differentiates the knowing Self from the Other it seeks to know. Such anthropological work is thus confounded with the structuring of social difference between the knowing anthropological Self and the ethnographic subject to be known, upon which anthropology as a discipline is based. If we accept that the structuring of anthropology as a discipline is indeed so predicated on the dualist structuring of anthropological Self and ethnographic Other, which is a permutation of official thought in general, then it is apparent that deep reconceptualization has implications for the integrity of anthropology as a discipline. How is this so?

An ambiguous type, neither 'primitive' nor 'modern' but partaking of both and likewise liminally situated between proletarian and farmer and other identities, 'the peasant' has a disruptive classificatory potential that threatens the absolute distinction between anthropological Self and ethnographic Other that structured classical anthropology. Modernist anthropology was faced with the historically given challenge of recognizing and accommodating 'the peasant' within the basic lineaments of its discourse and practice. As discussed earlier, modernist anthropology did indeed effectively contain the typologically disruptive potential of 'the peasant' by essentializing it as a categorically distinct Other. The danger inherent in its ambiguity as an anthropological category was neutralized by making the peasant an absolute category with the same logic of distinction—we-they, higher-lower, new-old, cultured-uncultured, modern-traditional, developed-underdeveloped—that marked the primitive.

This containment at work within the theory of peasants buttresses political and economic forms of domination and exploitation by participating in the reification of the inferior Other—*the* peasant. Containment fulfills this ideological mission not by stating falsehoods but by stating truths, indeed truths in whose creation it participates. In other words, containment is effective when it is able to constitute the types it essentializes. Containment thus works not by promoting false consciousness, that is, the hegemony of the dominant culture (although such hegemony may accompany containment) but instead by occupying intellectual space that might be filled by other images of rural communities—but communities in which, in these alternative versions of truth, there are no peasants. Such contrary images are disruptive, because they populate cultural and political landscapes with subjects that defy the essentializing power of official definitions of subjects so defined so as to *subjugate* them.[16]

A basic assumption running through anthropological literature on peasants is that they are socially, politically, and culturally dominated by nonpeasants. These relationships are seen as imposed on peasants by nonpeasants not only by force of law and police power but also by the force of custom, much of which is enacted as right and proper behavior by the dominated themselves. Such relationships are depicted in the writings of academics and intellectuals generally who call attention to the poverty, powerlessness, and general 'underdevelopment' of peasant society. As such, this literature would appear to be pro-peasant by informing intellectual and political projects that shift the balance of power, however little, in the favor of peasants.

But if we take seriously Bourdieu's (1984:176) depiction of intellectuals as one of the dominated fractions of the dominant class, then there is reason to pause and reconsider just how such seemingly pro-peasant literature is indeed pro-peasant. Even the most sympathetic writing about peasants, which arouses humanitarian sentiments toward them and "their" problems, nevertheless is produced within and consistent with relationships of domination. This structural condition shaping the context of its writing suggests that such literature is best regarded critically from a theoretical perspective that defines it not as ideological but instead as a literature that is constructive of the social categories, of the identities, about which it writes. Similar to ideology, the theory of hegemony assumes that preexisting classes are historical residues bound together in an inherently unstable relationship that class conflict would naturally dissolve were it not for the power of "dominant culture" (Williams 1977) to congeal class structure by clouding the social vision of the dominated classes.[17]

But in the case of 'the peasantry' we are, more often than not—certainly in Mexico—dealing with a hollow category, one that has amazingly little objective referent. Thus, whereas ideology, hegemony, and dominant culture impede self-consciousness of an objective social category, theories and other images of 'the peasantry' seek to contain social identities to a category from which they are escaping or to which they have never belonged. From the state's point of view, that is, from the point of view of official thinking, such social identities—those of the informal economy and all those with complex polyphonic selves—are getting out of bounds and thus must be constituted as proper subjects. And the first step in such a task is the construction or reconstruction of the category of their proper, official identity.

The theory of containment—of construction and constitution of social difference—has an appreciation of ideology, hegemony, and dominant culture, but it is an appreciation gained from historical examination of the formation of social identities by acts of state. *Acts* is taken here in both the sense of actions by agents and agencies of the state, such as law enforcement, and also of acts as the literature of the state—its laws, codes, regulations, licenses, and other texts, including textbooks. The simultaneous constructive and constitutive nature of official acts is revealed in the polysemy of *act,* which, according to *Webster's,* is both an action taken and "the formal product of a legislative body" or "a decision or determination of a sovereign, a legislative council, or a court of justice." A parallel semantics is present in *deed,* which has both the sense of an act, as in a good deed that is done, and of a deed to property, which thus constitutes the identity of a 'property owner,' just as, conversely, the absence of a deed constitutes, for example, a 'tenant.'

The theory of dominant culture is concerned with the effects of culture on consciousness and is thus a theory of construction but as such pays little attention to the ways in which culture informs and so forms identities, that is, to how these identities are constituted. These presumably hegemonic constructions are like the waters of a river, but where are these rivers destined to flow? Clearly, there cannot be rivers without banks to channel them. Thus, whereas identities are constructed as ideas, they are not embodied until constituted as social identities. This constituting is done in large part by embodying inscriptions such as the writing of constitutions, property laws, contract laws, religious laws, and so forth. These acts that so constitute identities are thus, as it were, inscribing channels in which run the identities so constituted, and in acting out these identities the actors carve more deeply these constituting channels, just as the water of a river scours the bed that contains it.[18]

True peasant identities have been constructed and constituted in various historical moments, but for the most part the peasant is no longer an identity supported by contemporary social conditions, which instead condition the widespread emergence of identities that although having superficial appearances of peasants are constituted in rather different ways. We are thus faced with a situation in which there are disparities between the constitution of such peoples and certain constructions elaborated of them. Such a situation, in which there is a marked disparity between construction and constitution, calls into question the identity, which lacks identity with reality.

I have been, borrowing Jameson's term, referring to such discontinuous images as strategies of containment. As used herein, strategies of containment come into play when the symmetry between construction and constitution breaks down as the latter, under the weight of historical contingency, moves out of alignment with the former. In such a circumstance, the continued constructing of images serves less to constitute the identities it defines and more to contain the new identities that have become historically constituted but not yet represented intellectually, such intellectual representation being the necessary precondition for organized political representation. As regards the social center of gravity of such containment, it is to be noted that contrary to dominant culture and hegemony, which are seen as emanating from intellectual work and cultural creativity in the upper classes, containment may be most effectively elaborated by critical intellectuals who are politically disposed to be the most pro-peasant.

Thus, the reifications of the peasant of, say, modernization theory certainly essentialized the peasant as a way of containing rural subalterns, but at least modernization theory, as does classic Marxism, marginalized peasants to the edges of history-making and foretold their inevitable demise. But more pro-peasant orientations of both the political left and right can be seen as consistent in their containment by theoretically insisting that peasants are here to stay. The point here is not that the thinking of modern radical peasantists has been distorted by dominant culture but instead that the social origin of containment is not class-specific.[19]

As noted earlier, strategies of containment come into play when the actual lived constitution of peoples no longer coincides with the cultural identities that have been constructed of them. Thus, peasants only "really exist" when there is no need for containment, that is, when the constructions of them fit the lives they live—as must have been the case in certain premodern moments, such as in feudal Europe, and in nondemocratic states that imposed jural definitions on peasants that were continuous and consistent with historically given identities. Such jurally coded differences have largely disappeared in modern nations, which now have national constitutions that permit them—without creating formal contradictions—to become signatories of, for example, the Universal Declaration of Human Rights of the United Nations. In such cases the recognition of the existence of peasants must be inscribed in some other literature, which thus officially comes to have the power not only to recognize difference but also to construct it.

This thesis can be restated as follows. Until the rise of the modern democratic capitalist and socialist states, European peasants were defined by the state or by customary law as a social type. Peasants were de jure just about everyone not included in one of the three estates. This legal classification was fundamental to the structure of difference and the domination of the peasants by elites who were similarly constituted. In the modern capitalist states this defining power, which is both an expression and a constituting component of political power—conferred by the power to name—is given over to the social sciences. The modern social science literature on *the* peasants as a social type is thus continuous with the former jural definitions of peasants in nonmodern states.[20]

The basic thesis is illustrated by the anthropology of peasants: Anthropological writing is a special kind of national literature that comes into being out of the tension between the modern colonial nation-state and its dependencies. It thus contrasts with other kinds of national literatures that define differences within and among the modern nation-states. Anthropology comes into its own in the latter phases of colonial expansion. During this period, anthropological literature constructs a sharp distinction between colonial Self and colonized Other as the difference between civilization and savagery-barbarism.

There are two phases to this consolidation of early classical anthropology. The first is the Victorian anthropology epitomized best by Frazer's *The Golden Bough* and Lewis Henry Morgan's comparative work, and the second is the late classical anthropology of the interwar period. The first is a grandly comparative compendium built out of items culled from the reports of explorers, missionaries, and colonial administrators; the second is based on the first-hand observations of an author examining a single society and presenting his observations and analysis in the form of a monograph.

In the post–World War II era the politico-spatial structure of formal colonialism breaks down and occasions a corresponding shift in anthropological writing as a national literature. When the structure of colonialism was firmly in place, the Other was firmly in place out there and, per Fabian (1983), "back there" temporally. But in the postcolonial era this firm distinction has largely disintegrated, as the Other moves in from the periphery and begins to penetrate into the core, threatening to dissolve the very difference between core/Self and periphery/Other. The task of anthropology as a national literature must shift accordingly.

Whereas for classical anthropology construction of the national anthropological Self was in Relationship to the 'primitive' ethnographic Other, which was out there in space and back in time, in the postcolonial era the Other is penetrating into the colonial centers. The lines of distinction are not only being redrawn in ever tighter circles around the Self, but what is worse, these distinctions are deteriorating, threatening the annihilation of this authorial, anthropological Self who can be constituted only in contradistinction to an ethnographic Other. At this moment anthropological attention turns from the Other per se to an obsession with the distinction between the threatened anthropological Self and the encroaching, disruptive Other. Having lost control of the Other, the anthropological Self becomes obsessed with Self-control, with *its* power to represent, and this Self-obsession manifests in the much commented on "literary turn" in contemporary anthropology (Sangren 1988).

This high degree of reflexivity in interpretive anthropology is an instance of Jameson's (1984) characterization of the postmodern condition as a piling of representations onto representations. This is a Self-obsession that is a permutation of a defensive nationalism. The Other is, as it were, clambering at the edge of the text to have its voice heard within it—to pass from being an object to become a subject—just as former colonials are immigrating to centers of the former empires. Their presence is an unavoidable reality that threatens the structuring of difference and power. The problem thus becomes one of border control, of containment, of shoring up the disintegrating structure of apartheids.

The debate about anthropology as texts centers on the issue of representation, of whose voices will appear in the texts and what they will say. This debate is a structural homologue of national immigration policy and practice that seeks to control who will enter the borders of the nation-state and in what status. Thus, as a national literature interpretive anthropology is a specialized kind of "print capital" that, like other forms of capital, serves as the media out of which distinction is constructed and difference constituted.[21] Anderson's (1983) thesis is that print capital was instrumental in the construction of the modern European nation-states, enabling each to be distinct from the others by producing a language and literature that define identities around which borders can be drawn. Contemporary reflexive anthropology performs a similar kind of border work and that is to reify, even as they are disintegrating, the borders between the national integrity of the domain in which anthropology as a discipline is situated and the alterity that surrounds it, penetrates into it, and disrupts it.

Interpretive anthropology is writing against, for example, Hanif Kureishi's film *Sammy and Rosie Get Laid,* which is a sort of nightmare scenario for the conventional ethnographer, for in this film colonial Others have taken up residence in a London that is in seeming chaos and in which the English are mostly absent.[22] In basing its project on the exotic Other, contemporary interpretive anthropology is the heir of the late classical ethnography of the interwar era. Interpretive anthropology is in this sense the trustee of this iconic Other, which it retains at the center of its gaze in a world that has gone crazy with diversity. But in the interim, other types—most notably the peasant—have come on the scene. How has this hybrid type, the peasant, which is part primitive and part civilized, been accommodated within anthropology? The answer is by a division of labor between interpretive anthropology and the various currents that identify with the natural sciences. Thus, whereas interpretive anthropology focuses on the truly exotic, the peasant is given over to positivist and materialist schools of anthropology that are less concerned with hermeneutic issues and more with applied ones. Whereas hermeneutic anthropology deals with the threatened integrity and authorial power of the anthropological (read national) Self, the applied branches are assigned responsibility for containing what is rightly felt to be the truly troublesome type—those peasants who on a number of occasions in the twentieth century, as in previous ones, have created major disruptions.

There are both left- and right-wing variants of this applied anthropology, all of which, except for certain romantic variants (Chapter 4), are dedicated in one way or another to eliminating the peasant from future history. When anthropologists began to write ethnographies of peasants, the implicit definition of the community of the Other tended to shift from ethnic groups or "tribes" to specific villages and towns. This is a humanizing advance. But the containment at work here is still formidable, for these are communities that are localized and depicted largely without connections to national and international milieus, except as recipients of cultural traits that 'diffuse' from 'donors.' The portrayal of such communities as 'bounded' is seen in retrospect as a tactic in the larger strategies of containment.[23] These bounded communities are admitted into modern history but only to affirm, as it were, that they are going to be developed out of existence by it. Their histories are not of concern, except to Wolf (1982) and a few others.

The exclusion of the peasant from the purview of interpretive anthropologists can be traced in the career of the recognized leader of the field, Clifford Geertz (1963), who first gained wide recognition in, as it were, the peasant rice paddies of Java but who later published the manifesto of contemporary hermeneutic anthropology (Geertz 1973b). Although his 1973 book *The Interpretation of Cultures* includes some entries in the index under "peasant societies," ten years later in *Local Knowledge* (Geertz 1983) there are none. The peasants have disappeared from his project to be replaced by Australian aborigines, Azandes, Yorubas, and so forth, who are now juxtaposed against Jane Austin, Fra Angelico, Giovanni Bellini, Nabokov, and others but with no mention of peasants or of peasant society.

Peasants are similarly absent in Geertz's more recent *Works and Lives: The Anthropologist as Author* (1988). They are also absent from the book that is generally considered to be the pivotal statement in the current debates about anthropological representation and hermeneutics, George Marcus and Michael Fischer's *Anthropology as Cultural Critique* (1986), as well as from the much-cited collection edited by James Clifford and Marcus, *Writing Culture: The Poetics and Politics of Ethnography* (1986), and the essays of Clifford, *The Predicament of Culture* (1988).

We can now restate the thesis. The peasant comes onto the anthropological stage in the 1950s and 1960s and threatens to dissolve the structure of anthropology as a distinct discipline. Two strategies emerge to contain this disruptive type. One is the applied, which essentializes the peasant as a type to exercise control of it within a social science modality; this has the effect of naturalizing and distancing the peasant in the mode of classical anthropology and "objective" dualist theory. The other strategy is to develop an interpretive anthropology that is more 'intellectual' and that is fascinated not with these disruptive others but instead with the anthropological Self and its power to write about itself writing about primitive others who pose no real threat because they have already passed from history.

Beyond Stated Definitions

The modernist anthropological sensibility, predicated on its dualist assumptions, was appropriate for a flat world of Euclydian space and railroad time and of vistas seen from the vantage point of a fixed, solitary subject in a space where lines converge at a single vanishing point. In such a world, distance in space is equated with distance in time. In such a world, modernist anthropology was reasonably successful at constructing a peasantry that was 'out there' geographically and 'back there' timewise. This sensibility is, however, giving way to one of high-velocity, high-volume communication that dissolves spatial distance and brings the distant into the present, into more intimate relationships that dissolve the former ways of distancing and differentiating Self from Other.

Good peasants, like all 'good' subalterns 'know their place.' But as I discuss at more length in Chapter 8, such types are becoming increasingly *displaced*. Displacement in the theory of practical anthropology is any intentional or unintentional movement that relocates subjects into geographic or social spaces and relocates their corresponding intellectual spaces such that their constructed identities as political beings are altered. A strategy of practical anthropology is to effect such displacements intentionally to give subalterns more power. But changes in identity, which are not necessarily empowering, also result from unintentional and forced displacement. And indeed, the number of displaced persons—most notably refugees, migrants, immigrants, exiles, and commuters—is ever larger both in absolute numbers and as percentages of the total global population. Such churning of communities affects social identities in ways that are not yet well reflected in anthropological theory (see Chapter 5 for a discussion of transnational communities and globalization).

In subsequent chapters I will examine what happens to modern dualist images of time and space, of Self and Other as they realign with contemporary hyperrealities. Just as official social categories and definitions of identity are elaborated by the state, so do contrary identities and definitions struggle to displace themselves, and indeed, official forms would not be necessary were it not for such resistance. In other words, just as there are official right and left modernist programs that foretell and seek to effect the disappearance of peasants from history, so are there champions of peasants on the right and the left. Although romantic resistance to official peasantology also tends to reify peasants, nevertheless precisely because it does oppose the official construction of the category, it provides clues for a yet deeper reconceptualization. It is with this purpose in mind that Chapter 4 examines such romantic reactions.

Notes

1. See Gouldner (1970:51–65) for middle-class theoretical assumptions about utility and social control.

2. In the *Principles of Sociology* (3 vols., 1876–1896), Spencer discusses how "the individual" becomes differentiated from group life and gains greater freedom in doing so. Spencer here established a basic theme that was later taken up by mid-twentieth-century modernization theorists. But as Gouldner (1970:64) notes, the free bourgeois individual who emerges with the passing of feudal society and champions the Rights of Man is an *impersonal* individual.

3. For a cautionary note against reification of the state, see Abrams (1988).

4. It is ironic that even as Potter and Potter reveal the arbitrariness of the category *peasant* in contemporary China, they tend to participate in its inscription and reification, among other ways, by titling their book *China's Peasants*.

5. See Roseberry (1989a:215–216) for oppositional models of peasants in anthropology.

6. For discussion of Communists' need to invoke the concept of hegemony, see Laclau and Mouffe (1985).

7. For Parsons and Weber, see Gouldner (1970:167–338) and Taylor (1979:3–41); for neoclassic economics, see Hunt (1992); and regarding Redfield, see Stocking (1989).

8. "His [Redfield's] early anthropological orientation clearly reflected Park's personal intellectual heritage, which was an amalgam of the pragmatism of John Dewey and William James, the sociological concepts of Georg Simmel, Ferdinand Tönnies, and William Graham Sumner, and the epistemological thought of Wilhelm Windelband" (Stocking 1989:231).

9. Redfield's references to the "disorganization" brought to traditional communities by modernization reveal his romantic disposition, but his is what might be called a realistic romanticism, for he accepts the passing of traditional society as inevitable but nevertheless mourns its demise.

10. See Wolf (1969:290–293) for a contrasting theory of a revolutionary "middle peasantry."

11. The introduction of this neologism—*peasantlike*—is warranted by the inertia of *the peasant*, which, although its referent has largely passed from history, continues to influence perception of *rural* peoples and their communities, which strictly speaking are neither rural nor peasant. Peasantlikes can thus be taken as variants of subalterns.

12. This discussion of Potter and Potter (1990) is taken from Kearney (1993a).

13. Indeed, Mitrany (1951) might as well have written a book titled *Capitalism Against the Peasant.*

14. Although I use Wolf and Stavenhagen's definitions here, which were state of the art in the 1960s and 1970s, their later work is important in moving toward a postpeasant discourse (see Chapter 5).

15. Kuhn (1970:137–138) notes that scientific paradigms are the most directly defined in introductory textbooks, which are the means whereby the bearers of those paradigms hope to socialize the next generation into their way of thinking.

16. Subjugate is an especially apropos term for such definitional control of 'peasant' subjects, since it is a dead metaphor that originally meant "to bring under the yoke."

17. See Roseberry (1989a:45, 75–76) for theories of dominant culture and hegemony against which a theory of constitution can be contrasted. Also see Comaroff and Comaroff (1991:19–27) for a discussion of hegemony.

18. Corrigan and Sayer's *The Great Arch* (1985) is perhaps the most extensive study of the development of difference by such complementary working of construction and constitution. See also Nagengast (1991).

19. Cf. Roseberry (1989a:45–49) for a discussion of how hegemony is not just top-down ideas.

20. In the former Soviet Union and in contemporary China, the literary, social science, and de jure definitions of peasants are combined to a far greater degree than is the case in the nominally democratic capitalist underdeveloped countries.

21. *Print capital* is Anderson's term (1983); for "forms of capital," see Bourdieu (1986).

22. Sammy is a Bengali immigrant living in London with his wife, Rosie, who is apparently Irish. At the beginning of the film Sammy's father arrives from India thinking he is going to die, and in an inversion of the typical desire to return to one's homeland to die, he opts to go to the former colonial center. As they walk about the neighborhood, they ignore everyday rioting and looting by resident West Indians. In this postcolonial world, the dual

structures of the colonial have disintegrated. Those who were peripheral occupy the center, and their destruction and reconstruction of it is taken as normal. Although the film is set in Britain, the British are largely absent from it.

23. Chapter 4 discusses shifts in contemporary ethnography away from images of bounded to those of unbounded communities. Note that "bounded" as used here is not to be confused with Wolf's (1957) reference to "closed corporate communities."

Chapter 4

Romantic Reactions to Modernist Peasant Studies

Whereas Chapter 3 reviewed the emergence of the concept of 'the peasant' within anthropology in relation to the social and historical contexts that brought it forth, this chapter examines changing historical-structural conditions that no longer support the peasant concept. In this contemporary context, the peasant has thus been losing potency as an anthropological category as the social and political conditions that brought it into the foreground of anthropological thinking change. This chapter and the next characterize the present historical moment as postdevelopmental.

The modernist construction of the peasantry in both its bourgeois and Leninist versions began to come into crisis in the 1960s and 1970s. This crisis was provoked by the end of developmentalism, which conditioned the elaboration of renewed romantic sensibilities among peasantists who are so disposed. In other words, whereas developmentalism conditioned modernist views of the peasant, contemporary pervasive stagnation in rural areas conditions the rise of new romantic images of peasants. Both are based on the dualist assumptions, but certain romantic ideas about rural society advance analysis toward nondualist views of a postdevelopment society.

Although these romantic ideas also reify peasants, in them are found seeds for reconceptualization. The modern notion of history as the development of nations (Chapter 3) is also now moribund. The crisis of development is therefore also a crisis in the idea of the nation-state that is reflected as a decay of the antinomies out of which both nation and peasant are constructed. It is this loosening of the structuring image of nations and their destinies that now makes possible the reconceptualization of peasants and of anthropology in general. This task is therefore pushed forward by a review of theoretical work that has critiqued the assumptions of developmentalism.

Chapter 3 explored the evolutionary, teleologic master narrative within which modernist images of 'the peasant,' like those of 'the primitive,' were constructed.

In this chapter we examine how the conceptual underpinnings of this dualist image of the West and the rest are undergoing an autodeconstruction, by which I mean any historical process within the socioeconomic context of the master narratives of an era that erodes their binary structure.

Autodeconstruction coincides with the emergence of new images and assumptions that are more consistent with the emerging socioeconomic realities. I use the prefix *auto* as a reminder that the reconceptualizations of which we speak are but ideas whose time, that is, their global infrastructural bases, is coming into being and weakening the possibility of containment. Autodeconstruction is a sociocultural current characteristic of contemporary history that is rising into consciousness as new forms of popular and global culture that dissolve distinctions between modern and traditional identities, as I examine in Chapter 5. It also arises into consciousness as contemporary philosophical and critical ideas, such as, for example, deconstructionism, that attack the logocentrism and metaphysical dualities of modern thought.

But whereas deconstructionism represents the manifestation of these trends in avant-garde philosophy and intellectual life, it is the task of anthropology to detect the changing social-historical contexts that are so reflected in philosophy and popular culture and to represent them theoretically in constructs that conform to the emergent social conditions. In this historical process of autodeconstruction not only are the modern social categories breaking up, but the binary structure upon which they are constructed is being reordered. Thus, the anthropological work of reconceptualization does not allow for the possibility of pouring new wine into old skins because the old skins no longer exist.

The peasant as a social type is highly coterminous with rural society, such that the historical and conceptual fate of the one is interwoven with that of the other. Accordingly, a reconceptualization of the principles of classification that define rural types that are alternatives to 'the peasant' also necessarily entails the reconceptualization of the notion of rural society, a task begun in Chapter 3 that I now continue. The contemporary social and economic conditions that are reflected culturally as deconstructive work have proceeded at a faster pace than their reflection in consciousness. These images of the countryside and of rural life are, after all, cultural sedimentations that have been laid down for over two or three thousand millennia. It is not surprising, therefore, that not just images of 'peasants' but the worldview that structures these images has a certain historical inertia.

But this inertia need not be seen as just some 'cultural lag' that will naturally catch up with actual social conditions. Instead, this discrepancy is in part actively maintained by the intellectual and political work of authors and other purveyors of official views that figure in the construction of images of the peasantry—images that are to some degree constitutive of the social categories, which thus, as it were, come to life. Such cultural dynamics were integral to the creation of difference in the past between 'peasant' and 'nonpeasant.' But the current historical moment is marked by an increasing disparity between images of peasant and the social conditions that shape such images. And as discussed earlier, it is in such moments that the persistent production of peasant images is seen not as lag but as containment.

Although the modernist discourse, with its urbancentric views of the country-side and country folk, dominates peasant studies, there are and always have been contrary views that extol the virtues of rural places and peoples. The Classic Greeks praised the bucolic virtues of Arcadia of ancient Greece, which, located in the Peloponnisos, was assumed to be an isolated region in which a proverbially simple and natural life prevailed. We can loosely identify such intellectual, aesthetic, and political currents as *romantic.* Whereas the modernist urbancentric views emphasize the backwardness and brutishness of rural life, romantic views depict a 'moral economy.' In *The Country and the City,* Raymond Williams (1973) reveals that such romantic critiques and nostalgia tend to be strongest during bad times. Romantic perspectives are, generally speaking, based on the same dualist structuring of space and time as are modernist perspectives; both elaborate what Roseberry (1989a:201) aptly calls "oppositional history" in which an earlier natural economy is eventually replaced by modern society. They differ only in the relative value they place on urban versus rural types, as they conceive them.

Whereas modernism in the form of, for example, applied anthropology seeks reconstruction of the countryside in the image of urban society, all forms of romantic reaction—as romantic is used herein—mount a critique and rejection of the idea that modern society, economy, and culture are universally progressive or desirable. Romantics desire to preserve the 'traditional' rural community or otherwise see it as having values and potential and a role in history that are unrecognized and unappreciated by modernizationists. For urban romantic intellectuals, this attitude is a reaction against the alienation, technocracy, individualism, or even the democracy of modern society. A common feature of romantic orientations toward the peasantry is that they have, as Roseberry (1989a:56) says, a tendency to depict "a relative homogeneous, undifferentiated traditional order." For some, such 'organic' cultures stand as a critique of the loneliness of compartmentalized urban lives.[1]

Extreme romantics see preservation or reconstitution of the rural community as a political goal to be attained by revolutionary programs. Such romantic peasantists are politically in opposition to modernizing projects of the state, which with few notable exceptions, such as Chinese agrarian policy through the Great Leap Forward, are designed to eliminate peasants by developing them into some other social type. But for other, more 'realistic' romantics as diverse as Redfield and Marx, the desirable human qualities of the organic rural community must of historical necessity give way to the destructive and creative forces of modern urban industrial society.[2] In both cases, as Raymond Williams points out, the idea of culture as an organic, traditional, more natural way of life appears "only in the wake of a revolution that destroyed forever its living remains" (Gorack 1988:52).

As for political leanings, romantic sensibilities, like peasant modernism, take left and right forms. Both romantic currents advance critiques about the progressive nature of modern urban industrial society to genuinely develop the countryside in ways superior to those of its organic culture and society. Whereas modernist ideas about the countryside see it as existing to be acted upon by the more dynamic modern urban society, romantic leftist views of peasant society see it not just as the passive victim of the forces of modern 'capitalist' society but as having the potential to play progressive roles in a transition to a postcapitalist society.

In the nineteenth and twentieth centuries, romantic ideas about rural life and peasants have been expressed in various populist philosophies and political programs. Peasant populism was the most developed in Russia. Central to the Going to the People and Land and Liberty movements of the 1870s was a vision of Russian development that could bypass a capitalist stage. The peasant commune was seen as a basis for developing a socialist democratic society in which petty commodity agricultural production rather than large-scale capitalist production would prevail. The Russian populists closely read Volume 1 of Marx's *Capital* but unlike Marx did not see the necessity for having to pass through a destructive phase of capitalist development. The existing peasant commune could instead provide a basis for socialism. Alexander Herzen was the first to popularize this idea that the Russian peasant commune, the *obshchina,* could serve as the foundation of an egalitarian, rural-based socialist society. This idea was "subsequently adopted by almost all the theorists of revolutionary populism in Russia" as an alternative to the capitalist route to socialism (Harding 1983:433).

Although for the most part they are permutations of the same basic structure that informs modernist assumptions, in the 1960s various romantic interpretations of rural society, especially left variants, began to dismantle its basic dualist worldview assumptions about development. A review of these recent romantic currents is useful, in that they enable us to envision yet deeper reconceptualization.

Right-Wing Romanticism

Right-wing romantics are, of all the theoretical dispositions, the most enamored of 'the traditional.' Right-wing ideas about rural society tend to be backward-looking reactions against contemporary society, which has undermined the old order. Thus, for example, in reaction to some of the social and philosophical aspects of the Enlightenment, Rousseau celebrated the noble savage and rural life in general. Rousseau, supported by the French nobility, was writing within a sociopolitical matrix that predisposed him to these ideas, just as it disposed Marie Antoinette to dress in lace versions of French peasant costumes and play as a shepherd with perfumed lambs in the gardens of Versailles at a time when the ancient regime was being undermined by the spread of capitalist relations.

For the nobility and those with aristocratic pretensions a rural society is a necessity, for how can there be a rural aristocracy without peasants. Such aristocratic dispositions to romantic constructions of a countryside also resonate with elite nationalist sentiments. In the nineteenth and twentieth centuries, conservative European nationalism often found expression as romantic populism, which sought to build a nation out of autochthonous natural and cultural resources of which the land—the countryside—and the peasants who populate it are the most basic resources, hence the linguistic resonances between 'country' and 'land' as nature and nation.

Such romantic sensibilities tend to project onto 'the peasantry' a backward-looking historical identity, the revival of which these romantics take up as a political project that is part of a greater nationalist project. Right-wing romantics tend to buttress romantic ideas and ideology with bourgeois social theory, especially varieties of neoclassical economics. Such synthesis is most apparent in the work of the Russian populist Alexsandr V. Chayanov.

Russian populism in the nineteenth century was predominantly leftist in proposing noncapitalist routes to a Russian socialism. But in the 1920s Chayanov's pro-peasant ideas, within the context of the Stalinist Soviet Union, assumed a right-wing stance in opposing forced collectivization. Chayanov's ideas were also consistent with right-wing dispositions in shifting emphasis from the commune to the peasant household as a unit of analysis. Thus, when Chayanov approached the perennial issue of social differentiation, he departed from the Leninist concern with class differentiation and class conflict to a neoclassical focus on the peasant household with its corresponding ideological resonances, although it appeared not as dominant ideology but instead as subversive to the Stalinist terror, of which Chayanov himself was a victim.

For Chayanov, social differentiation was the result not of enduring class relations but instead of phases in the life cycles of households. In this theoretical move of taking the household as his basic unit, he thus assumed a somewhat more social version of the individualism of hard-core utilitarianism. Although he was not a proponent of capitalist development, this modified methodological individualism of neoclassical economics, with a shunning of class analysis and a populist vision of 'the traditional family,' marked Chayanov as a right-wing romantic.

Chayanov was a paradigmatic peasantist in that he bracketed this type in the countryside and idealized it. Working within the tradition of nineteenth-century Russian populism, Chayanov sought to demonstrate the essential positive features of production organized by families within the context of peasant communes. The Chayanovians elaborate a peasantry that is imbued with a distinctive rationality. Although it borrows and modifies the basic modernist assumptions of neoclassical economics about the rational, maximizing individual, the Chayanovian theory of a peasant rationality is not an apologia for capitalist culture and economy but instead is a vision of the prerevolutionary Russian countryside as it was before the agony of forced collectivization. Thus, Chayanov was writing against Lenin and especially against Stalin and the collectivization of the New Economic Plan.

Lenin's main social unit was not 'community' but rural population. Whereas Lenin's modernism was apparent in his use of large populations and his concern with the power of the state to effect historical social change, Chayanov's romanticism predisposed him to a focus on small social units, examined ahistorically. He, even less than Lenin, did not extend his vision of what peasants are beyond the spheres of production and consumption, that is, he had little or no concern for peasants as social and cultural beings.

Robert Redfield is a romantic of a different kind who did much to lay the foundation for modernization theory, and in this regard the results of his work are consistent with right-wing modernism. But his basic disposition is that of an aristocratic romanticism. Aside from his prose style, the main indication of this is his implicit valuing of country over city, an attitude he shared with his father-in-law and founder of the Chicago school of urban sociology, Robert Park. Park (1915), like his colleague Louis Wirth, regarded urban problems such as crime, poverty, and violence as inherent in "the urban way of life" (Wirth 1951). Against such disorder and anonymity of the city, Redfield juxtaposed the "Little Community" with its rich web of integrated relationships and collective symbolic forms. There is in Redfield, as in Marx, a tragic quality that despairs of the inevitable erosion of the little community caused by the penetration of urban forces into the countryside with the inevitable "disorganization" such forces cause, a concern not shared by the more hard-core modernists. In his own way, Redfield was attempting to grapple with the complexity and differentiation in rural society. But in the end he essentialized "the Little Community" in a pastoral mode (Redfield 1956).

The works of James Scott, although definitely in a romantic mode, are difficult to categorize in terms of left-right leanings. In pointing out the innumerable ways in which economic value is extracted from them and the ways in which they resist such appropriation, Scott comes down on the side of the victims who are, compared to those who abuse them, the keepers of a 'moral economy.' But in attending almost exclusively to these "micro-technologies of resistance," Scott seems to deny the possibility of structural change that would liberate peasants from their adverse conditions. Thus, as in Chayanov's work, there is in Scott's a resonance with the unabashedly conservative, marginalist neoclassical microeconomists. Furthermore, Scott (1985:28) sees his work as a counter to "left-wing academic romance with wars of national liberation" (quoted by Gutmann 1993:77)

Left-Wing Romanticism

Although the right-romantic currents surveyed in the previous section erode the hegemonic modernist structuring of anthropological thinking about rural society, they were for the most part attempts to patch up the basic paradigm. Much deeper reconceptualization was, however, carried forward by a broad left-of-center intellectual current that emerged in the 1960s as a critique of both right- and left-wing modernist theories of development.

Dependency Theory

Just as 'peasants' appeared in modernization theory, they also appeared in the critique of modernization theory that came to be known as dependency theory, which called attention to the "de-developed" rural areas of the world. In terms of right and especially left theories of development, the Cuban Revolution of 1959 should not have happened. Like the Chinese Revolution of 1948, the Cuban Revolution occurred in a basically agrarian society with a large, impoverished rural population. According to the Marxist-Leninist orthodoxy adhered to by Latin American Communist Parties aligned with the Soviet Union, Latin American nations had to undergo capitalist development before conditions would ripen for transitions to socialism. From this point of view, the triumph of the Cuban Revolution and the establishment of a socialist government was an anomaly. In retrospect, it has often been noted that Cuba, whose economy was based on sugar production, was basically industrial, with the multitude of poor, underemployed sugarcane cutters actually more of a rural proletariat than a peasantry. Nevertheless, the revolution provoked a deep reassessment of prevailing ideas about Latin American history and development.

In the 1960s and 1970s, dependency theory was most accessible to North American readers in the early paradigmatic writings of Andre Gundar Frank (see especially 1967, 1969, 1979), Paul Baran (1957), and Dos Santos (1970).[3] The basic assumptions of dependency theory can be seen as a rejection of those of modernization theory; in rejecting them, dependency theory inverts them and takes them as its own. Indeed, it can be said that Frank, while a student at the University of Chicago, found modernization theory in the form of the Chicago School of Urban Sociology standing on its head and turned it right-side up.

Thus, although it began as a leftist critique of the developmentalism of the Latin American Communist Parties, to a great extent dependency theory is an inversion of the diffusionist assumptions of modernization theory, which posited an inexorable spread of the cultural and social traits of modernity into the backward countryside, transforming it into capitalist society. Dependency theory thus turned attention away from the 'diffusion' of modernity outward along the folk-urban continuum to an examination of the extraction of economic value from the 'periphery' and its 'accumulation' in the 'core' of the capitalist world system, a process that promoted the simultaneous de-development of the former and the growth of the latter.[4] Capitalist history is thus not a trend toward universal development but is instead, as occurred within local capitalist societies and economies, a process of economic and cultural differentiation now played out on a global scale. As such, dependency theory anticipated the present north-south structuring of postdevelopment discourse (see Chapter 5). Furthermore, developmentalism as ideology and policy is itself part of the mechanism of capitalist global differentiation.

The clearest expression of the Chicago paradigm of modernization, as worked out in anthropology, was Redfield's model of the "folk-urban continuum." We recall that the major assumption of the folk-urban continuum, and of modernization theory in general, was that 'underdevelopment' is the result of a historical lag whereby the modern poles of the world developed ahead of those that lack their dynamism. The underdeveloped areas are coming along but more slowly. Implicit here is the modernist assumption of *dualism,* namely, that the developed and underdeveloped areas of the world have been basically unconnected. The latter can, however, be helped to move forward in history by any form of intervention, for example, applied anthropology, that enhances the *diffusion* of modern traits from the developed areas (Chilcote and Edelstein 1986). This process would occur more rapidly were it not for barriers to the 'acceptance' of modernity, barriers that are found for the most part in the 'traditional' cultures and personality types prevalent in the underdeveloped societies.

The major deconstructive move of dependency theory was to reject the principle of dualism by historicizing underdevelopment within the context of global capitalism. Rather than being unconnected to Europe, Latin America was brought into its orb through conquest and colonialism. European powers imposed mercantilist and later imperialist policies on their colonies to extract economic value from them that was transferred back to Europe to underwrite its development at the expense of the colonies, which were simultaneously de-developed. Mines and plantations were worked by slaves and cheaply paid peasants. The silver, gold, and commodities so produced were exported to Europe and elsewhere, where profits were made that financed the economic development of Europe while the distortion of the colonial economies simultaneously de-developed them and brought about widespread poverty and misery that had not existed before the arrival of Europeans. This same analysis was also extended into the nineteenth and twentieth centuries when the United States replaced Europe as the main power, imposing relations of dependency on Latin America and benefiting from its exploitation.

The shortsightedness of both classical Marxist analysis and modernization theory was to assume that the juggernaut of European and North American capitalism would transform precapitalist societies in its own image everywhere it penetrated. Ironically, dependency theory, especially Frank's variety, was also seduced by a Eurocentric view of history. The main advance, however, of dependency theory was to initiate wide discussion of the way persistent 'backwardness' was linked to the development of the 'metropoles.' Backwardness and stagnation in the colonies and the postcolonial nations were seen not as modernization theory and classic Marxism saw them, as conditions of underdevelopment, but as resulting from systematic de-development brought about when merchant capital and later imperialism drained off wealth that fueled the development of Europe and North America and that still subsidizes their relatively high standards of living.

Dependency theory thus turned attention from the diffusion of the cultural traits of modernity from 'modern' to 'traditional' to the *extraction* of economic value from the 'satellites' to the 'metropoles' within the contexts of colonialism and neocolonialism. But in retrospect, this dismantling of modernist dualism is only partial, for a strong spatial residue of dualist thought is retained in the imagery of core and periphery but as poles that are mediated by mercantile and other forms of global capitalism. Certainly, for the colonial period this is an apt imagery, for colonialism did effect differentiation on a global scale. And to the high degree that colonial societies and economies were largely agrarian, this spatial differentiation was replicated in the global periphery as the opposition between city and country.

In addition to its partial deconstructive impact, dependency theory also effected considerable discursive displacement in that it was advanced primarily by Third World scholars. A conclusion of their analysis was that modernization was possible only by breaking out of foreign domination and establishing more progressive independent economic and political systems. Socialist or bourgeois revolutions were not only necessary but also most feasible in the peripheral countries. And dependency theorists effected further displacement by assuming that as in Cuba, China, and Vietnam, rural peoples—peasants—were destined to play major parts in such wars of national liberation.[5]

Rather than viewing them as passive subjects, dependency theory proposed that Third World peasants and proletarians were capable of being primary historical agents. In this regard it extended the work of Braudel, whose global social historiography decentered the "great men" of the West who are the subjects of conventional history.

In retrospect, it is possible to see the romantic dimensions of these ideas of the revolutionary power of rural peoples. Roseberry, for example, discusses how some Venezuelan leftists promoted rural guerrilla movements in the 1960s. But as in Mexico, Bolivia, and other Latin American countries, these movements did not attract the following leaders had hoped for. "One reason was that the movement romanticized and attempted to organize the peasantry during a decade when it was disappearing" (Roseberry 1989a:73).

From Dependency to Articulation

Dependency theory, when it came into discussions of 'development,' was a major step in the dismantling of the dualist assumptions of modernization theory. By showing that 'underdeveloped' areas were but the underbelly of 'developed' nations, dependency theorists furthered the possibilities of thinking globally, of seeing local history in terms of a "world system."[6]

But dependency theory is only a partial deconstruction of dualist anthropology, for its 'core' and 'periphery' are but permutations of the polar ends of the folk-urban continuum, a spatial opposition that also corresponds to the temporal distinction between anthropological Self and ethnographic Other—the one 'traditional,' the other 'modern.' Further movement in this direction was the task of a postdependency perspective that centered on concern with modes of production and how they are *articulated* in various configurations of development and nondevelopment.

This general body of articulation theory has been a major way station in the overall trend toward reconceptualization of the peasantry. As we will see later, articulation theory shifted attention away from dependency theory's primary concern with circulation of economic value to a concern with the production and accumulation of surplus. Furthermore, whereas dependency theory tended to see the modern world as one in which capitalism was nearly ubiquitous, articulation theory recognized complex interrelationships between capitalism and other modes of production. Underdeveloped areas were thus defined not just as instances of de-developed areas of the world capitalism system but instead as non-capitalist societies that were brought into being and maintained as such because of their integration with and subordination to capitalist economies.

Articulation is an apt term for such a relationship, since it implies the functional joining of two disparate entities such as arm and shoulder or thigh and hip. The anatomical metaphor of articulation was chosen as the preferred term to capture this type of reproduction of differentiation in which distinct modes of production, like bones connected at a joint, owe their differences to being combined in complementary functions (see Foster-Carter 1978; Kearney 1986a).

The germs of articulation theory are present in Marx's (1976 [1867]) discussion of the penetration of capitalist relations into noncapitalist societies from centers where it is already present in mature form. Central to this process is the progressive incorporation of noncapitalist labor into capitalist relations of production and exchange and the subsequent extraction of surplus value from those who expend such labor. In preliminary stages labor is only indirectly incorporated, or "formally subsumed," in Marx's terminology. He offers the example of how usurers advance money for raw materials or tools to primary producers who work with such resources at their own direction to produce a product that can be sold for cash, a large amount of which is paid back to the usurer at high interest, which "is just another name for surplus-value" (Marx 1976:1023). Another, deeper form of formal subsumption is effected by *"merchant's capital,* which commissions a number of immediate producers, then collects their produce and sells it, perhaps [like the usurer] making them advances in the form of raw materials, etc., or even money. It is this form that provides the soil from which modern capitalism has grown and here and there it still forms the transition to capitalism proper" (Marx 1976:1023, emphasis in original).

For Marx, such formal subsumption of labor in noncapitalist societies was a transitional phase in the development of industrial capitalism and real subsumption, that is, full proletarianization and a corresponding shift from absolute to relative surplus value (Marx 1976:1025). But by the 1970s it was increasingly apparent that what Marx and later orthodox Marxists regarded as "transitional" was actually fairly persistent and possibly an inherent feature of global capitalism. Furthermore, whereas Marx regarded formal subsumption—now read as articulation—as characteristic only of usury and merchant capitalism, the twentieth century offers numerous examples of labor from noncapitalist communities that is articulated with industrial capitalism, thus calling into question mature capitalism's ability to destroy noncapitalist modes of production. Also different from the original model of the subsumption of labor from noncapitalist communities is the now-recognized great importance of migration as the means whereby labor from the noncapitalist, usually 'peasant,' communities is delivered to industrial capital. Indeed, as revealed in examples offered later, it is migration that allows the articulation of 'peasant' communities with sites of industrial capital often at great distances from the home communities of the migrants and even in different nations.

When applied to peasant communities, this perspective took account of complexities of relations of production and processes of cultural reproduction not previously imagined by dependency theory, much less by ideas of peasants as part societies with part cultures. A review of contributions to articulation theory is useful, in that it has provided what is undoubtedly the most advantageous base from which to advance yet deeper reconceptualization of peasantry. Two types of contribution are noted here: One is to carry forward the dismantling of the dualism of core and periphery begun by dependency theory and world systems theory; the other is to move toward a more nuanced understanding of complex, internally differentiated subjects, often producing and reproducing under disparate and distantly separated sites and conditions, as discussed in Chapter 5.

Latin American Sources of Articulation Theory

Articulation theory shares with dependency theory the objective of explaining persistent underdevelopment in postcolonial countries, but the two differ with regard to the causes of this situation. The pivotal article here is Laclau's frequently cited "Feudalism and Capitalism in Latin America" (1971), which is the single most incisive critique of Frank's thesis of the development of underdevelopment as a result of the presumed early penetration of capitalism. Laclau's main points are, first, that Frank's analysis is confined to the sphere of circulation and is not sufficiently concerned with capitalism as a specific type of production. Capitalism is not, as Frank implies, synonymous with markets and commerce but instead has an essential characteristic as a mode of production, namely, wage labor. Laclau says that as a consequence of these oversights, Frank has rejected several interrelated Marxist concepts—namely, mode of production, surplus value, exploitation, and class analysis. Laclau shows how Frank distorts history by insisting that capitalist relations were introduced into Latin America at the very beginning of colonialism, thus denying the introduction and persistence of feudal relations.

There is no argument here about the transfer of wealth from the colonies to the colonial centers, from periphery to core, or from satellite to metropole, as Frank would say. Rather, the debate centers on the mechanisms of accumulation. On this issue Frank, focusing on circulation in the marketplace, falsely assumes that wealth is increased by exchange rather than by production by human labor.

Certainly, international exchange was a central feature of sixteenth- and seventeenth-century mercantilism, as it is of contemporary global relations, but the source of the commodities exchanged remains a question. If capitalist relations of production were dominant, then a proletarianized wage labor force would have to be the source of wealth created in the colonies, producing the surplus drained off through the conduits of markets. But in fact the persistence of pre-Columbian tributary systems that extracted goods and labor from indigenous communities, the institution of slavery and debt peonage, and the forced labor of nominally free populations were the dominant relations of production throughout Latin America until well into the twentieth century. And only in the twentieth century has extensive proletarianization taken place. But we have only recently begun to understand how proletarianization in de-developed areas and the resultant configuration of class relations in those areas differ from those of the industrial capitalist nations.

Dependency theory's main contribution was to present and defend the thesis of persistent de-development. Its weakness, however, was a failure to resolve the apparent paradox it posed, namely, the presence of a presumed pervasive capitalism with underdevelopment. But as Laclau and other critics have demonstrated, noncapitalist forms persisted into the twentieth century in close association with capitalist forms. Not only were they coexistent, but contrary to the dual economy thesis, they were intimately articulated. And contrary to the dependency thesis, aspects of feudalism were not only coexistent with capitalism but were perpetuated by virtue of this association.

Thus, Laclau reintroduced discussion of feudalism and in doing so raised the issue of the persistence of precapitalist or noncapitalist modes of production in general. But clearly, feudalism is dead in Latin America and the rest of the world. If feudalism is gone and capitalism has not filled the vast deserts of underdevelopment, what other noncapitalist forms then prevail? To answer this question we must escape from Eurocentric categories, of which even Laclau, with his attention to feudalism, was partially a prisoner. The route of escape was provided primarily by several currents of Marxist anthropology, expressed in the works of Stavenhagen and Wolf, who although essentializing, are also more cognizant than anyone else in the 1960s and 1970s of the problematic nature of 'the peasant.'[7]

> Indeed, one of the essential characteristics of peasant economies in the contemporary world is that peasant production is invariably found to be subordinated to the dominant economy. In the majority of cases, this is a capitalist economy. Subordination is manifested in various ways, but the principal result is the same: the peasant economy transfers net value to the capitalist sector; in other words it is exploited by the latter. (Stavenhagen 1978:31–32)

As noted earlier, Marx envisioned such formal subsumption as transitional, destined to disappear under the destructive but progressive power of capitalism to remake precapitalist societies in its own image within the context of imperialism. But conditions of persistent underdevelopment noted in the 1970s implied that such articulations were not transitional but were inherent in capitalism as a global system. Accordingly, these 'traditional' economies and their corresponding sociocultural forms were considered not to be surviving precapitalist forms but instead to be noncapitalist forms that were reproduced in the present precisely because of their subordination to capitalism.

Among the most comprehensive and incisive anthropological theorizations of peasant articulation is that of Angel Palerm (1980), who situates the changing and enduring relationship between peasant and nonpeasant "modes of production" within broad comparative historical-structural contexts. There is a strong romantic dimension to Palerm's analysis, in that he sees ongoing processes of repeasantization as driven by the dependence of capitalist agriculture on cheap labor produced in peasant communities. And with a certain ironic twist, he argues that such repeasantization is at times furthered by agrarian reform, which, although ostensibly intended to modernize peasants out of existence, renews the political and material bases for their preservation (Palerm 1980:182–183). Indeed, Palerm attributes the modern turn of anthropology to peasant studies in the 1950s and 1960s to the increased political significance of those studies and chides anthropologists for ignoring the long tradition of peasant studies in Europe that were provoked by similar political global- and national-level tensions present in the mid-twentieth century. His own distinctive contribution, however, was to enrich the *campesinista* (peasantist) perspective in Mexico through an elaboration of articulation theory.

French and African Sources
of Articulation Theory

Most of the debate over dependency theory and modes of production in Latin America took place among economists and sociologists who were writing about the countryside, peasants, and rural proletarians from their own urban experiences. But the modes of production debate was also advanced by French anthropologists who, as a result of their fieldwork in peripheral settings, had a more fine-grained, ethnographic view of rural areas.[8] Also influential here was Althusser's structural Marxism, which led him to ponder the articulation of the various instances of a capitalist formation (see Althusser 1977; Althusser and Balibar 1970). This concern appears to have disposed his students, Rey and Meillassoux, to rethink the relations between distinct modes of production. Also, Meillassoux notes that he was sensitized to this perspective by seeing African migrants in France: "Our research, which had begun in African villages, led us to the squalid and overcrowded dormitories of Paris suburbs where the very same men that we met in their places as proud peasants were converted into anonymous proletarians" (Meillassoux 1981:ix–x). As in Latin America, articulation theory in France was strongly influenced by anthropological studies of migration that forced consideration of peasants as complex subjects.[9]

As Klein (1980a) points out, there were various distinct forms of subsumption of less than fully proletarianized labor in the vastness of Africa, ranging from plantations to migration into the copper mines of Zambia; in West Africa peasant commodity production prevailed, and in southern Africa "hunger for labor converted large areas into labor reserves and strongly distorted the growth of others" (Klein 1980b:19).[10]

Another application of articulation theory to come out of Africa is Burawoy's (1976) comparison of the structure of apartheid in South Africa with Mexican farm labor in California. In the former case, the tribal "homelands" were artificially created and maintained as sites for the reproduction of labor absorbed in distant industries and services, whereas in the latter case, circular migrant farmworkers in California were produced in and retired back onto rural Mexican communities.[11] In both cases, participation in "modern capitalist" spheres allowed for the social and cultural reproduction of the seemingly "traditional noncapitalist" communities.

U.S. Sources of Articulation Theory

As noted earlier, the Vietnam War had a deep impact on U.S. anthropology, which came to see it as a "peasant war." Involvement of anthropologists in the antiwar movement in the late 1960s (Wakin 1992) paralleled the events in France in 1968 that influenced the emergence of articulation among French anthropologists. In the United States, early moves to reconceptualize the hegemonic Redfieldian notions of the peasantry are associated with the anthropology of Julian Steward (1902–1972), who in retrospect can be seen as disposed to question and dismantle anthropology's tendency to create primordial types and dualist "oppositional histories" (see Roseberry 1989a:213–217).

This antiabsolutism is apparent in the evolutionary typology with which Steward reorganized the *Handbook of South American Indians* (1946–1952; see Steward 1949:670–671). In this classification the most peripheral types—"the marginals"—owe their social and cultural forms to historical processes manifested through space, which originate in the urban centers of high civilization. The Andean climax areas are one end of a chain of interconnected adjacent superordinate-subordinate types, the other end of which are the marginals. Instead of seeing the contemporary hunter-gatherers as surviving primitive precursors of state civilizations and chiefdoms, Steward views them as peoples who have been pushed into peripheral areas on the fringes of the more complex types. In effect, Steward—whose early critical work on this issue has largely been ignored—relativized South American hunters and gatherers in a way that has only recently been attempted for African foragers (see Gordon 1992; Wilmsen 1989). Steward's multilineal evolutionism thus opened the possibility of histories other than those traced by modernization theorists, in which Western culture and its nation-states are the end point and motor force of development. Steward's students apparently acquired this sensibility and developed it into a distinctive North American concern with modes of production and their articulation that contrasts sharply with the Redfieldian folk-urban paradigm.

Ever prescient, the work of Eric Wolf, a student of Steward (see Lauria Perricelli 1989; Silverman 1979), is the bridge to images of the countryside that go beyond ideas of the 'traditional' peasant based on the dualist assumptions discussed earlier.[12] Of significance here is Wolf's reading of Marx in the early 1950s (Ghani 1987:356). Wolf, who is basically a productionist, brought to U.S. anthropology the concern with 'modes of production' noted earlier and thus introduced a Marxist counterpart to the 'little community' seen as a barrier against the spread of capitalist modernity into the countryside: Indeed, for Wolf the modern peasantry is formed largely by capitalism. But unlike Lenin and the modernizationists, Wolf does not seem to see an inevitable complete replacement of the peasant by the full development of capitalism, although he also does not seem to share romantic dispositions. Wolf's image of the countryside is more complex than that of any of the authors I have mentioned so far.

In the mid-1950s, in contrast to Redfield's lumping tendencies, Wolf (1955) provisionally proposed seven types of peasant communities, all of which are defined in terms of the "structural relations" whereby they are integrated with nonpeasant forms of production. Although they are all defined only in terms of productionist criteria, the range of production they participate in is fairly wide. In this theoretical landscape, the classic peasant is associated with only one socioeconomic type—the "closed corporate community"—which owes its existence to its relationships with other rural systems of production such as plantations, haciendas, open communities, and capitalist farming. Although the term *articulation* is not present in these writings, the concept is implicit and basic.

Wolf's model of the closed corporate community is comparable in its intellectual impact to Redfield's model of the peasant community with which it so markedly differs. Their main point of contrast is in the way the two authors conceive that their communities fit within the greater sociology of the countryside. Redfield situates his peasants at an intermediary point on the folk-urban continuum, where they are exposed to the traits of modernity that diffuse outward from the urban areas. The traditional society would give way before the penetration of urban traits were it not for the traditional culture—backwardness—that inhibits their acceptance. For Redfield, the traditional culture closes the modern out.

In somewhat of a similar vein, Wolf (1957, 1986) speaks of the "closed corporate peasant community," but it is closed only with respect to the penetration of outsiders and outside social forms; with respect to the extraction of value it is exceedingly open. Wolf develops this analysis without any recourse to "tradition"— indeed, the word is hardly in his vocabulary. Furthermore, Wolf's corporate peasant community, unlike Redfield's "little community," is brought into being by historical-structural forces (which in 1955 he referred to as "cultural structural"). Wolf's (1969:xiv) definition of peasants as people who are "existentially involved in cultivation and make autonomous decisions regarding the process of cultivation" is prototypical modernist-productionist peasant essentialism. However, if these local definitions are set within the greater body of Wolf's writing on the countryside, then we find in his texts observations that dissolve the brackets he has placed around the peasant.

With few exceptions, such as Wolf's work, the theoretical containment of 'peasants' to domains of agricultural production is consistent with the tendency to conceptualize them as members of local communities. The methodological practice of delimiting a single bounded community as the site of research was the dominant mode in which the conventional anthropological image of 'the peasant' was formed and doubtlessly contributed to the narrow definition of the peasant in terms of the domestic sphere. Certainly in Mesoamerica, highland Andean areas, and elsewhere, this tendency to see peasants as members of local communities was reinforced by the reality of closed corporate peasant communities. The fact that these communities were inhabited mostly by indigenous peoples made them especially attractive to anthropologists as research sites. Hence, several conditions coincided that added to other predispositions to define—to contain— 'peasants' as denizens of small, circumscribed life spaces.

But as noted earlier, for Wolf this closed community is but one type that contrasts with a variety of open peasant communities, open in the sense that they have more complex economic and social relations with other milieus and also in the sense that they are open to cultural forces and identities that are closed out of the indigenous corporate communities. Thus in 1957, Wolf anticipated a more recent concern with "unbounded" communities and units of analysis.[13] Wolf (1955:461) noted that "for the construction of this type" he relied on his own fieldwork in Puerto Rico. Subsequently, he described how peasant communes and sugar haciendas in Morelos, Mexico, are articulated through wage labor. This general paradigm reaches full maturity in his *Europe and the People Without History* (1982), which recounts how various noncapitalist types are incorporated into global capitalism.

Wolf's classic peasant writings do not consider either urban migration or nonagricultural economic activities, such as participation in the so-called informal economy. Nevertheless, the Wolfian peasant is an ambulatory type who gets around a great deal as he or she moves in and out of different spheres of production. Wolf's peasant is a mobile type whose natural history demands fieldwork in all of the various ecosystems within which he or she moves and reproduces. It is thus a testament to the complexity of Wolf's thinking that even as he articulates some of the most explicit versions of peasant essentialism, he is also one of the earliest and most consistent anthropologists to begin to deconstruct that very peasant essentialism in whose elaboration he has participated.

Wolfian anthropology deals with differentiation in ways rather unlike the Leninists, Chayanovians, and orthodox marginalists, who are all concerned with the tripartite socioeconomic categories defined with respect to a narrow conception of peasant production organized in terms of household units—small, medium, and large.[14] Wolfian peasants not only work in their domestic spheres, but also *labor* in a much wider economic universe that includes haciendas, mines, plantations, and so on, which are all sites of production with which the neoclassical peasantists do not concern themselves and would instead have peasants contained within their gardens and fields.

Wolf's de-essentializing work is also prefigured in his discussion of the formation in Mexico of the mestizo, that ambiguous social identity born of an indigenous mother and a European father. Wolf contrasts the mestizos of Mexico with the property-owning middle classes who "possessed a stake in constituted society."

> The mestizos, on the other hand, comprised both men who worked with their hands and men who worked with their wits. They shared not a common stake in society but the lack of such a stake; they shared a common condition of social alienation. Relegated to the edges of society, living in permanent insecurity, their reactions were akin not to the firmly anchored, substantial European middle classes but to the groups which Karl Marx called the "Lazarus-layers of the working class" and to the rootless, underemployed, unemployable intelligentsia-in-rags of post–1929 Europe who furnished the *condottiere* of the European Right and Left. In their common estrangement from society, the petty official, the political fixer, the hard-pressed rancher, the hungry priest, found a common denominator with the Indian bereft of the protection of his community, the artisan burning his midnight oil in poverty and religious devotion, the petty trader or cattle-rustler, the half-employed pauper of the streets, the ragamuffin of the Thieves' Market. Such men constituted neither a middle class nor a proletariat; they belonged to a social shadow-world. (Wolf 1959:242)

The mestizo is an ambiguous type who confounded colonial racial identities by being neither Indian nor European. But as Wolf describes him, he also does not conform to conventional social identities and instead belongs to a "shadow-world." By introducing this ambiguous, problematic type, Wolf opened the door to consideration of rural social complexity beyond standard structural types of identity, a complexity that makes typological essentialism untenable. Certainly, the mestizo was discussed by anthropologists prior to the appearance of *Sons of the Shaking Earth* in 1959.[15] But the mestizo was then characteristically essentialized as distinct from "Indian."

Once the mestizo as a type that resists essentializing is present in the anthropological literature, a next possible step would be the consideration of mestizo peasants. If mestizos are difficult to classify as social types, then what kind of peasants do they make? The answer would seem to be, typologically speaking, rather poor ones. This is an issue to which I will return, but first I note that most U.S. anthropologists working in Latin America finessed this challenge by working not in mestizo but in "Indian" peasant communities, which vis-à-vis Euro-modern types are unambiguously contrastive, or so they seem. The combined closed corporateness *and* Indian cultural identity of these communities resulted in a doubly determined essentialization of them as 'traditional': first as 'indigenous' and second as 'peasant.'

In Wolf's hands, articulation theory not only dismantles the distinction between the 'traditional' and the 'modern' by revealing how each is but the obverse of the other, in that both are bound into circuits of exchange that fuel their differentiation—the basic assumption of articulation theory—but goes further by illuminating the presumed spatial separation of development and de-development. And it does this by redirecting theoretical concern away from a nearly exclusive attention to circulation back to considerations of production and reproduction within historical and global contexts.

From Articulation to Disarticulated Economies

Alain de Janvry's (1981) *The Agrarian Question and Reformism in Latin America* can be read as a major contribution to de-essentialization of the peasant. Working with a modes of production perspective, de Janvry presents a model of "articulated" and "disarticulated economies." In de Janvry's model, the term *articulated economies* is a gloss for developed societies at the core of the world system in which a correspondence exists between the production of capital goods (Sector I) and the production of consumption goods (Sector II): "On the supply side, the economy is *sectorally articulated,* for linkages exist between productive sectors. An increase in the production of consumption goods creates an increase in the derived demand for capital goods" (de Janvry 1981:27, emphasis in original). The same is also true on the demand side, where "the necessary relation between the development of production and consumption capacities (i.e., between derived demand for capital goods and final demand for wage goods) implies a *social articulation* between capitalists and laborers" (de Janvry 1981:27–28, emphasis in original).

The two sectors are articulated in that consumption of wage goods (for the reproduction of the workforce) is paid for with wages that are earned in both sectors. The production of capital goods, which produce consumer goods, is also supported by this consumption. The result is social and sectoral articulation—that is, integration of the economy with social differentiation in a system that is more or less self-sufficient.

Sectorally and socially disarticulated economies are located in the periphery of the world capitalist system and are of two types: export enclave and import substitution. In these disarticulated economies, the counterparts of Sectors I and II are referred to as the "modern" and "traditional," respectively.

> Under *sectoral disarticulation,* forward linkages in the production of raw materials (plantations and mining) and backward linkages in industrial production (outward- and inward-oriented) do not exist. Industrialization under sectoral disarticulation thus implies external dependency for the import of capital goods and technology and places equilibrium in the balance of payments as a necessary constraint on the capacity to produce. The performance of the export sector and the nature of the terms of

trade on the international market are determinants of accumulation in the modern sector. (de Janvry 1981:33, emphasis in original)

This condition corresponds to social disarticulation in which the traditional sector does not have the consumption capacity to absorb the products of the modern sector. Rather than providing consumers, who can clear the shelves of commodities produced in the modern sector, the traditional sector functions primarily as a source of low wage labor for the externally oriented modern sector. The modern sector is thus dependent on the sale of luxury goods and export to developed nations in return for capital investment. This relation of "uneven exchange" results in the transfer of surplus from periphery to core, from disarticulated to articulated economies.

Within this model, a primary source of surplus accumulated in the modern sectors of peripheral and core nations is impoverished rural, small, noncapitalist agriculturists producing primarily for auto consumption. They are sources of cheap food and cheap labor, which are at the base of chains of accumulation. Because they are producing at an infrasubsistence level, these agriculturalists must enter wage labor markets as semiproletarianized workers who, because of their partial support from their own food production, are able to accept low wages— which translate into the accumulation of surplus transferred to the modern sector. De Janvry refers to this condition as functional dualism, which is most apparent in commercial agriculture where the rate of profit "is maintained by compensating for cheap food through the hiring of cheap agricultural labor. The hiring of semiproletarian rural workers at wages below subsistence costs is secured through *functional dualism with subsistence agriculture.* Subsistence agriculture thus becomes the ultimate embodiment of the contradictions of accumulation in the disarticulated economies" (de Janvry 1981:39, emphasis in original).[16]

Although conceptualized in dualist terms, de Janvry's model nevertheless advances beyond dualist economic and social concepts of city and country, of modern and traditional. Moreover, in his historical vision the distinction between them is constantly dissolving as the laws of motion of global capitalism eliminate the material bases of the traditional sector. De Janvry's historical sensibility is in this respect rather modernist in foreseeing a disappearance of difference between modern urban and traditional rural societies. But this is not a Redfieldian teleology in which the modern absorbs the traditional but instead is one in which impoverished rural traditional peoples are gradually reduced to an urban underclass. Class, for de Janvry, is the final arbiter of difference.

Several trends will ensure the eventual destruction of small producers as a rural type. First is population growth because of the economic value of children in peasant and semiproletarian households. Then there is the constant encroachment of commercial operations into the land occupied by subsistence producers. The combined pressures of population increase and reduced access to land compel small producers to intensify production to the point where ecological deterioration undermines capacity to produce. But "even though peasants are eliminated as food producers and transformed into a labor reserve, functional dualism is re-created in other forms in the course of its elimination" (de Janvry 1981:39). How? Rural-to-urban migration results in an ever-expanding informal sector, "which becomes a new source of subsidy for the maintenance and reproduction of labor power" (de Janvry 1981:40).

In addition to de Janvry's partial movement beyond dualist thinking, several germinal ideas are present in his vision of postpeasant futures that are helpful in reconceptualization. First, there is the introduction of ecological issues into the agrarian question. As we will see in Chapter 8, the coupling of ecological concerns with the theory of peasant society has been a major influence restructuring it. Ecological thinking, with its sensibility of complex interrelations between environment and human communities, is essentially nondualist. Second, there is de Janvry's vision of what in effect is a postpeasant society without development. In such a society, peasants will have been absorbed into the constantly expanding urban informal economy that becomes an increasingly important source of accumulation in disarticulated societies. At the same time, the peasantry that remains in the countryside "is forced onto more and more minute and eroded land plots, where it is of necessity increasingly semiproletarianized. And lack of employment opportunities blocks sufficient outmigration and perpetuates rural misery" (de Janvry 1981:121–122).

But these ideas are only hinted at in de Janvry's work, which basically is focused on the enduring issue of economic differentiation in agriculture conceived in dualist terms. Thus, although de Janvry makes intriguing mention of peasants and the informal sector in chapter 2 of his book, when he addresses economic class differentiation more closely he reverts to a conventional two-dimensional field of analysis summed up in a diagram (see de Janvry 1981:117, Figure 4.2) that is one of the most comprehensive and theoretically sophisticated representations of peasant differentiation in the history of peasant studies. But even so, it is only two-dimensional: One axis is "production income," and the other is "wage income," which corresponds to a distinction between land ownership and agricultural work, respectively. Although de Janvry's model of the decomposition of peasants is more complex than Lenin's, in the end, with respect to social (class) differentiation in the countryside, de Janvry is basically a Leninist. In this model, rural identities are unitary. Individuals are seen as belonging to either one type or the other or as being in motion between them.

Here one would like to see differentiation also charted in other dimensions, especially that of the informal economy. De Janvry's earlier prescient awareness about the growing importance of the informal economy is absent from this scheme, in which the inertia of the dualist conceptual framework—labor versus capital—prevails. And what about differentiation in other non-economic—cultural—dimensions? Also, the discussion of differentiation in this diagram is framed in terms of individuals. One would like to see a consideration of differentiation in terms of households and of communities as well. Clearly, that is too much for a single diagram. But we must see differentiation of individuals *and* households *and* communities as occurring within more complex, multidimensional spaces. When identity is so considered we will find that unitary subject identity of 'the peasant' has largely vanished (see Chapter 5).

To a great extent, appreciation of a more nuanced internal differentiation has been inhibited by the lack of categories to conceptualize it. The official categories of rural anthropology and economics are both symptom and cause of such categorical hegemony. It is through such categories that social scientists apprehend rural social reality even as they study it to inform policies that in turn reify the categories. Thus, data tend to be collected through categories that reify rural and urban identities, as well as unitary class identities. Dualist thinking is predisposed to binary either-or categories readily susceptible to coding for digital statistical manipulation. It is not the case that multiple dimensional coding and analysis of subject identities is impossible but rather that there is a correspondence between the needs to specify unambiguous identities for both official bureaucratic administrative purposes and the categories of identity of the social sciences, which, after all, share a common culture with the bureaucratic domain.

Thus, de Janvry (1981:109–114) develops a "typology of farm enterprises," but as with all such typologies they must coincide with the categories in which extant comparative data exist. The data de Janvry uses in the "empirical characterization of the rural class structure" in his model were collected by the Inter-American Committee for Agricultural Development. The data categories are Large Multifamily Farms, Medium Multifamily Farms, Family Farms, and Subfamily Farms. Each of these identities is a unitary subject position. Subjects may, of course, change from one category to another, but subjects are not conceived as occupying more than one position at a given time. But in de Janvry's typology, another type—the "semiproletarian" who is part peasant, part worker—is added. This term reflects considerable deconstructive movement but movement that occurs only along a unilineal historicity laden with Leninist assumptions about class differentiation in the countryside—that is, that the long-term trend in the development of capitalist agriculture is to dispossess and fully proletarianize most peasants. Indeed, this was to have been the historical mission of capitalist agriculture.

But given de Janvry's demonstration of the persistence and indeed the increase of rural misery and infrasubsistence agriculture in disarticulated economies, it would be as appropriate to refer to semipeasants.[17] Similarly, given the high degree to which semipeasants enter the informal economy, it would be as appropriate to refer to them as semi-informalized. Clearly, such a neologism is undesirable, but if it is, so then are other semis. The point here is that all such terms are burdened with residual dualist thinking. The emergence of the semiproletarian in the Leninist models is a partial recognition of the actual complexity of rural identities. As such, it is a progressive step in the reconceptualization of the peasantry. But it is a concept that reifies dualist thought even as it struggles to escape from it.

De Janvry's work is important to reconceptualization in that it partakes of both modernist and romantic sensibilities and as such tends to blur the boundaries between them (see Figure 4.1). He is modernist in foreseeing the power of capitalist society to eliminate peasants from history. Like Lenin, he sees capitalism as promoting a differentiation that destroys the peasantry. But at the same time he is romantic in that he does not see the forces of modernization in capitalist society developing the peasants out of existence through either modern agriculture or proletarianization. Instead, contrary to both such possibilities, demographic growth and environmental degradation in disarticulated economies result in a proliferation of the informal sector, that is, a growth of postpeasant urban and rural poverty. De Janvry sees peasants in semiproletarian form disappearing only when the contradictions of disarticulated economies are overcome, which is not likely in the near future. Thus, with respect to policy options, de Janvry bases recommendations on the assumption that the ongoing decomposition of the peasantry displaces class struggle toward proletarian issues. This implies the need to forge alliances "between workers and those segments of the peasantry that can be mobilized for this purpose" (de Janvry 1981:268).

Several observations can be made about the implicit assumptions of this recommendation. First, it is notable that after the advances de Janvry makes in de-essentializing 'the peasant' and undermining the dualist assumptions on which the concept is based, in the end he reverts to a marked reification. Identities are still unitary: Individuals are basically either peasants or proletarians; class consciousness condenses in primarily one or the other modality. Other modalities and forms for the expression of class consciousness are not considered. Suppressed here, for example, are de Janvry's earlier insightful observations about the growth of the informal economy. By pushing de Janvry's analysis of the growth and rural-urban spread of the informal economy to its political implications, one can arrive at a structural appreciation of the conditions that condition the recent proliferation in Latin America and elsewhere of the "new social movements" that organize along neither proletarian nor peasant lines and that indeed in certain ways incorporate and transcend such dualist arbiters of identity.[18] But in the end, de Janvry opts for a modified proletarianist position still partially predicated on dualist assumptions, although one that more completely than any other contextualizes the agrarian question in national and international contexts.

The work of Scott Cook on small-scale agricultural and craft producers in the Valley of Oaxaca, Mexico, is an excellent fine-grained ethnographic complement to de Janvry's macroeconomic model.[19] An enduring concern in Cook's work has been the social differentiation of small agricultural and nonagricultural producers, ranging from full-time peasants to peasant-artisans to piece workers to petty merchants to petty industrial capitalists. Cook's work is relevant to our two principal concerns, namely, movement beyond dualist thinking and the nexus of differentiation and social identity.

Just as de Janvry's work largely corrected dualist conceptions of national economies, Cook and Leigh Binford effect a similar critique at the level of small-scale agricultural and nonagricultural production. Marshaling considerable survey data, they reject Chayanovian-type models that posit distinct economic spheres for peasant and peasant-artisan producers as compared with capitalist economic enterprises. Whereas the dependency theorists saw capitalism as having penetrated early into the major industries of peripheral countries, Cook and Binford call attention to how it is deeply rooted in local small-scale production, which both articulationists and neoclassically oriented Chayanovian types characterize as noncapitalist economies.

Thus, in contrast to scores of investigators who have seen the Valley of Oaxaca and other comparable regions as populated with subsistence and petty commodity producers operating outside of capitalist relations, Cook and Binford see it as a single, complexly differentiated capitalist economy into which the smallest producers and merchants are organized. They are thus staunchly antidualist in rejecting the existence of distinct, articulated modes of production. Indeed, their research convincingly makes the case for the widespread presence of petty capitalist relations of production in various craft industries that exist in organic relationship with 'peasant' production.

> Appearances to the contrary, rural industrial wage laborers and petty merchant and industrial capitalists are concealed behind the residence lots (*solares*) of the region's villages, enclosed by walls of adobe, organ cactus, and thorn branches. The smallness of scale of capitalist enterprises, as indicated by low ratios of employees to employers, combined with low levels of capitalization, helps to explain why many visitors to the Valley treat its rural zones as bastions of subsistence and petty commodity production and as lacking capitalist development. (Cook and Binford 1990:112)

Contrary to such a view, Cook and Binford (1990:30) "argue for a complete rejection of dualistic thinking and for the acceptance of a unitarian commodity economy concept." In such an economy it is common for small petty commodity–producing households to achieve sufficient "endofamilial accumulation" to hire labor to weave, sew, do fieldwork, and so forth, and so to become petty capitalists. But this is a nickel and dime capitalism that within any particular household may last for only a generation or less. Such petty capitalism is, however, common and as such is an expression of distorted development in which the macro conditions do not allow for growth of these petty capitalist operations into more robust forms.

Although Cook and Binford do not make reference to de Janvry's (1981) model of peasant differentiation and disarticulated national economies, they arrive at similar conclusions regarding the structural depth of distorted development in Mexico in general and in Oaxaca in particular as a context in which poverty and extreme inequality persist. This is the greater macro context in which petty capitalists thrive but seldom grow. This is also the context in which dualists misperceive petty capitalists as exploited peasants and artisans, failing to realize that they are involved in the accumulation of surplus value within their own communities.

And herein lies the failure of so many class-based development and political programs that are directed at exploited "peasants" and "workers." Cook and Binford are adamant that class is a basic structural feature of such situations in that it is the basis of difference upon which the differential accumulation of value is effected. However, the complexity of economic relations yields no cleavage planes that clearly demarcate exploiter from exploited. Also, many exploited persons seek betterment of their situation by bootstrapping themselves into a position where they will be able to hire workers of their own. "Social relations of production, so readily distilled into classes by the social scientist, are lived concretely, often ambiguously, through complex vertical and horizontal ties of kinship, patronage, and dependency and [are] encompassed by discourses that develop around such factors as locality, kinship, and ethnicity along with class" (Cook and Binford 1990:228). Furthermore, ideas about private property, payment, and reward for hard work "serve to justify, legitimize, and, therefore, mask the multiple forms of exploitation of labor by capital" (Cook and Binford 1990:229). The perception of class is thus doubly blurred and obscured from consciousness: first by the multitasking of individuals and households that call to mind Wolf's complex identity of mestizo types noted earlier and second by "concepts, which are part and parcel of petty commodity economy [and that] meld into the hegemonic ideology of capitalism and reinforce the orthodox neoclassical view of income distribution" (Cook and Binford 1990:229).

Cook and Binford argue effectively that this sort of complex identity is not disposed to a clear politics of class. Because it is so contradictory within itself, it may in different political junctures lean either left or right. But over the long run it tends more to the right than to the left and thus participates in the overall reproduction of social relations in the distorted peripheral economy. In their discussion of political programs for overcoming distorted development in Oaxaca, Cook and Binford (1990) do not consider options other than those of conventional party politics and thus fail to carry forward the political implications of their social and cultural analysis. Advance on this front is dependent on a theory of the subject that corresponds to the refinements Cook and Binford make in class analysis. Such work, which entertains options other than party politics, is one of the tasks of Chapter 5, that develops a theory of subject identity that corresponds to the contradictory structuring of class Cook and Binford describe for Oaxaca.

In sum, like de Janvry's work, Cook and Binford's research advances our understanding of the complexities of class differentiation and its effects on political dispositions of subalterns in places like Oaxaca. Indeed, it is perhaps the most incisive ethnographic study of class in the history of peasant studies. Yet, like de

Janvry's model, considerable residual essentialization of unitary subjects and some structural dualism are still present in it.[20] But their work does significantly move analysis of class differentiation deeper into the identity of complexly constituted subjects.

Cook and Binford's (1990) work, like dependency theory, is fairly modernist in its insistence on the pervasiveness of capitalism, but it goes one step beyond dependency theory in this regard by tracing capitalist relations and ideology into the home workshop of petty producers. But the outwardly "peasant," precarious, and often ephemeral nature of this petty capitalism of distorted development *is distinct* from large-scale merchant and industrial capitalism. Furthermore, this global differentiation is, in their view, a structural feature of global capitalism and as such is consistent with romantic views of subalterns as distinct from those of modernists. Thus, Cook and Binford both reject peasant essentialism and affirm a specific kind of subaltern distinctiveness and therefore theoretically adopt a form of modified articulationism.

Whereas Cook and Binford examine articulation within households in the Valley of Oaxaca, J. V. Palerm (Palerm 1989, 1991; Palerm and Urquiola 1993) traces the growth of articulation within households in the Bajio region of central Mexico as they become incorporated into "binational communities" that are themselves components in a "binational system of agricultural production." The articulationist assumptions of Palerm's work are indicated by his use of such terms as *peasant* for people who are also migrant workers and of *binational system of agricultural production,* with an emphasis here on *binational* and *production* as opposed to consumption (integrated systems of capitalist and noncapitalist production are the hallmark of articulation theory).

One side of this system is California agriculture, which, with a heritage of large Spanish holdings, tends to be based on large corporate units that are now capital-intensive. But although highly capitalized and technologically advanced, California agriculture has remained labor-intensive and in different historical periods has drawn its labor primarily from 'peasant' communities throughout the Pacific Basin and most recently from communities in Mexico. Palerm and Urquiola (1993) take two communities as case studies: the town of Guadalupe in coastal central California and the municipality of Valle de Santiago in the state of Guanajuato. Migrant workers from Valle de Santiago began to migrate heavily to Guadalupe and other agricultural areas of California during the era of the 1941–1964 binational labor treaty between Mexico and the United States known as the *bracero* program, which allowed U.S. growers to hire temporary Mexican migrant workers. Palerm and Urquiola (1993:345) describe how, during this period and subsequently, "many Guanajuato families became firmly established in California rural/agricultural communities" but did so while maintaining "a home base in Mexico," thus forming "binational households" that span the border and whose members share incomes, pool resources, and provide mutual assistance.

Despite the great distance separating Valle de Santiago and Guadalupe and mounting obstacles created by the INS [Immigration and Naturalization Service] to discourage illegal border crossings, growing numbers of binational household members easily move back and forth across the border, not only seeking employment in the United States but also to attend weddings, baptisms, and other social gatherings on either side. Money, goods, and gifts flow with equal ease, and it becomes common practice, for example, for U.S. residents (legal and documented) to access private and public medical services in Mexico and, conversely, for immigrant workers to provide access to U.S. public services to dependents actually living in Mexico. (Palerm and Urquiola 1993:345)

Thus, the "peasants" of Valle de Santiago are actually fairly complex with respect to their patterns of production. Palerm and Urquiola (1993:331ff.) also describe how as agricultural producers they are deeply involved in state-directed agricultural projects and programs and are also involved in aspects of transnational agroindustrialization that, as discussed in Chapter 5, have modernized mechanical and biological farming technology and have greatly limited the autonomy of small producers to make production decisions. Thus, two of the basic components of 'peasants' (simple technology and autonomy of decisionmaking) have been greatly compromised. Palerm's work also points beyond articulation theory by hinting at the effects on identity of consumption in a global context, a theme explored in Chapter 7. But a fuller appreciation of such complexity requires letting go of the unitary subject upon which 'the peasant' is constructed.

The Legacy of Romantic Reactions

Articulation theory emerged in the 1970s as a response to the dualism of modernization and dependency theories, both of which dichotomize development and its antithesis, 'underdevelopment' in the case of the former and 'de-development' in the latter. Although articulation theory also largely reified this same basic dualism, it did underscore a much greater degree of differentiation than did dependency theory and talked not just about different levels of capitalist development and underdevelopment but also of capitalist and noncapitalist forms. The deconstructive significance of articulation theory lay not just in its image of the articulation of two distinct modes of production—thus joining them and dissolving the categorical distinction between them—but also in its concern with the articulation of capitalism with any number of noncapitalist modes of production, thus challenging the neat symmetry of dualist thought.

The discussion of articulation also made the issue of the essential identity of 'peasants' more complex and led debate past the dualistic positions of rural peoples as essentially either peasants or proletarians. Furthermore, developing along with studies of migration, it did much to enhance appreciation of the degree to which the distinctions between 'rural' and 'urban' and 'traditional' versus 'modern' were dissolved under the impact of long-distance labor migration. The basic economic and demographic relationships of articulation are indicated in Figures 4.1, 4.2, and 4.3.

We can begin discussion of Figure 4.1 with the domestic economy based on self-sufficient subsistence farming in which there is no articulation. In this situation free labor, P_n, is combined with seed and/or animal resources, sunshine, water, and soil to produce Y_n (subsistence income), which is consumed as R_n in the reproduction of the household, including P_n. In the case of an ideal Chayanovian household, R_n, the cost of reproduction of the domestic unit, is met almost entirely by Y_n such that the income and costs of the domestic unit, operating outside of capitalist relations, are in equilibrium—that is, the income from household production is adequate to cover the reproductive costs of the household and also to produce surplus sufficient to pay taxes. Thus,

$$Y_k = 0, R_k = 0, \text{ and } Y_n = R_n + T_n$$

For this situation to remain in demographic and economic equilibrium, Y_n must remain comparable to $R_n + T_n$, but should Y_n become less than $R_n + T_n$ (because of declining productivity, growing consumption, or both, possibly caused by population increase, loss of land, or both as a result of erosion or foreclosure), then equilibrium is upset and must be restored. If restoration of equilibrium is obtained by consumption of Y_k (income derived outside of the domestic economy) as a complement to Y_n, then reproduction is taking place under conditions of articulation in which there are two main opitions: migration out of the local area to sell labor power (P_k) for wages (Y_w) or expenditure of labor to produce petty commodities for cash income (Y_p) that sums to Y_k, which is expended as costs (E) to purchase, outside of the domestic economy, the items (food, tools, credit) that must be consumed as R_k to complement the infrasubsistence domestic R_n. Part of Y_k may also be used as T_k to supplement T_n, the inevitable taxes and rents peasants must pay.

The points of articulation occur in the labor and commodities markets, which are the sites at which net economic value is transferred from the domestic unit to recipients on the capitalist side of these transfer zones. The primary mechanism for accumulation of value so tranferred is labor exploitation (L) in wage labor markets where members of the household, working, for example, as migrant agricultural workers, are paid considerably less than the value added to commodities by their labor. Net transfer of value is also effected by unequal exchange (U) in the form of high prices typically paid by subalterns who are disadvantaged consumers because of limited purchasing power and reliance on usurious moneylenders. The total of L plus U minus the expenditure of R_s, which goes into the reproduction of the domestic unit, amounts to the surplus (S) that is accumulated from the domestic economy and transferred out of it. Under conditions of static articulation, the following relationships are typically present:

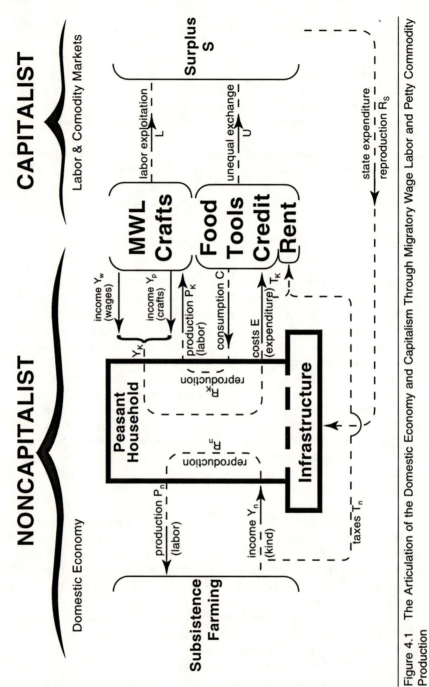

Figure 4.1   The Articulation of the Domestic Economy and Capitalism Through Migratory Wage Labor and Petty Commodity Production

Notation used in
Figures 4.1, 4.2, and 4.3

Y_n: noncapitalist (subsistence) income
Y_w: wage income
Y_p: petty commodity income
Y_k: capitalist-sector income
$$Y_k = Y_w + Y_p$$

R_n: noncapitalist cost of reproduction
R_k: capitalist reproduction
R_s: state reproduction
R: total reproduction cost of household
$$R = R_n + R_k + R_s$$

T: taxes (rent)
T_n: taxes on noncapitalist-sector income
T_k: taxes on capitalist-sector income
P: total production
P_n: noncapitalist production
P_k: production in capitalist sphere
$$P = P_n + P_k$$

C: consumption
E: monetary costs
L: labor exploitation (accumulation of surplus value)
U: unequal exchange
S: surplus accumulation
$$S = L + U$$

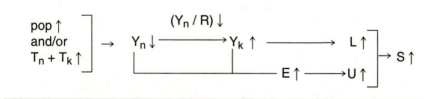

Figure 4.2 Increasing Articulation: Population Growth and Impoverishment Associated with Labor Intensification

$$Y_n < R \qquad Y_k = C \qquad \Delta pop = 0$$
$$Y_k < R \qquad E - C = U \qquad Y_n < P_n$$
$$Y_n + Y_k = R \qquad P_k - Y_k = L \qquad \text{(self-exploitation)}$$
$$L + U = S \qquad T_k \text{ negligible}$$
$$S > R_s$$

This situation can, however, be thrown out of equilibrium by population (pop) increase, an increase in T_n, or other changing conditions. Population increase may be either absolute or relative, relative population increase being the result, for example, of soil erosion or land concentration. In any event, increases in population or T_n translate into a decrease in Y_n, which translates into a necessary increase in Y_k occasioned by a fall in the ratio of Y_n to R. (R_k may also rise because of inflation, as was dramatically the case affecting consumers in Mexico in the 1980s.) The impact of this situation is that some member(s) of the household must seek increased income outside of the domestic sphere, thus articulating it with capitalist relations of production. Another dimension of this process is an increase in monetary expenditures (E), which most often are made from positions of comparative disadvantage as small consumers and that thus promote relations of unequal exchange (U) that serve to transfer economic surplus (S) from the domestic to the capitalist economy—the other main source of surplus extraction being the transfer of surplus value (L), which is extracted through wage labor.

Figure 4.3 schematizes relationships between domestic and capitalist economies through successive generations as this relationship is conceived by articulation theory. According to the logic, it is clearly in the interest of the latter to have the former perpetuated, since the rate of accumulation from the former to the latter is highest under conditions of perfect articulation in which labor is produced in the domestic economy, works in the capitalist economy, and retires in the domestic economy (first generation). Typically, after a generation of this pattern, circular migrants start to settle down within the "receiving" society and thus shift reproductive costs to it from the domestic ecocomy, a trend that continues into the third generation when most of the benefits of articulation are lost to the receiving economy, especially if remittances continue to the original sending community. The comparative efficiencies of these relationships for the receiving economy are L2 > L3 > L4 > L1.

Articulationists disagree with dependentists' assumption about the extensive degree to which capitalist relations have penetrated into peripheral societies and economies and have de-developed them in the process by the extension of capitalist forms of production and exchange. This thrust of articulation theory is consistent with romanticism, in that it affirms the persistence of the peripheral noncapitalist, nonmodern community. It is not, however, a full-blown romantic theory that asserts an intrinsic organic nature to the peripheral community, for articulation theory is a theory of capitalist underdevelopment that locates the logic of the persistence of the noncapitalist forms within the dynamics of the overarching system. But in its critique of the transformative power of modern capitalism in the periphery, articulation theory, like romanticism in general, celebrates the persistence of peripheral noncapitalist communities. And what is more, it is a theoretical perspective that informs the power of such peripheral communities to resist.

| NO MIGRATION | $Y_n = \beta B = \alpha(A + B + C)$ |
| | $L1 = 0$ |

CIRCULAR WAGE LABOR (first generation)	$Y_n < \alpha(A + C), Y_w > \alpha\beta$
	$Y_n + Y_w = \alpha(A + B + C)$
	$\beta B = \alpha B + L2 + Mac$
	$L2 = \beta B - \alpha B - Mac$
	$L2 > L1$

IMMIGRATION (second generation)	$Y_w = \alpha(A2 + B) + M_c, Y_n \rightarrow \alpha A1$
	$\beta B = \alpha(A2 + B) + M_c + L4$
	$L3 = \beta B - \alpha(A + B) - M_c$
	$L3 < L2$

IMMIGRATION (third generation)	$Y_w = \alpha(A + B + C)$
	$\beta B = \alpha(A + B + C) + L4$
	$L4 = \beta B - \alpha(A + B + C), \alpha C > M_c$
	$L4 < L3$

Summary: $L2 > L3 > L4 > L1$

M: remittance
L: labor exploitation (accumulation of surplus value)
  L1–4: generations/phases in L associated with degrees of articulation
    L1: no articulation
    L2: articulation, no immigration
    L3: articulation plus immigration, first generation
    L4: articulation plus immigration, second generation
  Lm: migrant L = L2
  Li: immigrant L = L3, L4
α, β, A, B, C, per Meillassoux (1981:52):
 A, a: the preproductive period of childhood
 B, b: the productive period of adulthood
 C, c: the postproductive period of old age
  α: annual consumption per head
  β: annual production per productive individual (in B)

Figure 4.3 Migration and Surplus

Articulation theory implies that peripheral types are varied and indigestible, that is, that capitalism as a global phenomenon does not just subsume developed and de-developed poles but instead that its inner workings generate and perpetuate noncapitalist forms. But whereas dependency theory saw these polar types as qualitatively different and separated by large spaces, articulation theory pointed out how they were combined in those living persons, the migrants, who shuttled back and forth between the two modes of production. Thus, whereas dependency theory saw capitalism as nearly pervasive in core and periphery, articulationists saw noncapitalist forms as structurally inherent within global capitalism.

But there is, of course, an inherent contradiction in talking about distinct modes of production in such cases where they are actually fused in the body and identity of persons. Nevertheless, with its appreciation of adaptation to multiple contexts, articulation theory anticipated later understanding of internal differentiation (Chapter 6). The attempt to deal with this problem led to the depiction of what might called hyphenated peasants, most notably the 'worker-peasant.' Ways to advance past this still residual dualism are suggested later, but the point here is that articulation theory nevertheless took a step beyond dependency theory in dismantling the dualism of developmentalism and depicting a periphery populated with identities that are more complex than those envisioned by either modernization or dependency theories. As such, it is a more complex theory of differentiation and identity that significantly moved forward reconceptualization of 'the peasant.'

Furthermore, articulation theory carried forward the two forms of intellectual displacement begun by dependency theory: It did this first by positing that peripheral peoples were not just the passive recipients of the benefits of modern societies but were instead sources of economic value that fueled the development of the metropoles, which in an economic sense were dependent on the peripheral societies. This is, of course, what dependency theory posited. But whereas dependency theory was concerned primarily with the accumulation and transfer of value, mainly through unequal long-distance commercial exchange, articulation theory highlighted the production of surplus value by rural subalterns and the actual movement of peripheral peoples into the metropoles where they deliver surplus value and in doing so draw the periphery into the core, thus in part dissolving the distinction between them—core and periphery, as it were, becoming embodied in the migrant worker who reproduces by shuttling between them.

The fact that dependency theory was advanced by intellectuals in the periphery constituted its second form of displacement. These Third World intellectuals thus challenged the intellectual hegemony of North American and Western European elite intellectuals in the developmental discourse. But whereas dependency theory significantly displaced the discourse to the periphery and to the left, it too was dominated by urban intellectual elites. In contrast, some currents of articulation theory were associated with grassroots articulation in its—articulation's—second meaning having to do with expression, a theme taken up in Chapter 8.

Sustainability or Stagnation?

The recent emergence of concerns with sustainable agriculture and sustainable development is de facto recognition of the failure of both right and left versions of developmentalism to bring about the major transformations in 'underdeveloped' areas of the world they foresaw in the 1950s and 1960s (Redclift 1987). Resource management (McCay and Acheson 1987), an aspect of sustainable development, has also become somewhat of a growth industry in contemporary applied anthropology. The rhetorical forms of these new specialties—for example, 'appropriate technology' and 'management'—suggest strong residues of developmentalism but a developmentalism that has come up against the ecological limits of modernization as conceived in its classical forms.

Interest in sustainable agriculture as an approach to development tends to be located on the right side of the political spectrum but with considerable blurring of that distinction, having, for example, found support from both the World Bank and the Sandinista government. And it blurs even more the distinction between modernist and romantic visions of development and in this regard is a right-of-center counterpart to articulationism. Indeed, theories and models of sustainable development propose combining 'appropriate' modern technologies, cultigens, and social forms with time-tested 'traditional' counterparts to avoid the environmental degradation and social disasters so often associated with unmitigated modernist approaches of nineteenth-century reforms and the so-called First and Second Green Revolutions.[21] In its concern with how the traditional and the modern are combined, thinking about sustainability is comparable to articulationism, indeed, both intellectual currents have come to share a common ground that does much to dissolve, or at least confound, left-right distinctions in addition to the one between the modern and the romantic (see Figure 4.4).

Some currents of sustainability, such as those advanced by Altieri (1995), tend to be romantic and populist in extolling the knowledge of "traditional" peoples to manage their ecosystems. Rather than deeply reconceptualizing modernization theory, more right-wing and liberal ideas about sustainability—such as those advanced by, for example, Gliessman (1990) and Netting (1993)—discard evolutionary modernizationist assumptions about totally transforming communities but retain a basic concern with theoretical-methodological individualism, that is, a focus on individuals and households as the primary social units engaging in small-scale horticultural and craft production. More populist forms, such as the programs of the Interamerican Foundation (Blayney and Bendahmane 1988), tend to be concerned with larger social units such as producer cooperatives. But in both currents, as in ecological anthropology in general, primary attention is given to relationships between the local environment *and* the culture of local communities rather than to relationships between broader economic and political conditions at regional, national, and global levels, as is characteristic of articulation theory. Thus, although there is convergence between the two intellectual

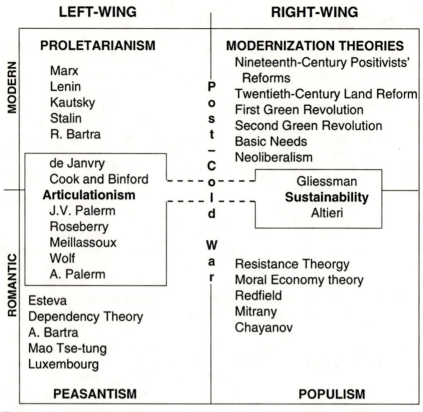

Figure 4.4   Intellectual-Political Dispositions Toward "Rural" Communities

currents in both dimensions, it is most apparent in the blurring of the distinction between the modern and the romantic (Mitchell 1991).

Much sustainability thinking and policy is markedly romantic in a sense that takes it beyond peasant romanticism to a rediscovery and reevaluation of the primitive, now reconfigured as the 'indigene.' In contrast to the *primitive,* a term that implies a form that existed in the distant past and was doomed to disappear from history, 'indigenous peoples' are the living descendents of the original inhabitants of environments. The continuity of their existence in these landscapes over hundreds and thousands of years, often without causing environmental degradation, suggests that they have 'traditional' knowledge and practices that have allowed them to manage ecosystems without destroying their biodiversity and their capacity to support human inhabitants. Thus, the cultural and biotic resources of indigenous peoples serve as correctives to the disastrous ecological imbalances provoked by modern societies. Programs working to promote sustainability interact with ethnicity in ways rather different from modernist approaches. In both its left and right versions, this reevaluation of the indigene is a de facto recognition not only of the persistent inability of the modern nation-state to digest ethnicity into modern society but, furthermore, of the inadvisability of doing so for the welfare of humanity.

The politics of sustainability as enacted in policy initiatives is deeply contradictory in ways that imply a confounding of conventional left-right perspectives. The reevaluation of indigenous peoples' knowledge of how to live in harmony with natural ecosystems is, from a left-romantic perspective, a progressive movement. Furthermore, the term *peoples* in *indigenous peoples* links sustainability as a movement to the political aspirations of indigenous peoples to defend their cultural and political autonomy against the designs of the modern nation-state to make them disappear from history, whether by assimilation or some other form of ethnocide. The global environmental movement has thus become linked to the defense of the human rights and the self-determination of indigenous peoples in ways that perhaps no one foresaw before 1970 (see Chapter 8).

But the apparent enthusiasm for these postdevelopmentalism projects shown by interests with essentially conservative dispositions should give left-leaning promoters of sustainability cause for concern. For one need not be cynical to see in official support of sustainable development and appropriate technology a de facto recognition that rural poverty in the Third World is not going to be developed out of existence. All peoples will not be brought up to the comfort level of the affluent classes and must therefore adapt to conditions of persistent poverty in ways that are not ecologically, economically, or politically disruptive. "They" must therefore learn to use solar cookers instead of cooking with gas, to use organic compost instead of expensive chemical fertilizer, and so on. In other words, the subtext of right-wing support for sustainable development says "we've got the benefits of development, but there aren't enough resources to go around, so you'll have to accept the principle that less is more. Furthermore, you'll have to find ways of doing this in the countryside so you don't continue to migrate into the cities and disrupt them. And while you're adapting to nondeveloping economies in the countryside, you must do so in ways that don't eliminate the forests that produce the oxygen we breathe." In other words, the de facto project of such right romantics is to sustain existing relations of inequality.

A basic contradiction for proponents of left-leaning postdevelopment thinking is that simple productionist approaches to the realities of environmental and technological limitations to economic growth align them willy-nilly with elitist First Worlders who are disposed to ensuring that rural subalterns are stabilized in the countryside in ways that are neither environmentally nor politically disruptive. But apart from this contradiction, we are concerned here with appreciating how contemporary ideas and politics about sustainable development reflect a dissolution of the modern dual structuring of the opposition not only between modern and romantic but also between left and right.

For example, entangled with concerns about appropriate technology and sustainable development are debates over "management of the commons." The basic theoretical and philosophical issue here centers on the question of whether humans are by nature capable of collectively maintaining communal resources such as forests, fisheries, and pastures. Classic right-wing perspectives, based on assumptions of humans as self-seeking individuals, argue that resources held in common will be degraded as individuals attempt to maximize their short-term gain to the long-term detriment of the communal resource base (see, e.g., Hardin 1968). Traditional leftists take the opposite view. For our purposes here, it is notable that numerous diverse philosophical and political tendencies converge in debates about commons management and sustainability in general so as to blur the conventional distinctions between left and right and between modern and romantic. For example, Garrett Hardin has substantially modified his original position on the tragedy of the commons and is now dialoging with Kropotkinites, "ecofreaks," and proponents of deep ecology—all of whom find common ground (pun intended) in their mutual concerns with sustainability (see Hardin 1993; McCay and Acheson 1987).

The intellectual retooling entailed in this reconfigured sociology of knowledge has been greatest for those, such as Hardin, who formally premised their social theory on a view of the person as a rational choice–making, maximizing, consuming individual whose isolated self-interested actions summed to the motor force of open-ended capitalist development.[22] But a world populated with such individuals appears to be inimical to sustainability. In this present postdevelopment context attention from many different political and theoretical quarters is focusing on 'indigenous peoples,' many of whom are reconceptualized 'peasants' who in this new intellectual political field are lumped with 'tribals,' 'horticulturalists,' and 'foragers' with whom, in terms of the former productionist criteria, they contrast.

Beyond Dualist Theory

Figure 4.4 represents the intellectual field in which major conventional positions on peasant society are arrayed. This two-dimensional ordering of theoretical and political dispositions toward peasant society suggests certain patternings to debates, alliances, and oppositions among people imbued with these various sensibilities. On purely formal grounds, inspection of this structuring of peasant discourse would suggest that the most intense and acrimonious debates would be between positions that cross two, rather than just one, dimensions of this field.

Such debates are, in the terms of this classification, doubly determined, suggesting that the intellectual and political stakes are higher than those in debates that cross just one dimension. Such indeed is the patterning of the intensity of intellectual warfare waged between, for example, classical Marxists (proletarianists) and Chayanovians. This structuring of discourse also explains, for example, the vehement denunciation of Marx by a self-appointed right-wing romantic defender of peasants such as Mitrany (1951). And although ostensibly engaging in intellectual warfare from entrenched positions on both sides of the divide between capitalism and socialism-communism, classical Marxists—for example, those of the Third International—had little of a deep structural nature to disagree with when engaging modernizationists. Although their local discourses were based on different assumptions about human nature and history, the two groups agreed on the progressive nature of capitalism and its inevitable destruction of the peasantry, a process they both sought to accelerate. Certainly, the classical Marxists looked beyond underdevelopment and the demise of the peasantry to a postcapitalist world. But this was to be an industrially developed socialist world formed at some point in the future. Meanwhile, capitalism had a historical mission to fulfill.

Debates between modernists and romantics on the left are more intense than those of the right. Nowhere is this more true than in Mexico, where a sharp debate raged between *proletarianistas* and *campesinistas* about the essential nature of the Mexican peasantry. The basic issue concerned the historical role to be played by the peasantry as determined by its inherent class nature. *Proletarianistas,* such as Roger Bartra (see, e.g., 1976, 1993), saw the peasants as destined to be dissolved into the urban and rural working class where as such they would be predisposed to advance progressive revolutionary political programs. In contrast, peasants were seen as at odds with proletarians since the former, as consumers, favored a politics of low-priced food, whereas the latter, as producers, supported high prices. For the *proletarianistas* the resolution of this contradiction would be the absorption of peasants into the working class. But the *campesinistas'* (e.g., A. Bartra 1979; Esteva 1978, 1983) understanding of the dynamics of Mexican agriculture was that the peasantry would not be completely displaced by capitalist production and that it had further progressive roles to play in Mexican history.

The classical Marxist critique of dependency theory was more intense than that which it leveled at right-wing modernizationists. But of all the debates suggested by Figure 4.4, the one that caused the greatest expenditure of ink was the one initiated by dependency theorists against the assumptions of modernization theory. This debate was only secondarily about peasants per se, but it did oppose two radically different interpretations of the role of capitalism in the 'development'—or 'the development of underdevelopment,' as some dependency theorists were wont to say—in areas of large peasant populations.

As discussed earlier, the dependency critique of capitalist development was basically an inversion of all the basic postulates of modernization theory. But as intense as this debate was, it was contained well within the parameters of the common discourse, the structure of which is now apparent. Both the social time and social space of this discursive structure are flat, that is, two-dimensional (see Figure 4.4). It is in this two-dimensional intellectual space that all major theories of the peasantry are constructed upon binary categorical structural oppositions:

peasant-proletarian, urban-rural, core-periphery, present-past, modern-traditional, production-consumption, active-passive, open-closed. This is the intellectual geography inhabited by peasants conceived as 'individuals.'

The major debates in peasant studies have been about the essential nature of this individual as a social type and the kinds of communities in which he or she lives. These debates have served to reify not only official variations of this type but also the official mode of categorization that generates these types. Thus, even as modernists and romantic peasantists or proletarianists fight over which is the true basic type, they collaborate in perpetuation of the structure of the discourse within which they debate.

Figure 4.4 is organized to indicate the historical movement whereby the basic binary structuring of the sociology and content of knowledge of peasant society has been autodeconstructing. In Figure 4.4 historical time is represented as moving simultaneously from top and bottom toward the horizontal midline, while a comparable movement has also taken place in a convergence from the left and right toward the vertical midline. The intersection of the two midlines is the vanishing point where the peasant concept is disappearing from intellectual history.

With respect to the left-right axis, we have seen that the modern opposition between left and right theories of the peasantry emerged within the global Cold War context of East-West confrontation. But as discussed earlier, just as this left-right, East-West opposition has dissolved into a post–Cold War environment in which the geopolitical forces in which 'the peasant' emerged within anthropology no longer exist, so also have we seen an erosion of the distinction between modernist and romantic views of history. These two sensibilities have not however, come to a common ground, but instead the unilinear image of history upon which both of them were based has given way to postdevelopment images that envision the possibility of history moving in other directions. Articulationism, although continuing in part to reify the opposition between proletarian and peasant, considerably dissolved the spatial and ontological assumptions upon which both proletarianism and peasantism were predicated. Similarly, the modernization theories that informed both phases of the Green Revolution, designed to eliminate rural poverty, have been largely superseded by a discourse of sustainability that is a tacit recognition of the persistence of nondevelopment and that occupies a discursive space comparable to and merging with the somewhat earlier articulationism.

The classical peasant is one who produces a surplus agricultural product, some fraction of which is appropriated by nonpeasant types who exert political control over these direct producers. In Wolf's (1955) state-of-the-art article "Types of Latin American Peasantry," all of the seven types he provisionally enumerates are surplus-producing.

But throughout the contemporary world this classical type, defined as such by productionist criteria, has given way demographically to types that not only do not directly produce a surplus agricultural product but that do not directly produce enough of an agricultural product for their own reproduction. It appears that at some point in recent history a threshold was crossed whereby the classical surplus-producing peasant community types have largely evolved to communities of 'infrasubsistence' peasants (see, e.g., Reyes Osorio et al. 1974), which represent a contradiction in terms in that such units produce less than they consume. Such types figure in the older agrarian literature as "small peasants" who are typically defined as making up the deficits in their own production by working for large peasants or farmers for wages. But the term *infrasubsistence* signals a discursive shift to a type that often, through migration, enters wage work at sites of capitalist production far from the sites of peasant production and reproduction. Articulation theory thus considerably expanded the spatiality of agrarian issues to national and transnational contexts. But more important, the terms *infrasubsistence* and *articulation* signal the theorization of a more complex subject than the monovocal peasant.

The increasing predominance of these infrasubsistence types is associated with the contemporary moment that is aptly characterized as postdevelopment. Our task herein is to depict and account for such nonpeasants. In doing so, we shall continue to move away from productionist criteria of rural social types. Said differently, as peasant production as the defining feature of peasant economy and society diminishes, so is it appropriate that productionism recede from its central position in the realm of theory. But a de-emphasis on production as a condition shaping identity need not be a capitulation to neoclassical circulationist economic assumptions about the rational choice–making individual. Rather, the challenge is to rethink the dualist structure upon which the opposition between production and circulation is based. This task is taken up in Chapter 5, but what is of note here is the way in which articulation theory has given us the basis to conceive the possibility of such a theoretical breakthrough.

Marx saw the articulation of modes of production in colonial settings as transitory, enduring only until the superior force of capitalist relations annihilated the precapitalist mode. But now we can view the concept of articulation itself as transitory between classical analyses of modes of production considered in isolation and the present state of theory in which the recognized complexity and diversity of conditions of capitalist and noncapitalist production defy reduction to discreet modes populated by unitary subjects, such as 'proletarians' or 'peasants,' or by their hybrid offspring, such as 'peasant-workers.' The modes of production debate was a response to the disintegration of the classical one-dimensional typology of differentiation and as such can be seen as an attempt to retain the classical types even as it in effect served to advance their dismantlement.

Fuller anthropological treatment of these semiproletarians and semipeasants must, in addition to exploring their economic and productionist nature, also inquire more deeply into their cultural and social identity. Here it is useful to recall Wolf's characterization of the mestizo, discussed previously. Indeed, a fully anthropological treatment of such types, who seem to have largely replaced peasants, has much to gain from the reconceptualization already advanced by Wolf, A. Palerm, Roseberry, de Janvry, Cook and Binford, and other articulationists. A feature common in their work, especially Wolf's, is an appreciation of the way the complexity of the identity of such peoples is derived from an awareness that they move about a great deal geographically and also in and out of different social, economic, and cultural spaces.

Articulation theory made important contributions to the move away from dualist thinking about peasants. Although not expressed in such terms, articulation theories were in effect elaborated as critiques of the various one-way road metaphors. By pointing out the interdependence of capitalist and noncapitalist forms of production, articulation theory in effect elaborated two-way linkages between developed and underdeveloped agriculture, which instead of transforming one into the other served to perpetuate both. In keeping with the road metaphors, articulation theory converted the former one-way routes from peasant to modern into two-way routes by which the modern also leads to the traditional. Lenin saw the demise of peasant society under the progressive development of rural capitalism as occuring by way of either the "farmer road" or the "junker road." The history of 'underdeveloped' areas has not, however, followed only these two routes but has also been going down other roads to postpeasant societies.

To more accurately employ this road metaphor, we should perhaps now speak of freeways and freeway interchanges where multilane interstates and international routes converge. Whereas the original road metaphors were one-way routes, it is possible on a freeway network to start from different points and arrive at many near and distant ones. This freeway road metaphor also facilitates thinking about two other features of rural differentiation. Not only is it possible to arrive at many different destinations on such a highway system, but such multidirectional means of communication are themselves part of the process of complex differentiation. Freeways share with other high-volume, high-velocity, high-tech means of communication the promotion of mass culture even as they also promote the internal differentiation of the subjects who travel along them between distant and disparate sites of residence, work, education, recreation, and consumption, where different facets of their identity are reproduced.

Such wide variance in interpretations of the essential nature of 'the peasantry' exists because it is an inherently ambiguous category that resists typology. It is betwixt and between a number of other categories without having any firm, clearly demarcated identity of its own. Indeed, this categorical marginality, this ambiguity is its singular most defining feature. Furthermore, it is precisely this ambiguity, this marginality that makes the peasantry the prototypical postdevelopmental social type. Clarification of this ambiguity will not be achieved by further proliferation of hyphenated types, the hyphen being but a sign of dual thinking, but instead by critical reassessment of the dualist thinking that spawns these hyphenated types. Such an exercise leads inexorably to a discarding of modernist and romantic categories and discourses of both the left and the right and with them identities they defined, such as the peasant.

Notes

1. See, for example, Stocking (1989:234) on romantic impulses to retrieve a 'genuine culture.'

2. Marx's ambivalence toward the peasantry has often been noted. In his *The Eighteenth Brumaire of Louis Bonaparte* (1963), he regards French peasants as acting politically in their own self-disinterest and as generally politically reactionary. But in his writings on precapitalist modes of production, such as the *Philosophical Manuscripts,* he regards pre-capitalists modes of production in general as having positive human qualities that are destroyed by the penetration of capitalist society and economy.

3. In the United States, elaborations and critiques of dependency theory appeared mainly in the journal *Latin American Perspectives,* which was founded in 1974. For a review of the growth of dependency theory and subsequent political-economic approaches that involved turning attention to the periphery, see Chilcote (1974, 1981), and Harding (1976); regarding the "periphery" and the "peripheral situation," see Appadurai (1986), and Nugent (1988), respectively.

4. Redfield is perhaps the first to speak of "the peripheral community" in *The Folk Culture of Yucatan* (1941:xvii, xix).

5. Although he is not a dependency theorist, Wolf's *Peasant Wars of the Twentieth Century* (1969) well illustrates such historical roles assumed by Third World subalterns.

6. Although world system theory (Wallerstein 1976) continues to invoke dependency theory's imagery of "core" and "periphery," it does advance dissolution of this dualism with its addition of the "semiperiphery," which is poised between the polar terms.

7. Stavenhagen has also been leading the way in introducing human rights, ethnicity, and the politics of indigenous peoples into the discursive spaces peasant studies occupy (see Chapter 7).

8. See Foster-Carter (1978) for a general overview of articulation theory with special attention to its French sources.

9. This attention to migration, which is intimately related to history, was an antidote to the ahistorical "scientific" precepts and practice of Althusserian structural Marxist anthropology.

10. Most of the studies presented in Klein (1980b) employ an articulation perspective to explore particular African cases.

11. See Kearney (1986a) on Mixtec and African migrant labor as typical examples of spatial separation of production and reproduction. Nagengast's (1991) case from Poland is in some ways a more complex example, in that her 'worker-peasants' are not migrants but commuters who live on their farmsteads and take the bus to the factory.

12. Wolf's doctoral dissertation was one component of a larger research project on communities in Puerto Rico organized by Julian Steward in which different students each examined a distinct type of community; see Lauria Perricelli (1989) for analysis of the contributions and limitations of this project.

13. In a manner similar to the way in which Wolf calls attention to unbounded local communities, Basch, Glick Schiller, and Szanton Blanc (1994) explore and critique hegemonic constructions of "ethnic group," "race," "nation," and other bounded models of social science.

14. Wolf does invoke a tripartite scheme on at least one occasion, but unlike the Leninists Wolf sees the "middle peasantry" as structurally predisposed to remain traditional and as also potentially the most revolutionary (Wolf 1969:290–293).

15. The socially ambiguous mestizo first appears in Mexican literature as a picaresque character in Fernández de Lizardi's novel *El periquillo sarniento* (1949 [1816]). El Periquillo defies being typed as he wanders in the interstices of colonial society.

16. Such a relationship between the "traditional" and "modern" sectors is what has more commonly been referred to as the articulation of modes of production. But by referring to the articulation and disarticulation of sectors, de Janvry has preempted the use of articulation in this other sense. In any event, de Janvry rejects "the concepts of a peasant (or simple commodity) mode or production articulated to capitalism. Peasants are to be seen instead as a class or fraction of a class within different modes of production" (1981:106). In other words, the position taken is that capitalism is pervasive in Latin America, and therefore no other modes exist that can be articulated with it. Nevertheless, the structured relationship between peasant and nonpeasant that de Janvry defines is comparable to the modes of production perspective as discussed in this chapter.

17. De Janvry's model of differentiation is unlike Lenin's in that de Janvry, in looking at Latin America, sees an "extraordinary numerical importance" of *external* semiproletarians who earn income outside of agriculture but also engage in subsistence agriculture, that is, under conditions of functional dualism (de Janvry 1981:116).

18. De Janvry's book was state of the art when published in 1981 and as such was unable to reflect on the multifocus urban movements that grew rapidly in Mexico City following the 1985 earthquake.

19. Most of Cook's work of over twenty years is compiled and synthesized in Cook and Binford (1990).

20. Such residual dualism takes the form of a distinction between "rural" and "urban," which are assumed to be distinct socioeconomic spaces. Also, Cook and Binford's (1990) primary attention to the economic materiality of class reveals a theoretical favoring of aspects of production in shaping consciousness over the role of consumption of cultural signs and symbols. Such a materialist bias is predicated on an implicit base-superstructure distinction in which there is little concern with their dialectical interaction. Cook and Binford do refer in passing to the "hegemonic ideology of capitalism," but the image here is of a distinctly top-down model of domination.

21. The First Green Revolution, devised originally in Mexico, was oriented toward large-scale industrial agriculture. In response to the severe rural dislocations it caused, it was repackaged for dissemination to small producers but generally with little success. Such programs were, however, a major movement toward the philosophy of sustainability among small producers (see Figure 4.4).

22. This deep revision of theoretical individualism conservative modernists such as Hardin have come to within the context of the failure of developmentalism is comparable to the modification of the same neoclassical economic assumptions of rational choice held by marginalist economists confronted by unanticipated patterns of Third World migration in the 1960s and 1970s (Kearney 1986b:334–335).

Chapter 5

Beyond Peasant Studies: Changing Social Fields of Identity and Theory

Whereas Chapter 4 examined theoretical reactions in the 1970s and 1980s to the modernist vision of peasant society and its demise, this chapter turns to contemporary global conditions affecting the formation of peasantlike identities and theoretical representations of them. These conditions include a deepening of the crisis of "development," a realignment in the present post–Cold War period of global political tensions from an East-West to a North-South polarity, and a continued decay of rural versus urban social and spatial distinctions. Furthermore, these trends are occurring as expressions of deepening transnationalization and globalization of communities, economies, and identities.

Nineteenth-century liberalism, of which cultural anthropology is in great part an heir, was explicitly productionist in its analyses and prescriptions for the peasant. Accordingly, its reforms centered on breaking the traditional "backward" forms of production that bound peasant communities. The central plank of such liberal projects is usually land reforms, which are intended to create material and jural conditions that will promote 'development' in a broad sense. But now in the late twentieth century, as we survey the wreckage of rural society in Latin America, Southeast Asia, Africa, India, and elsewhere, the failure of the liberal-reformist policies is starkly apparent. The corresponding productionist agrarian policies of the Eastern bloc have fared little better. We should expect that the failure of the liberal reformist policies of rural development should also affect the anthropological perspectives that share the same intellectual heritage and assumptions, based as they both are on the same dualist premises discussed in Chapter 3.

Developmentalism was a reflex of modernism. The death of modernism spelled the death of developmentalism. We now have sufficient historical perspective to perceive developmentalism as an idea of an urban intellectual minority in the Western metropoles who sought to have the world remade in their image. Recent history has, however, deemed it fit to move in other directions.

Chapters 6 and 7 outline characteristics of postdevelopment rural society as I see it. The central theme is the failure of developmentalism and how rural society will continue to be nonmodern and at the same time be nontraditional. This postdevelopmental society will also have characteristics that differ from the classical anthropological images of 'the peasantry.' To the degree that this kind of postdevelopmental 'rural' society is already present in much of the world, we can sketch its main outline and the social types that inhabit it. Although largely a world devoid of development in the grand scheme, it is not a world conducive to the formation or perpetuation of peasants.

Within the discourse of developmentalism, 'peasant' is virtually synonymous with 'traditional,' whose definition is predicated on the semantically saturated opposition to 'modern.' Although the term *peasant* has been fairly immune from deconstructive analysis, this is not so of 'tradition' and 'modern,' which have recently undergone considerable critical scrutiny (e.g., Comaroff and Comaroff 1993; Hobsbawm and Ranger 1983). The point here is that to the degree that the peasant is traditional, the decay of the opposition between *traditional* and *modern* is also a decay of the *peasant*.

Postdevelopment

To summarize this chapter and anticipate the next, we can note the basic assumptions of a theory of postdevelopment society, the seeds of which are found in the romantic currents reviewed in Chapter 4. It is convenient to do so in terms of several worldview universals (Kearney 1984).

Time and Causality

Contrary to the teleology of developmentalism, postdevelopmental theory is nonteleological. In this sense it is comparable to modern biology, which recognizes the reality and possibility of extinction and global disaster but which also affirms that constant diversification and differentiation take place as new microniches are created and filled. Anthropology must now recognize that as in biology, history does not necessarily mean progress and that postdevelopmentalism may take forms such as Calcutta, Lagos, Los Angeles, and Brasilia and the hinterlands with which they are continuous.

The empirical basis for the opposed types—traditional-modern, Great Tradition–Little Tradition, socialist-capitalist, peasant-proletarian—as structured pairs is being dissolved by history, for history, like biological evolution, is a process in which sharp demarcations are rare and gradations and diversity are the rule. For this reason dualist thought is most comfortable with synchrony in which absolute differences can be seized upon to the exclusion of the continua in which they reside. Historiography is thus corrosive of dualist, synchronic thought, which naturally resists it.[1] Accordingly, historical anthropological approaches to the peasantry carry within them a disposition to question the validity of this highly reified type. This is apparent in what can appropriately be called Wolfian anthropology, which even as it has explored the formation and variations of 'peasant types' and in doing so has reified them, has also, by explicating their historically contingent nature and complexity, done much to reveal the virtual nonexistence of any contemporary persons or communities that are actual referents of this highly abstract term.

Space

Elsewhere (Kearney 1984) I have argued that cognition of space occurs prior to images of time. Accordingly, time is distorted in ethnography per Fabian because the location of the Other in geographic and social spaces is the primary concern. In the space of modernity, modern and traditional communities were distinct and spatially separated. In a globalized world, they interpenetrate and in doing so dissolve the distinction between them (Gupta and Ferguson 1992; Kearney 1991).

One instance of this interpenetration is the way in which horizontal spatial differentiation between city (center) and country (periphery) is transforming into high-density population centers with increased vertical differentiation in which the more affluent classes live and work in high-rise apartment buildings, condominiums, and corporate centers and abandon the streets to the poor and homeless, many of whom are immigrants and migrants from outlying areas. In these megalopolises the polarity of rural-traditional versus urban-modern implodes with respect to life spaces.

Nowhere is this more apparent than in the spatial dynamics of Brasilia. Planned as the ultimate "modernist city" that was to be an engine of modernity and development in the center of the Amazon basin (Holston 1989), within a decade after its completion it was surrounded by an immense shantytown of poor rural migrants that has displaced its social, economic, and cultural center of gravity and neutralized the planners' futuristic vision of the city. And although very differently organized, the "global cities" Sassen (1991) describes (Tokyo, New York, London) are also reorderings of the bipolar national spaces of modernity, integrated as they are transnational spaces in terms of production, finance, labor, and information.

Discourses on peasants were constructed in a two-dimensional space that is now dissolving under the influences of transnationalism and globalization, which are the ground of a different spatiality in which the distinction between centers and peripheries is eroding (Kearney 1995b).[2] The flat space of modernity had an East-West axis; it was a space of centers and peripheries. But in a globalized world, as in astronomy, there are no distinct centers that are primary reference points.[3] This centerless space is comparable to the space of ecology and environmentalism, in which ecotones and gradual transitions are more common than sharp boundaries and distinct centers and in which species are formed out of complex adaptive interactions situated in networks of relationships that radiate far beyond local living spaces. And indeed it has been in the context of global environmental concerns that the former East-West alignment of the Cold War has been reorienting along a North-South axis in which the central issues are the global differential distribution of resources, whereby net economic value flows from the poor areas of the tropics to the developed northern midlatitude regions, and the implications of such patterns of production and consumption for the sustainability of ecosystems.

Later I discuss transnational communities that are socially unbounded and composed of social and communications networks that include, in addition to face-to-face communication, electronic and other media. One additional aspect of such communities bears mentioning, and this is the ways in which productive activities in them become partially or completely cognitively detached from geographic space and are reconstituted in hyperspaces (Jameson 1984). As I use the term herein, a *hyperspace* is socially constructed, it is not anchored permanently in a specific locale, and it is inhabited mainly by strangers. Furthermore, it has a certain universal quality that is independent of any specific locale in which it might occur. International airports are one example, as are shopping malls, the facilities of international hotel and fast-food chains, and housing subdivisions. Agroindustrial production is another.

Thus, commercial farming throughout northwest Mexico, California, Oregon, and Washington is one continuous system marked by a uniformity that is imposed onto and obliterates local landscapes and communities as distinct locales. Such a free-floating social and geographic landscape, so detached from a permanent local place, has a sameness to it comparable to the sameness of its chemical fertilizers, pesticides, and uniform genetically engineered crops. Referring to migrant Mixtec workers in the hyperspace of California corporate agriculture, Besserer notes that for them spatial referents are based not on local geography but on the hyperspaces of production. Thus, one worker told him, "Yes, well I don't know where we could have been because we were working in tomatoes"; and asked where his sons were, another man said, "They went to the oranges" (Besserer 1993:11, my translation).

In order to do research and political work it is necessary to bracket social fields and to enter them in search of social identities that reside and reproduce therein. Transnational corporate agriculture appears to be one field that can be bracketed justifiably for purposes of research. But the point is that many different internally differentiated types come together in this general field of activity. As we dissect it we find that it has no essential core, that there is no such individual as the "transnational agriculturist." What we do have is a system of production, distribution, and consumption in which a number of internally differentiated persons, corporations, and agencies come together and articulate facets of their identities to produce and reproduce in a transnational hyperspace. It is in such hyperspace, detached from a bounded geographic place, that transnational communities are situated.

Classification and the Self

In contrast to the unitary modern Self of epistemology, science, and political philosophy, the nonmodernist Self is internally differentiated (see Chapter 6). Anthropology has both humanized and othered the people it has studied. It has othered them by classifying them as exotic and then presuming to speak for them. But the processes of transnationalization and global homogenization with differentiation have done much to dissolve the infrastructural bases of the differences noted and to no small degree reified by anthropology. Classifying people as peasants, proletarians, indígenas, etc., has been one form of this othering.

What is now called for is anthropological theory that reflects the complexity and depth of contemporary patterns of difference and differentiation but that does so in ways that do not exoticise 'others' but instead depict the intimate ways in which 'they' and 'we' are imbricated in global contexts that determine all of our identities. It is not sufficient to construct images of these environments as two-dimensional—history-making versus passive, developed versus backward, core versus periphery, capitalist versus noncapitalist, North versus South, and so forth. For we live in social fields formed and deformed by forces far more complex than is suggested by these binary polarities. The point here is that the dualist conceptual underpinnings of modernist anthropology are dissolving and with them identities such as indígenas and peasants as easily objectifiable Others.

The maturation of articulation theory was largely the result of the study of labor migration from peripheral areas to sites of capitalist production. And herein lies another major difference between dependency and articulation theory. Whereas dependency theory took global regions and nations as its primary units of analysis, articulation theory focused its analysis at the level of the local community, the household, and even that primary site of neoclassical analysis—the individual. The latter two units especially present themselves as most amenable for the study of migration because of its diffuse and noncorporate nature. As territorially based entities, communities cannot, apart from continental drift, migrate; only the households and individuals within them can migrate to participate in different, spatially separated forms of production.

But the appearance of the individual as theoretically important in articulation theory should not be read as constituting some convergence with the methodological individualism of modernization theory. For the individual as a unit of analysis as conceived by articulation theory is not just the rational choice–making individual of liberal humanism but instead, as is consistent with articulation theory's primary attention to production, is a working individual whose identity and consciousness are embodied in a body that works to produce value in complex and varied ways at sites that are linked by migration.

In the final analysis it is specific men and women who migrate between domestic and capitalist sites of production and who, in doing so, overcome the spatial distinction between them. But in addition to such real subsumption of labor made possible by migration are the complex and varied forms of formal subsumption that take place in the lives of individual migrants both in their rural communities and when they participate in urban informal economic activities. This type of analysis, to which we were led by articulation theory, points our attention not just to the global and regional differentiation effected by capitalist relations of exchange (per dependency theory) but also to the internal differentiation of function that occurs within the identity of individual ambiguous migrant types (see Chapter 6). Such migrant persons shuttle back and forth between the apparent poles of development and underdevelopment and knit them together into a seamless fabric that is both developed and underdeveloped and yet, when taken as a whole, is neither.

Until the twentieth century, all civilizations were based on a structural dichotomy of urban and rural, of city and country. However, as discussed earlier, what we see in the late twentieth century is the collapse of that primordial structuring, although at a global level the remnants of this structure linger on as the distinction between developed and de-developed nations. But even this difference is being leveled by the combined effects of transnational corporations and transmigrants, which increasingly move persons, value, information, and "stuff" around the globe at increased volumes and velocities.

Whereas scholars, ranging from Marx to Chayanov and from Mao to neoliberals, who sought to make sense out of the agrarian issue limited their analyses to a presumed 'rural' arena within which agrarian types are located, the kind of analysis now required encompasses nonrural, nonpeasant types as well and in so subsuming both kinds effectively dissolves the categorical distinctions between them. With the dissolution of the opposition between rural and urban, much of the opposition between developed and underdeveloped is dissolved and with it the opposition between peasant and nonpeasant.

This kind of analysis extends the sort of typological analysis begun by Wolf and the articulationists. Whereas they focused on the types and in doing so tended to reify them, I focus on the spaces—the margins—between the types. Whereas they dwelled on external differentiation, I am also concerned with internal differentiation. In the former case the differences—the margins—are external to the social types, but in the latter the margins are inside of those types and move with them as they migrate through geographic spaces and hyperspaces.

From Articulation to Networks to Reticula

The network is an image that enables us to theorize the postpeasant subject and other complexly internally differentiated identities. The difference between theories of internal and external differentiation is that in the latter the subject, is the node in a network of relationships. In contrast, in the case of the internally differentiated subject, the nodes of networks are internal to the subject and constitute it. To the degree that these nodes result from informal networking on the part of the subject, such networking constitutes subjects' identities distinct from those that are officially constructed.

It is to such transcendence of the official construction of community that *transnational,* in the second sense, refers—that is, the construction of subaltern identity autonomous of the official categories of the nation-state and its disciplines. We can trace the development of concern with this trend from an earlier movement in the history of anthropology when its definition of community coincided with the boundaries inscribed by the state. Such was the case of Mesoamerican ethnographies written from the 1940s through the 1980s. Indeed, the appropriateness of the *municipio* as a natural unit of analysis was spelled out by Sol Tax in 1937 and was later reiterated by others (see Hewitt de Alcántara 1984:193). No clearer expression can be found of the correspondence between the anthropological and the official constructions and containments of community.

But what concerns us here is the decomposition of that correspondence between anthropological and official constructions of community. With respect to the Guatemalan case, the bounded *municipios* Tax and others wrote about and in part, per Anderson (1983), "invented" have become transnationalized by the migration to Mexico, Los Angeles, and Florida of tens of thousands of refugees—that is, survivors—from the recent and still smoldering Guatemalan civil war. As with transnational 'peasant' communities in general, their demographic, social, and cultural reproduction occurs primarily outside of the original national space.[4]

A reflection in anthropological literature of the unbounding and de-essentializing of Mesoamerican 'peasant' communities is apparent in the history of the Harvard project in Zinacantan, Chiapas. From its founding up through the mid–1980s, Vogt (e.g., 1970) and other Harvard ethnographers depicted Zinacantan as a closed community of maize cultivators (see Vogt 1978). But by the late 1980s, Cancian (1987, 1992; cf. 1965) was documenting widespread proletarianization associated with migratory wage labor. And more recently, Cancian and Brown (1994) and Collier (1994a, 1994b) have described a deep and growing insertion of Zinacantecans into global economic relations and a corresponding disappearance of the classical peasant way of life and identity (see also Kearney 1986a, 1991).

Anthropological studies of migration have been overwhelmingly framed within issues of development and underdevelopment of rural communities (Kearney 1986b), but for the most part they have not been linked to the debates over the status of peasants as a social category. Recent theoretical advances in the anthropology of migration are, however, relevant to the reconceptualization of peasants. As originally formalized, the basic assumptions of migration theory were predicated on a thoroughly dualist structuring, the clearest and most comprehensive expression of which was spelled out over a hundred years ago in Ravenstein's (1976 [1885]) "laws of migration."

Basic to this thinking is the assumption that migration is the movement of populations through geographic space organized by polar nodes that "push" and "pull" migrants. Thus, migrants may be pushed from "sending" areas and pulled by "receiving" ones. This imagery is one of a bipolar force field in which individuals move and are distributed much like iron filings in a magnetic field. This model was also used to conceptualize subsequent anthropological studies of rural-urban migration, similarly conceived in "bipolar terms" (Rouse 1992a:26). Largely a reflection of the massive one-way movements of emigrants from Europe to the Americas in the nineteenth and early twentieth centuries, this bipolar model is an inadequate representation of much contemporary migration, which reconfigures the spatial constitution of communities and has implications for how we conceptualize social types such as 'peasants,' 'workers,' and 'migrants.'

Two developments are relevant. One is the increased attention to the cultural dimensions of migration and to the identity of migrants as opposed to a previous preoccupation with migration as primarily a demographic process. The other development in migration studies is the emergence of nonbinary theoretical perspectives that in effect deconstruct the dualism inherent in the classical models. Notable here are concepts such as a "transnational sociocultural system" (Sutton 1987), the "transnational community" (Kearney and Nagengast 1989), "transnationalism" and "transmigrants" (Glick Schiller, Basch, and Blanc-Szanton 1992), and the "deterritorialized nation-state" (Basch, Glick Schiller, and Szanton Blanc 1994).[5] All of these concepts shift thinking about migration from a primary concern with demographic issues of individuals moving through bipolar spaces in a time frame assumed to be progressive to other ways of conceiving migration that are not predicated on modernist assumptions about time, space, and social identity. Indeed, change in any one of these dimensions implies and is implied by changes in any other.

To a great extent, the reconceptualization of migration has been stimulated by an increased awareness of the multidirectionality of movement. Often as not, 'rural'-to-'urban' movement is accompanied by comparable flows in the opposite direction, as is often true with transnational migration. Furthermore, considerable movement occurs among multiple sites, not just between two. The most common fields of migration are thus not bipolar and unidirectional but instead are multipolar with complex flows among the poles. Such new images of migration imply a reconceptualization of the identity and consciousness of migrants as historical subjects. Briefly, let us take the case of so-called peasants who engage in circular migration in and out of peasant agriculture, wage labor in commercial agriculture, and urban activities. When considered by dualist thinking they are conceptualized as hyphenated types, such as the 'peasant-worker.' But in their lived reality they share structural features with the 'commuters' who each day jam expressways, trains, and buses, although such 'migrants' differ from 'commuters' in that they travel farther and stay at their destinations longer.

Migration is also significant for reconceptualization because of its power to transform not only the subject identity of migrants but also the official categories that contain subject identity. Thus, migration allows partial escape from the subject identity that is constructed and contained by the state with its laws and literatures that limit the identities and movements of people and keep them in their place. This is particularly true of "illegal" transnational migrants and especially of illegal migrants working in the informal economy who doubly defy the state. Thus, to the high degree that migration globally is associated with movement into informal economies, such migration corrodes standard identities, such as that of 'the peasant' (discussed later). Similarly, at the international level much migration dissolves the spatial structure of neocolonialism, which depends on a separation of colonial self and colonized other, and intersperses the self and the other in interpenetrating spaces (Gupta 1992; Kearney 1991).

Reconsideration of the identity of peasants as migrating persons implies similar rethinking of their communities. In modernist anthropology imagery, peasants are located mainly in bounded "little communities" (Redfield 1956) and "closed corporate communities" (Wolf 1957). But recently, ethnographic research on transnational migration has come to appreciate the great degree to which such communities have become unbounded (see Basch, Glick Schiller, and Szanton Blanc 1994; Gupta and Ferguson 1992) and as such require novel imagery that represents the complexity of their spatial distributions and sociocultural dynamics.

Central to the development of articulation theory was the growing awareness among field anthropologists of the economic importance of migrant wage labor in the reproduction of ostensibly peasant households and communities. Case after case demonstrated that what at first glance appeared to be very 'traditional' local rural communities were in fact maintained in great measure by migrant remittances, often earned in a different nation (Kearney 1986). Whereas articulation theory, like the variants of dependency theory that preceded it, was discussed and debated largely in the abstract, field anthropologists were confronted with the task of making sense not only of the complex productive relations in which peasant migrant workers engaged but also of their solutions to cultural reproduction under such complex regimes. Out of this work came an appreciation of the diverse and complex patterns of production and consumption in these *transnational communities*.

Several ideas are basic to this concept. First, there is the implication that this kind of community is transnational in the historical sense of transcending the defining power of the state to impose its categories of identity upon persons who are members of such a community (Kearney 1991). Second, in contrast to the focus on production in the articulation model held over from the various peasantist and proletarianist positions of which it was a fusion, the idea of the transnational community gives equal weight to *consumption* broadly defined to include cultural consumption (see Chapter 7). Such consumption takes place through transnational networks that are, to mix metaphors, the nerves and vessels of the transnational community. Things flow through these networks—namely, persons, things, values, signs, and information.

Communities conceived as networks in the microsociological sense are of little use for the issues with which we are concerned here. Of more value is network in the sense of a communication network, as a component of communication. The human medium of the social network, namely, face-to-face communication, is now augmented in most places by electronic communication, which more than face-to-face communication dissolves the spatial boundaries of rural communities. To the degree that personal identity is constructed from the consumption of information, the consumption of information as generated and channeled by extensive networks shapes the identity of their members in correspondingly distinctive ways. The networks that structure persons in transnational communities thus literally inform their members differently than does the shaping power of, for example, a closed corporate community.

Similar in conception to the transnational network is Rouse's (1988, 1991) notion of "migrant circuits." Like network, circuit connotes the flow of things through it. But network is arguably a preferable metaphor because of its resonance with "communication networks" through which information flows, which in turn inform subjects who are in the network. Moreover, "transnational networks" contrast with the usual meaning of social networks in network theory, which emphasizes links between persons as opposed to the idea that people move—migrate—through spaces inflated by the networks. The ethnography of such transnational networks defines spaces and forms of production and consumption that belie the neat dualist distinction of spatially separated but articulated modes. Thus, whereas the imagery of articulation supports a distinction between "rural" and "urban," reconsideration of migration as occurring within transnational communities formed of social and communication networks carries forward the conceptual dismantling of the rural-urban distinction and also advances migration theory from a concern with the migration of bodies to include migration and transmigration of signs and other values that move through and are transformed within networks. Furthermore, the ethnographic subjects who inhabit and are constituted within such networks are powerfully deconstructive of the opposition between peasant and proletarian, the primary social types associated with the standard spaces.

The metaphor of articulation is incompatible with that of network. Articulation speaks of 'poles' and 'centers,' whereas networks lack centers. Also, whereas articulation theory can at best only deal clumsily with complex subjects by treating them as hyphenated individuals, the image of network lends itself to the ethnography of communities composed of internally differentiated persons. And in addition to adequately representing complex migratory subjects, networks well represent communities of such subjects.

There is, first, the limitless capacity of networks to extend themselves spatially. Migrant networks, for example, may have their historical origin in some 'traditional' spatially localized and socially bounded corporate community, but as they spread, offspring communities condense that are spatially distant from the original parent community but that are yet components of a larger transnational community that subsumes parent and offspring communities (Kearney and Nagengast 1989). These networks lack spatial beginnings and ends that might correspond, for example, to a head or a tail. Furthermore, they are without formal internal structure. Thus, the social morphology of networks is like an amoeba, a creature with complex internal differentiation but without distinct cells and organs that correspond to the social components of corporate communities. Also, unlike official communities, which are bound to delimited spaces, amoebas can extend themselves in any and all directions.

Network also points to an active process of self-differentiation, in that as a verb it suggests a creative, ad hoc sociality in which persons tactically articulate facets of their identity with complementary facets of other persons—they network. Networking thus allows the person to escape the 'mechanical solidarity' of traditional communities. But the networks so formed are not instances of that modernist polar opposite of traditional social organization, namely, 'organic solidarity.' To the contrary, the complexly internally differentiated subjects of these networks have escaped the individualized monochrome identities of the modern subject— the butcher, the baker, and the candlestick maker.

Regarding electronic communication, much attention has been given to the impact of the penetration of electronic mass media into the countryside and its impact on local and national culture (Kearney 1995b). The working assumption of theories of modernization is that consumption of mass culture erodes local traditional society and facilitates the spread of modernity.

But somewhat of an internal contradiction exists in these assumptions of the effects of mass culture, and it resides in the difference between electronic and print media. Theories of literateness, in opposing two qualitatively different kinds of society—the oral versus the literate—are variations of the unilinear, dualist master narrative (e.g., Goody 1987; Ong 1982). But with respect to literateness, which is a major indicator of 'modernity,' cultural processes in subaltern communities appear to be leading not to greater literateness but instead to access to electronically mediated information located in global spaces that implodes into rural communities. Ease of access to these means of communication, which do not require that the user be literate, are thus enabling peasantlike communities to segue between a literate modernity and an oral-based tradition into a third sociocultural space not envisioned by theories of literateness and modernization.

Also comparable to the impact of mass media on rural communities is that of user-friendly recording and transmission devices—camcorders, videocassette players, tape recorders, telephones, teleconferencing, money orders, electronic banking, faxes, electronic mail, photographic cameras—all of which extend networks spatially while also compressing their social density. Furthermore, as communication systems, networks channel the flow not only of persons and information but also of value. As migrants travel through their networks from various sites of economic, social, and cultural production, consumption, and reproduction, they often carry cash on their persons, or they may transmit money electronically or by mail. And, of course, they carry within them embodied labor power that for the most part is reproduced within their networks and sold outside of them. Indeed, the direct generation, transmission, and consumption of signs, symbols, and value through these media are variations of the communication dynamics of networks, of which the migration of persons is a primary form.

For ease of exposition we may, as earlier, distinguish internally generated signs, symbols, and values that flow through transnational communities from the contents of mass media. But it must be understood that no such distinction between internal and mass culture is made when members of transnational communities consume the cultural materials made available to them within their networks. Such omnivorous consumption affects internal social differentiation within the transnational community and between that community and the social fields in which it is located in ways rather different from the production and consumption of 'traditional culture' within closed peasant communities. Furthermore, the spread of popular and mass culture into peasantlike communities increasingly dissolves the distinction between "Great" and "Little Traditions" that was central to the Redfieldan model of peasant society and culture.

Vignette 5.1

I (mk) am sitting at my kitchen table in California drinking coffee with a committee of men appointed by the authorities of San Jerónimo Progreso in Oaxaca. Most of the members of the committee work in the San Joaquin Valley of central California. Their assignment is to assess heads of migrant families from San Jerónimo residing in California eighty dollars toward the purchase of a satellite dish and relay transmitter to bring television reception to San Jerónimo. They have come to collect my contribution. I realize that we are participating in the fusion of the San Jerónimo migrant network with global media networks.[6]

Network theory is predominantly sociological. But the reconceptualization with which we are concerned deals with both social relations and identity formed in more complex and extensive spaces than are usually envisioned with the imagery of networks. Furthermore, *network* is a term rarely used in conjunction with class and class analysis, which are central to this project. Therefore, as a metaphor that retains the advances imagined with networks but enables thinking of yet more complex identities and relationships, I propose the term *reticulum*.

Reticulum, which is derived from the Latin for network, is a biological term that is appropriate for anthropological use in this age of transnationalism and globalization. In biology, according to *Webster's Collegiate Dictionary,* tenth edition, a reticulum cell is "one of the branched anastomosing reticuloendothelial cells that form an intricate interstitial network ramifying through other tissues and organs." Such is the form of globalizing reticula that ramify into nations, communities, and many other social bodies and spaces. Deleuze and Guattari (1987) propose a similar imagery with their "rhizome," which, unlike a tree or its roots, "connects any point to any other point, and its traits are not necessarily linked to traits of the same nature." The rhisome is "unlike a structure, which is defined by a set of points and positions, with binary relations between the points and biunivocal relationships between the positions" (Deleuze and Guattari 1987:21).

Such connections made by reticula and rhisomes are like those of a hypertext, in which words are not classified in a hierarchical index but instead have direct intratextual links.[7] I employ the reticulum again in Chapter 8 to enable thinking about value, power, and politics. But the prior theoretical work on networks is what makes such reconceptualization possible.

Globalization and Differentiation

In *Peasants (1966)*, Wolf identifies four "domains" that organize the incorporation of peasants into wider contexts and effect the transfer of their surplus production (see Chapter 6). On the basis of recent widespread trends in the international organization of agriculture, it is now appropriate to add a fifth type to Wolf's four domains. The term most descriptive of this new domain is *agroindustrialization.*

Briefly, agroindustrialization combines an increased role of transnational corporations in the financing, production, distribution, marketing, and consumption of agricultural products with increased use of petrochemicals and other advanced technologies, increased environmental damage, and an increase in complex forms of subsumption of 'peasant labor' in agricultural production so organized (see, e.g., Barkin 1990; Feder 1977; Gates 1993; Kearney 1980; Wright 1990). Furthermore, these conditions imply

> that the internationalization of agroindustry production and the agroindustrialization of local communities has spawned several modes of externally (e.g., internationally) controlled economic integration in local peasant societies. . . . This may occur through production contracting with peasant communities and farmers, labor contracting with farm workers, technological packaging for agricultural commodities, and by imposing international control over quality and variety for local agricultural production in peasant communities. (Carlos n.d.:2)

The growth of agroindustrialization necessitates a reconsideration of the role and identities of peasants and the state as conventionally conceived as actors in agricultural production. This analysis is particularly relevant to small producers of commercial crops, but it also applies to any small producer who relies on commercial inputs, such as commercial seed, chemical fertilizers, or herbicides.

Let us look first at peasants and then at the state. In the classical images of the peasant as an autonomous producer, peasants use simple technology to grow crops they themselves consume, possibly selling any excess. But the ethnography of agroindustrialization demonstrates how the production activities of seemingly autonomous small producers are shaped less by their own decisions than by the sociology, economics, and technology of production and consumption far from the sites where they actually produce. Thus, for example, some supermarket and fast-food chains in the United States contract with producers in Mexico to deliver specified varieties of vegetables with certain quality standards. The production of these varieties thus entails the purchase of a seed and petrochemical package that will ensure delivery of the specified product and quality. Similar arrangements are found in sugar production in which small producers are financed by the refineries to which they sell their crop, thus effectively working as wage laborers on their own land (Gudeman 1978).

Indeed, managers of transnational agricultural corporations are not as concerned with ownership of land as domestic capitalist farmers are. Rather, a tendency of agroindustrialization seems to be a shift away from ownership of land as a means of control of production to control of other aspects of production, especially finance and technical expertise—including patents of genetically altered cultigens. In such contract production arrangements the highest-risk area, namely, crop production, is shifted to the actual producer, who in effect has agreed to deliver a future. But the point here is that there is no primary locus or essential value for transnational agriculture (discussed later). Instead, production, like consumption, is dispersed in transnational spaces of which agricultural fields and orchards are but one of numerous kinds of sites in the overall process.

The growth of agroindustrialization necessitates a reconsideration of the agrarian question as conventionally conceptualized in terms of peasants and farmers gaining access to land, agricultural technology and extension, and capital. In land reform programs, the state typically assumes primary responsibility for the redistribution of these inputs within the national context. In contrast, in agroindustrialization, allocation of these inputs is assumed by corporations that are both upstream and downstream, with respect to inputs and outputs, from the actual sites of production that are the terrain of peasants as usually conceived. Thus, the dynamics of agrarian issues are significantly displaced from the national context, in which the state is the main actor, to a transnational context, in which corporations are the major players.

Formerly, in the closed corporate communities of highland Mesoamerica, local culture and society evolved along with endemic varieties of cultigens, often selected over centuries in local environmental microniches. Thus, in addition to having its own distinctive 'customs,' each of these communities is also a living germ plasma bank. In Oaxaca, for example—which is no doubt the region where the most productive of all grains, maize, was domesticated—hundreds of local varieties of "Indian corn" and beans are still preserved in small towns and hamlets. But even in these communities, which are populated mostly by infrasubsistence cultivators who consume what they produce, aspects of agroindustrialization are penetrating. These aspects are often introduced by circular migrants who have worked in high-tech commercial production where they have come to know commercial herbicides, pesticides, fertilizers, seed varieties, irrigation equipment, and so forth, which they then introduce into their own small subsistence operations, thus breaking the insularity of the local complex of cultural practices and genetic resources.

Whereas the older complexes of 'traditional' knowledge, practice, technology, and indigenous cultigens were relatively self-contained within their own local niches, the penetration of agroindustry effects several displacements. First, there is the obvious breaking down of the insularity and integrity of the local complexes of knowledge, practice, technology, and germ plasma as local producers become more dependent on the research and development capabilities of their agroindustry counterparts. Furthermore, the use of these alien inputs tends to increase dependence on them as local knowledge and dispositions to work in former ways are lost.

Vignette 5.2

San Jerónimo: Eutíquio is cultivating a hillside of black beans that are infested with a leaf-eating insect. I must make a trip to Oaxaca City, and he beseeches me to bring him a bottle of *Tamarón,* a neurotoxic pesticide known to kill farmworkers exposed to it. He knows it is effective because he has seen it used in commercial agriculture. I decline to buy it, but he says that if I don't he will make a special trip to get it. I relent. It is packed like a small bomb inside two boxes and foam rubber. When I deliver it he pours some into a bucket, adds water, stirs it, and then pours the mix into the tank of an old hand pump backpack sprayer. We hike to his field, and he begins to walk up and down the rows, pumping and spraying the deadly mixture. He is wearing a short-sleeved shirt, light cotton pants with the cuffs rolled up, and sandals. I stay upwind of the spray, which a light breeze carries away. On one of his passes I notice that the pumping mechanism is leaking, and the liquid is dripping onto the backs of his legs. We try to repair the leaking gasket with a strip of palm frond, but when we leave the field the back of his pants is wet with the liquid.

But the most irrevocable form of dependence on the new ways results from the extinction of local genetic resources as they are replaced with alien cultigens. I also want to underscore here that this growing dependence is mediated by migrants who shuttle back and forth between wage labor in commercial agroindustry and their own increasingly agroindustrialized subsistence production. Whereas articulation theory would see these as two distinct but joined systems of production, a global perspective sees them as aspects of a transnational system with a dynamic of differentiation that defies conventional distinctions between "peasant-traditional-subsistence" and "farmer-modern-commercial." Indeed, agroindustrialization effects an autodeconstruction of these paired opposites and constitutes new identities arrayed in systems of difference and distinction that are, if not always global, certainly transnational.

The transcendence of articulation is apparent in, for example, the circulation and conversion of economic value within the transnational networks in which transmigrants from indigenous communities participate. Thus, a portion of the wages earned by transmigrants in commercial agroindustry is spent to purchase petrochemicals and other industrial inputs for their own subsistence or small commercial production. The product so produced is consumed in the reproduction of the transmigrants so that they and other members of their families can sell labor power to commercial agroindustry, thus closing the circle through which value circulates and is accumulated on the wage-labor side of the cycle.

This reticulum in which value is formed, circulates, and is transformed and accumulated can be imagined as a field in which polarities are multiple and attenuated, in contrast with the dual structuring of articulation theory and the even more absolute dualism of dependency and modernization theories. Indeed, the dualities are dissolved into the identity of the transmigrant who differentially produces and reproduces within the transnational space of agroindustrialization in which 'peasant' and 'commercial' farmer are reconfigured as internally differentiated identities, various facets of which connect with facets of other persons situated at other positions within and outside of this transnational space.

From Modern Structures to Global Complexity

The plan for 'reconceptualizing the peasantry' we have followed in the preceding chapters has been to identify emergent trends in the anthropology of peasant society that are responses to changes in the objects—peasants and peasant society—of this anthropology and that are also responses to the more general changing world context within which this anthropology itself is situated. As a way of summing up these trends in the anthropology of peasants, we can consider them to be elements of an emergent global discourse associated with the fourth, contemporary period in the history of anthropology as outlined in Chapter 2, which contrasts with the modern anthropological discourse, which is waning. I stress "emergent" so as not to appear to be positing the existence of a well-formed paradigm. But these ideas are in the air in varying degrees, and if I have reified them somewhat, perhaps vindication lies in having breathed more life into them, to have nudged them along "into reality," so to speak. But I suspect that this nudge is but a ripple on a sea change of tidal wave proportion that is taking place as I write.

If a restructuring of the general sociological basis of anthropological knowledge as I have just outlined is indeed occurring, then it should be possible to outline the emergent anthropological discourse that is the general conceptual environment within which "the peasantry" can be, and indeed is being, reconceptualized. The form and content of this emergent discourse can be suggested by its keywords (Williams 1984), which contrast with the language of peasant studies associated with the fading modern period of anthropology. We have encountered most of them in previous chapters, but to consolidate this reconceptualization we can pull them together to reveal how they contrast with the discourse within which 'the peasant' was situated and given meaning in the second half of the twentieth century.

To designate the anthropological discourse that is waning I referred to it, in Chapter 2, as "modern" and identified the one that is being born as "global." This identification of contrasting epistemes might well open me to charges of replicating the very kind of metaphysical dualism I argue is autodeconstructing. In defense, it must be said that these two discourses do not exist in a relation of structural opposition such that, like metaphysical categories—for example, good-evil, truth-falsity—each owes its semantic existence to the other. Instead, these contrasting discourses exist in a relationship of evolutionary succession, such that whereas the latter is dependent on the former as its antecedent, the former has no dependency on the latter and indeed is annihilated by it. Also, unlike metaphysical oppositions—which are sharply dichotomous—but like evolutionary succession, the latter of these two discourses flows out of the former with no sharp discontinuity. Its emergence is only partial, and my depiction of it is a first attempt to sketch its broad outline and in doing so to assist its birth. Figure 5.1 lists the keywords of the two discourses and locates them in their respective discursive spaces.

Some of the terms of Figure 5.1 have been mentioned previously, whereas others remain to be examined in subsequent chapters. It is, however, convenient to pull them together at this point. Within the modern discourse the idea of development is teleological and eschatological in its almost biblical assumptions of progress and salvation through technological innovation and economic growth that would spread from developed centers to peripheral, backward areas. In contrast, in the global discourse it is possible for history to stagnate and even retrogress with respect to the material and social indicators of development. This worldview, which is more ecological and is influenced by chaos theory, relativizes human affairs within an intellectual framework that also subsumes other species, many of which do not fare well in the evolutionary long run. This perspective is informed by contemporary declines in living conditions in communities around the world as their life support systems are increasingly stressed by growing populations and shrinking resource bases. These problems are currently seen not as specific to peripheral areas but as global in extent and origin and necessitating international solutions.

With the decline of the Cold War, ideological rhetoric about capitalism versus communism as the cause of and cure for such problems has given way to concerns about the quality of life in a fundamentally global capitalist world but one in which there is considerable concern with the social, economic, and cultural rights that have to do with basic quality of life as spelled out in the Universal Dec-

MODERN DISCOURSE	GLOBAL DISCOURSE
Development	Diversification and Homogeneity
Teleology	Probability, Chance
Eschatology	Ecology
Centery-Periphery	Globalization
Structure	Complexity and Chaos
Communism-Capitalism	Quality of Life
East-West	North-South
Political Democracy	Social Democracy
Individual Human Rights	Collective Human Rights
Production	Consumption and Reproduction
Base-Superstructure	General Value
Agrarian Reform	New Social Movements
Farming	Gardening
Nation-State	Nongovernmental Organizations and Multinational Corporations
Cultural Homogenization	Cultural Differentiation
Acculturation/Assimilation	Ethnicity
Folk Culture	Popular and Mass Culture
Little Community	Transnational Community
Bounded Social Organization	Networks, Reticula
Individuals	Polybians
Peasants	Subalterns

Figure 5.1   Modern and Global Discourses of Anthropology

laration of Human Rights, as opposed to, for example, the much narrower definition of human rights in the Bill of Rights of the U.S. Constitution. Whereas developmentalism was obsessed with economic production, in the new discourse concern with production is tempered by a concern to change patterns of consumption having to do with the distribution of the world's resources and the environmental impact of consumption. Central to this issue is the differential consumption of global resources by "overdeveloped" northern nations compared to the poorer southern ones. Tension over this issue has now largely replaced the former rivalry between the capitalist West and the communist East.

Furthermore, whereas modernist left-wing theories of peasants emphasized relations and forms of production in shaping identity, consumption of material and especially symbolic artifacts and information is of central concern in the global discourse (Kearney 1995a). Such appreciation of the effect of consumption of both material and symbolic forms of value in turn diminishes any firm distinction between base and superstructure (see Chapter 7 for a discussion of the theory of general value).

In the former discourse the central peasant issue was agrarian reform, which in the new has been largely eclipsed by the broader issues concerning human rights and quality of life. Furthermore, there is a corresponding displacement of political activities by postpeasant subalterns into other political arenas and an enactment of them not as domestic party politics but as new social movements, which often displace the sites of political work from the space of the nation-state to international contexts in which nongovernmental organizations are playing growing roles (see Chapter 8). Whereas classical peasants were seen as subsistence farmers, the increasingly infrasubsistence production activities of peasantlike people are often better characterized as gardening, an activity that has manifold social, economic, and geographic variants and is increasingly becoming an object of anthropological research.

Modernist assumptions about the inevitability of acculturation and assimilation of "traditional" peoples have largely given way to concern with ongoing, typically complex cultural differentiation, often manifesting dramatically as ethnicity and indeed often in seeming contradiction with, on the one hand, the decline of local folk cultures and, on the other, the spread of popular culture and mass media of communication. It is within this context that the subaltern emerges, first announced by Gramsci in the early twentieth century and becoming established as a major category within anthropology at the beginning of the twenty-first century. But we now realize that the subaltern is a type of internally differentiated polybian, a social category that, to be understood, requires a reconceptualization of classification.

Figure 5.2 depicts the contrast between the modern and global discourses (Figure 5.1) in relation to both the history of classification in anthropology and the recent and ongoing emergence of postmodern concepts and theory in related disciplines. Within anthropology the articulation phase of the agrarian debate (Chapter 4) is transitional between the binary classification characteristic of the modern and earlier phases of anthropological thought and the emergent reticular classification of the current global period. Whereas binary classification is based on a hierarchically branching binary logic of either-or, social types defined by articulation theory were attributed ambiguous both-and identities that were disruptive of the neat logic of binary thinking. But such theoretical types and the logic that defines them are best thought of as a way station on the road to appreciation of the yet greater complexity of polybians. Whereas articulated identities are imagined as existing in distinct dual fields (e.g., modes of production), polybians are formed within complex reticula that in terms of positions, classification, connections, and flows have more in common with hypertexts than with hierarchical branching structures.

The appearance of reticular classification in anthropology at this time is driven largely by the ethnography of complex communities in global and transnational contexts (Kearney 1995b). But its appearance is also stimulated by comparable developments in related disciplines, which have seen much reconceptualization of

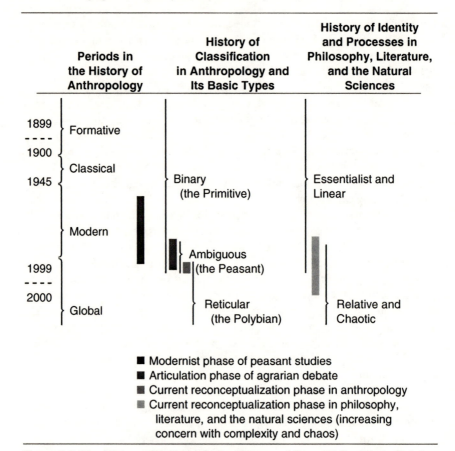

Figure 5.2 The History of Anthropological Theory of Peasant Society in Relation to the History of Anthropology and of Identity

modern concepts of identity and processes. In the humanities, most notably literary theory and philosophy, this transition is associated with postmodern thought, whereas in physics, biology, and other natural sciences it is associated with concern with complex and chaotic phenomena conventional scientific theory, mathematics, and methods are unable to deal with in other than trivial ways.

Thus, just as the social sciences typically adopt their metaphors and models from the natural sciences, anthropology is ripe to employ concepts and theories of complexity and chaos now common in the natural sciences (see, e.g., Casti 1994; Gleick 1987). It is therefore to be expected that concepts based on an appreciation of the complexity of identities and the intricacy of social and communication networks and the flows of persons, information, value, and so forth, through them should replace the teleology of development and the static, mechanistic assumptions of structuralism. This is not say that structured entities and relationships do not exist but that when they do they are more likely to be emergent from complexity than to have been generated from prior ontlogical structures of a Platonic, Saussurian, Durkheimian, or Chomskian type.

Notes

1. Historical studies focusing on the agency of proletarians and peasants appeared in the 1970s and 1980s as critiques of and alternatives to the ahistoric models inspired by French structuralist anthropology. See especially Wolf (1982), and Thompson's (1978) critique of Althusser.

2. Redfield's folk-urban continuum and the diffusionist ideas from which it was derived were, like articulation theory, early anticipations of this decay of bipolar space, but they were nevertheless basically polar models.

3. For several years in the mid–1980s, a Paraguayan political exile who was the founder of the Paraguayan League of Catholic Peasant Unions lived with my family in southern California. Accustomed to the sharp distinction between urban center and rural hinterland of the Latin American cities of his youth, he had a very modern notion of space. On numerous occasions driving to events in Hollywood, Santa Monica, Burbank, and other areas in the vast megalopolis of greater Los Angeles, he would invariably ask, "*¿Cuando llegamos al centro?*" to which my invariable reply was "*aquí no hay centros.*"

4. See Chapter 8 for the way the plight of these displaced persons has been a force affecting the discursive displacement in Mesoamerican anthropology from a primary concern with local peasant society to a concern with human rights.

5. See also Kearney (1986a, 1986b) on migrant "networks" and Rouse (1988, 1991) on "migrant circuits," which are discussed later.

6. Taken from field notes, March 1992.

7. It is interesting that one of the foremost peasantists in Mexico, Roger Bartra, has recently employed an innovative metaphor of networks (Bartra 1992; see Kearney 1993b) in a general discussion of political power.

Chapter 6

Differentiation and Identity

Whereas Chapter 5 explored the outlines of rural society after 'development,' this chapter shifts to the kinds of subjects that inhabit such nontraditional, nondeveloped spaces and in doing so returns to the main issue in peasant studies—namely, social differentiation of the peasantry. The basic theme of this chapter is that there are two intersecting global trends. One is an inexorable cultural homogenization mediated mainly by migration, transnational capital, electronic means of communication, and the spread of mass culture as discussed in Chapter 5. The other trend is the proliferation and diversification of social types that arise and fill ever increasing new social niches. This trend toward micro-social differentiation is contrary to the overall global trend of increasing extinction of biological species.

These new micro-social niches provide the social ecology for the increased social differentiation that is most pronounced as internal rather than external differentiation. This heightened internal differentiation demands a rethinking of the sociology and culture (consciousness) of complex subjects and of the constitution of communities. In the case of so-called peasant identities and communities, such reconceptualization can proceed by identifying third terms that have appeared and are appearing in the margins between the categorical oppositions (Chapter 3) upon which the peasant was constructed in the modern era from the residue of traditional society. Whereas peasants were constructed as permutations of the individual, the reconceptualized subject is an internally differentiated person. The collective forms of these identities are reticula and transnational unbounded communities (Chapter 5) and new social movements (Chapter 8).

The thrust of my argument so far is that effective reconceptualization of the peasant requires not just a substitution of another social category for the one whose intellectual and political potency has become exhausted but a reconceptualization of the principles that structure such categories. For it is not just the case that the classificatory power of 'the peasant' as a term has become exhausted but that the conventional principles of classification that define that social type no longer adequately reflect the social fields within which social identities are formed, including the anthropological Self and its relationships to ethnographic Others.

Indeed, reconceptualization of the anthropological Self is necessary to a general reconceptualization of the dualist structuring of anthropological thought within which the peasant was defined. This dissolving of the binary categories of modern thought is comparable to bringing social theory into line with contemporary astronomical cosmology, which has effected what amounts to a second Copernican Revolution. The first Copernican Revolution changed the polarity of creation by repositioning humans from the center toward the periphery of the solar system. However, the idea of a center, the sun, as an absolute point of central reference was retained. But now earth and sun are seen as on the edge of not only a galaxy but a galaxy that has no clear relationship to the center of the universe in which there are more stars than grains of sand on all the beaches on the earth. The anthropological counterpart of this deconstruction of the bipolarity of Copernican astronomy is now occurring, but it is driven not by the development of social science but by the emergence of internally differentiated selves who defy assignment to any of the unitary social identities in the repertoire of humanist social thought.

One indication of the need for critical reconceptualization of the anthropological categories, such as peasant, is their high degree of isomorphism with both official and popular images. In biology, the similarity of closely related forms is explained by their descent from a common ancestor. Similarly, the lack of contrast between folk and anthropological images of the peasant is the result of their derivation from common origins. The anthropological concept is thus insufficiently displaced from its object to gain critical perspective on it. There has, in other words, been no Copernican Revolution. And this lack of conceptual difference between anthropological thought and its object—the peasant—functions not so much to understand that object as to construct it.

The basic argument here is that the strategic point at which to reconceptualize modern social thought is the sites where images of its self are culturally constructed so as to become socially constituted. It is here, at this bedrock of worldview, that the deep structuring of social identities is formed, social identities that come into official consciousness as unitary social subjects—the peasant, the proletarian, the farmer, and so forth—all of which are permutations, are types of the prototypic self that is constructed as the individual.

From Individual to Person

Etymologically, 'individual' refers to a core unit of subject identity that is *indivisible*. The individual of modern, presumably nontheistic thought is usually regarded as situated within political, social, and philosophical discourses that are distinct from religious ones. But upon closer examination we find that this cultural category so basic to bourgeois humanism is historically derived from prior metaphysical ideas about the human 'soul,' which is identified in theological discourse as the essential kernel of human identity. This culturally coded specification of human identity that underlies modern humanism is thus historically derived from prior ethno-categories in Western culture that distinguish the 'material' forms of creation from the 'spiritual.'

The subject, or in the parlance of worldview theory, the self of modern humanism is thus not unlike the disembodied spiritual essence of religious metaphysics with which it is historically continuous. Thus, ideas about what a 'peasant' is are informed by classificatory prior attributes of what a 'human individual' is. Given the deep cognitive potency of this ethno-category, underlying as it does the culturally specific definition of 'human' in modern thought, any reconceptualization of social types as defined by social science that does not query the individual runs the risk of having left unexamined a basic assumption and imagery upon which social theory is constructed.

As a modern social type, the peasant was figured as a kind of individual, which is the prototype of all modern types such as the proletariat, the bourgeoisie, the middle class, and so forth. I have neither the space nor the need to review the genealogy of the individual as the prototypical social type of modern society in general and of capitalism in particular. Let it suffice to note that the individual is called forth along with and by the emergent modern nation-state and the particular sociocultural differentiation effected by capitalism. Whereas the latter called the individual into being by its distinctive division of labor, which is also a division of community into classes of those individuals, the state baptized these identities with official seals and registers that as marks on paper reinforced marks made on the bodies so identified.[1]

The unitary individual as the molecular social unit of the nation-state is, as a classificatory category, an absolute, nonambiguous identity. The primary semantic dimension of this identity is citizenship, which is an officially recognized either-or status. The identity *citizenship* is secondarily classified into mutually exclusive, nonambiguous subidentities that are, for example, consistent with the categories used in census enumeration. The particular 'individual' is thus defined as the intersection of a series of nonambiguous dimensions that are laid onto populations.

These social dimensions are binary and as such are, in this structural form, consistent with and permutations of deeper dual structural principles that underlie them and that are basic to the construction of nationhood as a social identity defined by its binary opposition to the nations and peoples with which it contrasts. Thus, just as the state is concerned to define its nationhood unambiguously vis-à-vis the other nations with which it contrasts, so does it internally seek to define its subjects unambiguously as unitary identities. The individual thus becomes naturalized and is received so prefigured by anthropology, which uncritically accepts the individual as its elemental social unit—although anthropology is far less susceptible to such reification than is sociology and especially neoclassical economics, which celebrates the individual as a fetish.

The emergence, with the growth of capitalist society, of the individual as a basic unit of social theory was a deeply progressive development that made possible the conception of "the Rights of Man" and all subsequent developments in the philosophy of individual human rights. But as I have discussed earlier, the emergence of the individual within capitalist society was facilitated by the official inscribing of that type of identity onto the citizens of modern nations. Indeed, central to the idea of modernization is the freeing of latent individuals who are held captive within the limiting confines of traditional society. Thus it is that when official thought regards traditional peoples, it treats them as individuals. The peasant is regarded by official thought as an individual who must be made to take his or her place among other unique citizens who exist or who are coming into being.

Recently, an alternative definition of 'human' has been forming within critical social science discourse that amounts to a partial dismantling of the dualistic mental-materialist metaphysics of modern social science, derivative as it is from prior theological discourse. We can help to nudge this reconceptualization, this alternative to 'the individual,' into consciousness by naming it. And the term that suggests itself is *person*. 'Person' can thus be taken as a cognitive particle upon which condense the attributes of self that are being brought into consciousness by contemporary history. 'Person' is appearing as a term resulting from and reflecting the autodeconstruction of the essentialized individual of modern thought.[2]

That 'person' is the term of choice to carry forward the project of overcoming the dualism inherent in the 'individual' of modern thought is suggested by its contemporary polysemy, which recovers the unity of the subject. For person is self in both the abstract sense of a legal, thinking person and also in the sense of palpable, feeling, moving flesh. The self so cognized assists in bringing the body into cultural anthropology, and indeed the body has recently emerged as a focal topic of anthropological investigation.[3] But this is a body with a mind, although not a mind that is like 'software,' which has an ontology and a dynamic apart from the 'hardware' it directs. Rather, the person as conceived herein is a seamless being. Such a theorization of the person offers to subsume and surpass the opposition within anthropology between the symbolic and interpretive and the positivistic and empirical natural science approaches.[4]

This dismantling of the structured distinction between the 'objective' and 'subjective' aspects of the modern individual is effected by a practical anthropology that displaces anthropological work from a sociology of knowledge, in which the anthropological Self attempts to know ethnographic Others, to a position in the social field in which both Self and Other are located and relativized, thus negating the distinction between them—*distinction* used here in both its epistemological and social class senses. To the degree that anthropology is predicated on a definition of ethnographic Others as basically objects—as in objective and empirical—

anthropological theory unself-consciously replicates implicit dualist worldview assumptions of the folk tradition within which it developed.

The forces of globalization and transnationalism that are now eroding the colonial situation (Kearney 1995b) are also undermining the historical basis for a distinction between the anthropological Self and the ethnographic Other, a distinction that structured the social field within which the opposition between positivist and interpretive anthropology was formed. It is beyond the scope of this chapter to explore how this opposition between interpretive and scientific anthropology is predicated on the same basic worldview assumptions out of which the dualist individual—imagined as 'mind' and 'body'—is constructed, but it must be realized that the full reconceptualization of anthropology required by the reconceptualization of its social identities must address this unacceptable situation in which the discipline is split into two incompatible and competing camps. The challenge of this problem for the development of anthropology is comparable to the search for a unified field theory in physics.

Internal Versus External Differentiation

Reconceptualization of the individual does not necessarily call for the individual to be discarded but instead for its status to be changed from empirical object to analytic category, which is not completely without theoretical value once it has become so relativized in the history of anthropology. It thus assumes a status comparable to, say, atoms, which at one stage in the history of physics were assumed to be elemental particles. But as protons and electrons were found to be subatomic particles, so in turn were yet smaller particles and forces hypothesized to account for events unexplainable with recourse only to the grosser entities. This trend from larger to more discrete units of analysis is characteristic of the development of science in general.[5]

In anthropology, the individual has presented a barrier especially resistant to reduction to the equivalent of subatomic particles. But this barrier must be surpassed, for the individual has about as much analytic usefulness to anthropology as the unit *word* does in linguistics; both are folk categories. Theoretical movement beyond this barrier is prefigured in role theory and psychoanalysis, both of which map facets or areas of individual identity. But both are inadequate for our purposes. Role theory as a component of George Herbert Mead's sociology is couched in a discourse that is largely devoid of the structural and historical dimensions demanded by an anthropology of "peasants" and complex transnational subjects. Roles in sociological analysis are primarily just that, identities the individual takes on while he "struts and frets his hour upon the stage." But the essentialized individual is like the constructed identity of the nation of which he or she is a microcosmic replication: "one nation indivisible."[6] Psychoanalysis has similar limitations, for its goal is to uncover and then dispel internal divisions in the psyche, which can be taken as a gloss for the individual. It thus seeks to reconstitute the category I seek to relativize.

The individual is given 'his' identity largely by the nation-state of which 'he' is a citizen. Indeed, the modern nation-state is constituted by and of individuals, and as such an official category the individual contains, in both senses of the term, the subject positions within it. An internally differentiated subject is contrary to the kind of mechanical differentiation the state is concerned to define and document and to replicate with its birth registries, passports, passbooks, licenses, certificates, credentials, diplomas, and so forth. For it is by documenting that it constructs and replicates. But internal differentiation threatens to erode, to weaken this categorizing power and therefore the authority of the state. The internally differentiated subject defies categorization and therefore documentation. And since documentation is the prerequisite of governance, the internally differentiated subject is categorically subversive of the power of the state to perpetuate the differentiation that is inscribed in its official categories.[7]

In social analysis based on the individual, the task is given as finding a classification scheme that approximates and distinguishes types of individuals. But the extent and complexity of the internally differentiated individual make such a task nearly futile. The subject does not disappear, but it is more complex than previously theorized. Foucault was wrong regarding the disappearance of the subject—it is the individual that disappears, evaporates. That a theory of internal differentiation should appear now is indicative of historical changes that call it forth as an alternative to the official subject, the individual.[8]

The internally differentiated subject is a *transforming* entity whose fluid identity is suspect and illegitimate, like that of the quick-change artist or con artist. A first approximation to denote the identities of complex transforming types such as migrants, who move back and forth from 'peasant' to 'proletarian' life spaces, is to speak of them as amphibians (*amphi*, both, + *bios*, mode of life). But biological amphibians, which spend part of their lives in water and part on land, are but dual creatures, whereas the kinds of categorical migrants with which we are dealing move in and out of multiple niches and are therefore more correctly called *polybians* (*poly*, many). The polybian is rather like a chameleon, which can adjust its color to match that of its immediate environment. But unlike such protective coloration, which is but skin-deep, polybians adapt their being to different modes of existence as they opportunistically move in and out of different life spaces. Thus, unlike the amphibian and Haraway's (1985) cyborgs, which combine two forms in one body and are therefore subversive of dually structured identities, polybians transcend dualism.

To describe a polybian locally and ahistorically he or she might indeed appear in one context—perhaps at one moment in his or her life—as a peasant, in another as a plantation worker, and in others as a petty merchant or an urban slum dweller. Each of these identities is reified as the polybian's essential nature by theories of external differentiation in concert with methodologies that are ahistorical and local in their scope.

But these slippery creatures defy constructed social bounds; they cross out of their "proper" places and enter into marginal spaces. And by populating these border areas they threaten normal social categories that the state has a responsibility to maintain. The state responds to these violators of boundaries, these "illegals," these "aliens" by denying them official recognition, by saying to them in effect that you will be this or that or nothing. By means of its border guards, its census enumerators, its recorders of vital statistics, and its rural sociologists and anthropologists, the modern state ensures the replication of the 'rural' social order in properly differentiated form and, furthermore, the proper differentiation of 'rural' versus 'urban' things, spaces, and persons.[9]

The polybian, by migrating without documents across social categorical borders, defies the documenting power of the state to impose unitary identities. Here is the basis of a subversive power far greater than recognized by theories of subversion and resistance based on implicit assumptions of the unitary undifferentiated subject.

Whereas 'illegal' transnational migration among different modes of production is perhaps the most dramatic transgression of official and existential boundaries, tens of millions of categorical subversives in the former Third World—itself a designation of an ambiguous place—defy classificatory and regulatory laws by working in the so-called informal economy. In countries such as Mexico, where official rates of unemployment run as impossibly high as 20 percent, such unlicensed and untaxed petty entrepreneurs are the lifeblood of the economy, but it is an economy that is out of control in an official sense (Tokman 1992). The same can be said of the extensive black markets that came into being in the final days of the Soviet Union and that allow for minimalist subsistence in the current postperestroika economy that has not yet made the fabled transition to modern capitalism. And another case with more clearly transnational dimensions is that of the extensive smuggling networks in Poland, which have made that country a major conduit for unofficial economic exchange between Western Europe and the states of the former Soviet Union.

Revolutionary theory envisions a double transformation: first, a structural transformation in relations of production and cultural superstructure and second, a transformation of the subject—the 'new person' who comes to occupy the new revolutionary subject position. But this theory of revolution accepts and indeed reifies the structure of the field within which revolution occurs; it is the same bipolar field within which unitary subjects are arrayed as they existed before the revolution.

Such is not, however, the case in the transformation of identity effected by the polybian, who embodies a sort of primary subversion that seeks not, like secondary subversion, to move subjects from one unitary social category to another that has more power or value but that instead seeks to escape a confining social identity by dissolving the principles that define categories. Conventional subversion of, say, a Stalinist kind is insidious in the literal sense that it "sits within" the official scheme of classification, whereas polybians situate themselves outside of not just the categories of the official scheme of classification but outside of its structure of classification.

The social categorical subversive power of polybians is thus better said to be immanent, in that it is constituted within the complex social field in which they live. But unlike the teleological assumptions of classical Marxist analysis, which also assumes that its own critical and subversive power is inherent within capitalist society and its workings, polybians defy such essentialism and therefore do not of necessity point to a radically different future.[10] As often as not living in, but not always adapting to and surviving in, severely degraded and polluted environments, the polybian has no essential teleology of salvation, of development. For among the binary cultural constructions its existence calls into question is that between culture and nature, that is, between human and nonhuman. Somalians starving to death by the thousands in 1993 in a man-made famine associated with the collapse of their nation-state are coevals with life-forms being made extinct by the man-made collapse of ecosystems in Amazonia. As environmental degradation overwhelms the adaptive ability of tropical rain forest species, so does historical contingency often overwhelm the creative abilities of polybians to improve the quality of their lives and even to survive biologically, thus mocking modernist assumptions of 'development' and progress.

A definitional dialectic is at work between the official categories and those of popular speech and personal identity. That the state has the power to rule, to order, and to maintain order depends in great part on the correspondence between the official categories and lived popular identities. The obverse implication is that resistance to the ordering power of the powers that be depends on and is derived from the subjugated subjects' ability to take on alternate definitions of self and to articulate and enact them.

The practical limitations, possibilities, and pitfalls of such projects are taken up in Chapter 8, which examines the transformative potential of several new social movements emerging in formerly peasant communities and how the highly internally differentiated social identities they articulate defy the power of the state to categorize and thus constitute them as *just* peasants, with all that identity implies with respect to being rustic, backward, ignorant, inarticulate, and passive subjects of the state and other forms of higher authority. But what concerns us here is the degree to which institutionalized anthropology has been a servant of state policy—in all the multiple senses of that term that have to do with control and policing of rural peoples—by constructing identities in accord with the identities the state constructs for its subjects. Such collaboration is not undertaken by choice and indeed may even be done by critical anthropologists who intentionally oppose the state and its allied interests, which control and appropriate value from peasants and other subalterns. The collaboration comes instead from the felt necessity to speak of and for 'peasants' but to do so in terms that have already been sedimented into general discourse by having been defined and validated by official and unofficial usage. The most obvious case of this is, as exemplified in Chapter 4, the use of official data—that is, data that have been first defined and then, as it were, brought to life by being collected.

Implied in the use of *person* as an alternative for the *individual* as a category for reconceptualizing 'peasants' is a corresponding reconceptualization of the communities composed of such persons. To the degree to which the person represents a species difference to the individual, such persons will cohere to a comparable degree in suprapersonal forms that must be represented politically and ethnographically in ways distinct from bounded communities presumed to be composed of peasants as individuals.

'Peasants' of officially identifiable communities regularly enumerate their individual members and otherwise keep track of the community's membership. And to no small degree, such official acts constitute the community. But it is an anthropological error, commonly committed, to assume that such lists adequately correspond to the community as a system of production, consumption, and communication within which identities are formed and reproduced. "Adequately," in this context, must be specified. Indeed, communities so constituted do indeed have objective realities as groups of individuals. But if by adequate we mean a conception of community that subsumes the folk definition and contextualizes it and its object, then the official definition is found wanting.

Major movement in the conceptual opening up of bounded, closed peasant communities was made by articulation theory, which revealed the degree to which such communities reproduce by participating in distant and distinct forms of production. But even as articulation theory opened up the imagery of the bounded community and extended its locus in space, it also reified the inherent dualist disposition of conventional anthropology, for it is always two modes of production that are so articulated. But as noted in Chapter 4, articulation theory effected considerable deconstructive movement. This momentum is now being carried forward by terms that transcend the residual dualism of articulation theory.

Decline of Class Identity and Increase in Class Difference

The peasant of contemporary anthropology is, as discussed in Chapter 2, the categorically troublesome third member of the taxonomy of classes constructed by nineteenth-century political economy, which endures in the late twentieth century. In nineteenth-century thinking the main referents of 'peasants' were various rural peoples in Europe and the British Isles. But in the twentieth century, when anthropology became concerned with peasants, the term, which belongs to the European context, was applied to referents found mainly in the Third World. The modern concept of peasant was thus applied to a historical context different from the one in which it originated.

What concerns us now, in what is arguably a third historical phase, is the enduring scientific validity of a social category that is so removed from the moment of its original construction. To address this concern, two confounded issues must be disentangled. The first is the validity of social class as a principle of classification; the other is the imputed class nature of peasants.

In recent years, several major theoretical issues concerning 'peasants' have dominated anthropological discussion of rural peoples. Each of these issues, to which we now turn, can be seen as a response to a dawning awareness of the precariousness of the peasant concept. The research and debates focused on these issues have carried forward the dismantling of the peasant concept even as they have served to freeze it, to contain it by the reificatory power of theory. These debates do serve, however, as a platform to better conceptualize the social fields within which the internally differentiated subject is constituted.

Value, Differentiation, Community, and Autonomy

Transnational migration and agroindustrialization are powerful forces dissolving spatial, social, and conceptual distinctions—rural-urban, peasant-proletarian, autonomy-dependence, traditional-modern—upon which the peasant as a social identity and anthropological category depends. Research and writing about these two forms of globalization have for the most part existed as separate but parallel discourses, but they are beginning to merge.[11] Further advances in theory that is able to deal with the integration of transnational migration and agroindustrialization will depend on concepts, images, and research that adequately addresses two basic issues: class and consciousness *and* autonomy of decisionmaking.

Class and Consciousness

The links between small producers and agroindustry, the impact of massive migration and occupational diversity, and the consumption and production of mass and popular culture all combine to promote internal differentiation that erodes any possible single, unitary subject position as a basis of subjective class identity. Indeed, the thrust of the argument herein is that categories such as *the peasant* and *the proletarian,* as both analytic categories and subject identities, have virtually disappeared as meaningful bases upon which a self-consciousness of class membership might condense. I have, however, taken this observation not as a demonstration of the nonexistence of class as a formative dimension of identity but rather as a demonstration of the impotence of class, as a basic dimension of identity, to inform *subject identity*—in other words, to be reflected in consciousness as class consciousness, as a sense of class membership.

Indeed, through the theory of internal differentiation we are brought to the conclusion that there is little to no subjective basis for a socially and politically meaningful sense of peasant identity. It is in such a situation that the category *peasant* is retained in history, not so much as a deeply subjectively experienced identity but instead as an official category of containment perpetuated by official nonpeasant discourses about presumed peasants.

This analysis does not, however, lead to a discarding of class as *the* fundamental dimension for the analysis of subjective identity. To the contrary, this low saliency of class consciousness requires a reconsideration of class as an objective basis of differentiation and of the ways in which this differentiation is not so much reflected but rather refracted in consciousness, in some cases as alienation and anomie and in others as ethnicity and the motive force of new social movements (see Chapter 8).

Land, labor power, finance capital, the household, the transnational corporation, and the person are all complexly articulated in transnational spaces that do not correspond to the classical categories. For example, the identity of a transnational migrant 'peasant-worker' of Oaxaca is as complex as the corporate identity of a transnational corporation. Both present conceptual and theoretical problems to the state with respect to their legal definition and control, but of the two, the transnational person is more problematic.

States have developed definitions—indeed, have facilitated the development of workable definitions—of the transnational corporation as a legal entity. But the state encounters a contradiction in the case of transnational persons, who they want to contain as individuals, as nationals. The contradiction arises from the inconsistency in the actual lived identity of such persons as transnationals and their official identities as citizens. Just as the transnational corporation has escaped the confines of the nation-state since World War II, so to a great extent have migratory peasantlike persons. But legal definitions of personhood have not evolved to a degree comparable to that in the recent evolution of the transnational corporation as a legal person. Such a lack of coincidence between formal legal and other textual definitions of social identity and actual lived identities is what I have defined as containment. Similarly, to the degree that transnational migrants escape the constitutive power of the state, reconceptualization of their identity is possible.

Studies dealing with the decomposition of peasant communities have tended to focus on proletarianization. But when the work histories of persons within transnational networks and circuits are examined, it is apparent that many of them participate heavily in so-called informal economies. In productionist terms, this is a nebulous social world populated with ambiguous types who are not engaged on a full-time basis in either peasant production or wage labor but who are nevertheless economically active most of their waking hours.

People so engaged earn money in many diverse ways limited only by their ingenuity. A partial list might include such activities as street vending, shoe shining, washing windshields of cars stopped at intersections, babysitting, sewing, rag picking, playing street music, making gadgets, maid work, gardening, day laboring, hauling, prostitution, loan sharking, production and sale of narcotics and crafts, and so forth. In some directions these 'informal activities' fade into criminality as defined by the state, whereas in others they slide into another conceptual morass summed up variously as 'lumpen,' 'homeless,' or 'derelict.' And many such polybians appear at certain moments to be fairly peasant, if those particular moments are bracketed off from the other diverse moments of their lives.

Such complexity of identity is even more apparent when we look at the families of these polybians. It is often possible to find rather peasantlike persons, especially older, nonmigrating folks who tend gardens and animals as part of an economic and sociocultural strategy of family reproduction. Contemporary polybious families are unlikely to reproduce the peasant identities of such "old folks" in coming generations. Examination of the lives of persons and families who work in the informal economy also as often as not leads us back into the 'peasantry' and the 'working class.' But in doing so these lives invariably reveal a spuriousness to such distinctions that rather than being essential identities are rather like hats one puts on or takes off according to the job of the moment. These varied ways of making a living are tactics in more complex economic strategies that nullify attempts to classify subjects and their communities on the basis of the standard productionist types.

Such multiple, varied identities are knit together by reticula that are the fabric and texture of informal relationships that defy the pigeonholing work of official constructions of univocal subject identity. The proliferation of informal economic activity and of informal network social relationships in general, which was discussed in Chapter 4, is the social ground on which internally differentiated subjects are formed. Or taking such subjects as our point of reference, it is their networking activity that constitutes the informal economy. Seen as such, the challenge the state faces in regulating the informal economy is not merely regulating individuals who are operating without licenses. Rather, to be effective in suppressing the informal economy, the state must suppress the complex internal differentiation of subjects that is formed in communities of reticula.

The Limits of Rational Actor Theory

Both historical-structural and microcognitive approaches to peasants emphasize autonomy of rational decisionmaking as a characteristic of peasants. However, agroindustrialization and migration (Chapter 5) require reconsideration of this basic feature of peasant essentialism. Indeed, if autonomy of decisionmaking concerning production is a defining characteristic of peasants, then the decrease of such autonomy under the pressure of agroindustrialization implies the decline of peasants. Much recent ethnographic and economic research on small producers who produce for markets well illustrates their loss of autonomy regarding production decisions as they become incorporated into agroindustrial relations.[12]

Earlier I discussed how production decisions are made by buyers and banks who control the finance capital that pays the cost of production. But the context of 'decisionmaking' is even more complex when migration is taken into account whereby the small producer moves in and out of distant and diverse social and geographic fields in which different facets of his or her identity are brought to light but that are rarely, if ever, studied in their totality by students of decisionmaking.[13] In contrast to their lived social complexity, the assumptions about social identity decisionmaking research brings to 'peasant' producers are predicated on the unitary, rational, maximizing individual largely contained to the sphere of agricultural production and to the maximization of economic value.

Several possible reconceptualizations of agricultural decisionmaking are suggested by these considerations. First, research should be refocused from the unitary *individual* as the psychological focus of decisionmaking to the various submolecular elements of identity of which the person is composed, each of which must be followed, as the person migrates, into the social fields that call forth particular aspects of the person. In other words, ethnographic research on decisionmaking concerning agricultural production is inseparable from the ethnographies of the other social fields in which the small part-time producer lives and that are often more important to biological and social reproduction than is agricultural production. Indeed, in such cases, research on agricultural decisionmaking should be dispersed throughout the transnational community in which the person lives. To do otherwise confines research primarily to a community erroneously assumed to be local, bounded, and rural and also to agricultural production and thus essentializes 'peasants' and contains them to the officially recognized spaces and identities.

As a strategy that is manageable, decisionmaking must of necessity impose such containment on subjects that otherwise present impossible complexity that is not amenable to the formal Aristotelian classification and binary logic of decisionmaking theory. Indeed, a fundamental contradiction exists here between this style of formal classification and analysis, which is the basis of official knowledge and political management, and the lived, physical and cognitive life of polybians. Given the complexity of polybians' experience as shaped by life in transnational communities, it is undoubtedly mathematically and logically impossible to model their decisionmaking except in trivial ways. The challenge to decisionmaking research presented by this complexity is comparable to that faced by projects in artificial intelligence.

Rational actor theory, largely an offshoot of neoclassical economic theory of the rational maximizing individual, employs a narrow definition of value based on a calculus of desire. In this model the rational individual makes trade-offs between binary choices such as cost and gain, pleasure and pain, work and leisure, and stigma and prestige. The theory assumes that decisions are made as either-or choices with an eye to some sort of bottom line, as on a profit and loss sheet. But when this dualistic style of theory is set aside, other possible ends of production and consumption become apparent. Rather than perceiving 'individuals' as maximizers of the desired, we can regard then as transformers of value and power who themselves become transformed in the process. This theoretical move de-essentializes the maximizing individual who is contained in dualist thinking and instead queries the effects of production and consumption of value on the formation of identity. I take up these issues in the remaining two chapters.

Notes

1. Although they do not deal specifically with the appearance of the modern individual, Corrigan and Sayer (1985) reveal the cultural and institutional contexts that brought it into being in England; compare Sagan (1985) who examines the emergence of individualism out of kinship-based societies.

2. Among references to personhood in anthropology, see Geertz (1973a), and Sullivan (1990).

3. One such indication of the appearance of the body on the theoretical horizon is the attention focused on it at the 1990 Annual Meeting of the American Ethnological Society, which was devoted to "the Body in Society and Culture."

4. Bourdieu's (1977) concept of "habitus" similarly transcends the theoretical dualism of mind and body.

5. "Without doubt the general trend in semiological-grammatological theory, as in modern science, points toward ever more minimal units: word → sign (signified/ signifier) → phoneme (mytheme) → distinctive features → trace → arche-trace" (Leitch 1983:28).

6. It is beyond the scope of this book, but a fruitful line of investigation would be to examine the ways in which the construction of the indivisible bounded subject—the individual—was coterminous with the construction of the modern nation conceived as bounded and indivisible (see Basch, Glick Schiller, and Szanton Blanc 1994).

7. It is therefore not surprising, as Rouse (1992b) notes, that one of the common first acts of Mexican peasants who rose up in the Mexican Revolution was to burn local archives.

8. In her discussion of how each "social agent" is located in a number of "subject positions," each of which "is itself the locus of multiple possible constructions," Mouffe (1988:90) basically identifies what I have been calling internal differentiation. And in her analysis of the complex multiple positionality of subjects she, to my mind, also justifiably rejects efforts to reduce the formation of subjective identity and political predisposition to a single primary class position. But at this point, I fear, she makes the egregious post-Marxist error of rejecting class as the primary dimension of difference. What must be rejected are simplistic definitions of class based solely on positionality in production processes. Instead, class analysis must be widened to encompass the overall differential distribution of general value in society, as discussed in Chapters 7 and 8.

9. The neologism *polybian* is somewhat similar to the Gramscian term *subaltern*, which the Subaltern Studies Group has employed to effect a displacement of the historical point of view and perspective from elites to the Indian subaltern classes (Guha and Spivak 1988). But this displacement involves only a minimal reconceptualization of the structuring of identity, of the subject. In contrast, the concept of the polybian is a new theory of the subject. Furthermore, whereas subalterns are class-specific types, namely, urban poor and peasants, polybians may occupy any class position. Nevertheless, the appreciation of the complexity of subject identity shown by the Subaltern Studies Group does point toward the idea of internal differentiation, which is the defining structural feature of the polybian.

Furthermore, whereas the Subaltern Studies Group has criticized official historiography for its distortions and erasures of subaltern subjects from history (see, e.g., Guha 1988), I am herein more concerned with the constituting power of official and popular intellectual work to shape categories of identity.

10. See Eagleton (1991:131) for discussion of "immanent critiques" as currents in contemporary philosophy and criticism that are conscious intellectual counterparts of the lived subaltern subversion of categories identified herein.

11. For examples of such merging, see Besserer (1993), and Zabin et al. (1993).

12. Case studies are increasingly illustrating this trend: see Barkin (1978), Cancian (1992), Collier (1994a, 1994b), Early (n.d.), Gates (1993), and Gudeman (1978).

13. This analysis calls attention to how the position of presumed peasants in economic fields beyond local household and community obviates much presumed autonomy of decisionmaking. This contextual critique of rational actor theory complements Bourdieu's (1990:46) critique of its assumptions of "ultra finalist subjectivism" and a "mechanistic determinism."

Chapter 7

From Modes of Production to Consumption of Modes: Class, Value, Power, and Resistance

Peasant studies, in addition to splitting into the dichotomies discussed in previous chapters—right versus left, modern versus romantic, peasantist versus proletarianist—also divide into approaches that favor infrastructural versus superstructural forces in the shaping of identity. This chapter explores emergent possibilities for a synthesis and transcendence of this opposition between perspectives that favor the production of economic value over consumption of culture in the shaping of identity and does so through a theory of general value, power, and class that is applicable to complex subjects in complex social fields. The platform for the analysis of such subjects was provided by articulation theory, which points the way to the transcendence of its residual dualism, a transcendence made possible by the theory of general value. With the final passing of articulation theory, the peasant passes as a useful theoretical category.

In addition to *class*, perhaps the most primary and yet the most abstract and indefinite categories of social theory are *value* and *power*. The former underlies economics and the latter political science, and together they consistitue the substance of political economy. The classical political economy of Ricardo and Adam Smith gave more or less equal attention to each of these categories, but with the fragmentation of reality effected by disciplinary specialization this unity of purpose was split apart. Only in the Marxist tradition has there been much concern to preserve it, and even there this is true more often in name than in practice.

Each of these two highly polysemous terms denotes and connotes a wide range of meanings that span some of the main antinomies of social science, which, as discussed in Chapter 3, are the conceptual armature on which images of social fields and identities such as 'the peasant' are constructed. Thus, both value and power have material and abstract referents that lie within the 'infrastructure' and 'superstructure,' respectively, of a total social formation. Economic value inheres in material artifacts and also in the immateriality of sublime creations, such as fine art and music, such that their identities are inseparable from their aesthetic value.

The transcedent nature of 'power' is comparable. Power is equally at home in the most material disciplines, such as physics and engineering, where it is considered an aspect of matter, and indeed power as 'energy' is convertible into matter and vice versa. But power becomes detached from this materiality as it is metaphorically appropriated by political science. It is first assumed to be associated with institutions and offices but later takes on a more abstract form, such as Weber's notion of charisma, and then becomes yet more sublimated by Foucault's equating power with knowledge.

These two terms, value and power, have had rather parallel but separate histories in the disciplines that have formed around them, and as each has matured it has appreciably dissolved the materialist-idealist opposition they both span. Anthropology is the discipline most disposed toward a synthesis of economic value and political power, since it contains both within its working vocabulary. Articulation theory, situated largely in a political economy in which the economic overshadows the political, deals primarily with economic value. But a major step toward synthesis occurs within articulation theory as developed by Meillassoux (1981:xi, 50–56), who is concerned with "human energy" as a general concept that subsumes labor power.

Further movement in this direction is now possible by combining these two terms. Such synthesis of their respective semantic loadings yields insight into the nexus of social organization and identity that is greater than the sum of their respective meanings. By combining the theoretical potential of each of these terms, yet further advance into the analysis of identity formation in complex social fields is possible.

The central issue here, as always, is differentiation, but it is a differentiation that is a result of and is largely coterminous with the differential distribution of value and power within social fields. Value and power may be considered aspects of some social, cultural, political force or energy for which we yet have no name. Semantic approximation of this something can be achieved, however crudely, by *value-power*, and indeed this hyphenated term can be seen as a provisional expression that announces the imminent emergence into consciousness of a unified theory of value, power, class, and identity that is yet to be concretized with the term that will denote it. Movement in this direction can be made by tracing the recent history of theory centered on these three terms—value, power, and class.

A fourth term has also figured prominently in recent anthropological discourse on peasants, and that is *resistance*. This, too, is a term in need of reconceptualization, but it brings forth with it advances in the theorization of the nexus of *value-power-class* and its relationship to social identity. In brief, the argument presented here is that these four terms, both in the abstract and as components of living communities, are mutually self-constituting, such that consideration of any one entails consideration of all. I shall start with class.

Class

In *Hegemony and Socialist Strategy* Laclau and Mouffe (1985) consolidate and deepen doubts and criticisms of class as a source of conscious social identity to the point of total rejection of class analysis as a basis of developing political strategy. They build their case on the history—or perhaps better said on the nonhistory—of class politics in modern Europe. At all critical moments of potential rupture of the reigning regimes of power from 1848 to 1968, class politics failed to bring about decisive transformation.

In brief, their argument is that the failure of proletarian mobilization has been rationalized away by invoking theories of dominant culture that cloud the consciousness that would otherwise emerge within the working class; consequently, forms of vanguardism are necessary to develop counterhegemonic culture that accurately reflects proletarian interests. But, argue Laclau and Mouffe, such counterhegemony lacks a structural base (class) to which it conforms. Hence, class analysis is false. Laclau and Mouffe do not seem to go one step further and argue that class analysis is even a form of false consciousness that by clouding the thinking of revolutionaries dissipates their efforts into counterproductive strategies and thus functions to buttress the structuring of inequality.

Because of the failure of a revolutionary class consciousness to inform social movements, Laclau and Mouffe (1985) argue for discarding political strategy based on class analysis in favor of analyses of what they consider to be far more complex constellations of popular identities and political movements and their respective forms of multivocal consciousness. To meet the political needs of such persons and to mobilize them into collective actions, democratic new social movements must be built that correspond to these complex identities.

Whereas Laclau and Mouffe develop an analysis of new social movements as an alternative to working-class politics, I am concerned with comparable "new" political arenas and forms among 'peasant' communities. But I am not as ready so Laclau and Mouffe to reject class analysis as a basis for thinking about social forms to advance political objectives. Concern with complex differentiation need not and should not obviate the fundamental material bases of social differentiation whereby persons occupy different positions in systems of production of value and the differential distribution and consumption of that value. Although the complex multivocality of internal and external differentiation suppresses class consciousness, social scientists should not therefore fail to attend to the very real class differentiation that underlies so many other forms of difference. In other words, the lack of reflection of the realities of class in popular consciousness should not be taken as a justification for dispensing with class analysis. To the contrary, this lack of reflection should be foregrounded as a research priority that is central to the issue of social differentiation.

Thus, in arriving at their conclusion that class analysis is false, Laclau and Mouffe are both right and wrong. Certainly, for their main case, modern Europe, they are right about the failure of class consciousness to mobilize decisive political movements. But from this valid observation they leap to an abandonment of the materialism of historical materialism, which is a far more serious issue. And indeed, this is the disastrous end point to which their analysis of hegemony has led them. They have thrown the baby out with the bathwater. By underscoring the general absence of class consciousness, they have precipitously concluded that class does not exist. They can arrive at this conclusion only by confounding the two phenomenal levels of class Marx took pains to distinguish: class as defined by social relations of production and consumption—that is, class *in itself*—versus class as the awareness in consciousness of one's identity so formed, that is, class *for itself.*

Laclau and Mouffe are disillusioned with this latter dimension of class and, I hasten to add, with good reason. They do make a compelling case against class-based party politics in favor of movements organized around issues that are uppermost in the minds of oppressed people. But what, in the final analysis—and it is the task of theory to answer this question—do people struggle for? This question can be more sharply focused: For what do internally differentiated subjects—formed within complex political fields where they occupy multiple, often unconnected subject positions—struggle? The answer is suggested by studies of *resistance,* which in their own way are as revisionist as Laclau and Mouffe's study and which emerge in more or less the same intellectual spaces. Like the hegemony debate, it is also possible to read resistance theory in two directions: forward toward its object, 'peasants,' and backward toward the dispositions of its authors.

Resistance

Perhaps the most cited recent book in peasant studies, one published the same year as Laclau and Mouffe's, is James Scott's *Weapons of the Weak: Everyday Forms of Peasant Resistance* (1985), which gave considerable new currency to 'resistance.' Following Scott's lead, the resistance literature, unlike Laclau and Mouffe, does not write off class but, to the contrary, brings it into political science and secondarily into anthropology and history in unexpected ways.[1] It stresses that resistance occurs at many diverse sites where individual peasants compete with their class superiors for nickel and dime quanta of diverse forms of economic value. Resistance thus serves both to minimize the loss of value to the peasant, for example, through ingenious ways of deceiving landlords and tax collectors, and to appropriate value in the possessions of other classes, for example, through poaching and petty theft.

As do Laclau and Mouffe, the resistance writers have an antistructural bias and in this sense are ambivalent about class.[2] On one hand they emphasize that resistance takes place at points where peasants confront other classes, but on the other, the detailed documentation of the diverse microsites where resistance is enacted dissolves any illusion of neat class boundaries carved into relations of production. Whatever class potential may be present among peasants is not enhanced by their use of resistance, and indeed in many cases the sociology of resistance seems to have a problematic relationship with solidarity. Resistance theory thus makes class theory respectable by domesticating it, by defanging it and situating it within a functionalist framework. Thus, the problem resistance theory presents to practical anthropology is that in a typical postmodern move, it effectively causes the political subject who seeks coherent structural goals to disappear. Political action is dissipated at a thousand microsites of opposition and so becomes woven into the fabric of domination without changing it. Resistance is but an aspect of perennial oppression.[3]

Although the resistance and critical hegemony literatures come to a similar position regarding the ineffectiveness of class to promote consolidated political action, the former has concealed within it a more radical theoretical vision, and this is its assumption that resistance is at base micro-level class warfare waged mainly over multiple forms of value in the spheres of production and consumption. As Scott puts it,

> Class conflict is, first and foremost, a struggle over the appropriation of work, property, production, and taxes. Consumption, from this perspective, is both the goal and the outcome of resistance and counter-resistance. Petty thefts of grain or pilfering on the threshing floor may seem like trivial "coping" mechanisms from one vantage point, but from a broader view of class relations, how the harvest is actually divided belongs at the center. (Scott 1989:8)

This observation reveals the kernel of value theory present in resistance theory: At each of the manifold sites of resistance there is the possibility of acquiring value or of mitigating its loss. But when the multiple sites and modes of resistance that are described are summed, it is apparent that the struggle over value is not limited to these economic forms (in the usual sense of what is economic) but is also waged over immaterial forms of value and the capacity to create them. Scott refers to such competition as "symbolic resistance," by means of which "the poor [reject] the categories the rich attempt to impose upon them" (Scott 1985:236). This, the least developed part of Scott's work on resistance, refers to Willis's study of the *penetrations* working-class people make into what in structuralist terms is considered to be dominant ideology.

In *Learning to Labour* (1977) Willis elaborates a two-part thesis of how symbolic resistance is contained and actually functions in the overall reproduction of class differences. The first part of this thesis is that the working-class lads Willis studied are cognizant that the socialization to which the schools subject them channels them into the same dead-end jobs their fathers have. This consciousness of the workings of the reproduction of class differences causes them to resist schooling, which they intuit as an agent of their oppression.

But the irony of this form of resistance is that it is informed by a penetration that is only partial. For what the lads do not comprehend is that by resisting schooling they deny themselves, if we may use Bourdieu's terminology, access to the cultural capital that would enable them to seek other than blue-collar jobs. It is thus by resisting that they replicate the identities of their fathers. In a form of subtle jujitsu, the 'system' uses the resisters' own momentum to bring them down. This perverse dialectic of resistance, resulting from partial penetrations, is the least developed dimension of the now abundant literature on 'peasant resistance.'

Progress in the class dynamics of peasant resistance can be made by exploring such contradictory aspects of what Scott calls symbolic resistance. In doing so, it becomes apparent that much of what is identified as "traditional culture" is in fact very contemporary forms and practices of resistance informed by partial penetrations that, obeying the perverse logic noted just above, are integral to the reproduction of 'peasant' culture. Far from being a survivor from a different historical era, 'traditional' culture (read resistance culture) is reproduced by the creative defensive efforts of oppressed people in the here and now. Scott is aware of how the traditional is synonymous with resistance, but what remains to be developed is the perverse dialectic whereby resistance is integral to the reproduction of class difference.

The students of resistance have focused on resistance against class superiors and the state. But an aspect of resistance they have failed to address adequately is the way in which it tends to be generalized by the resisting subject to coequals and those below him or her in a general struggle for value that is waged as both direct and indirect struggle in the form of, for example, cutthroat competition and gossip. Such a war of each against all in a "Limited Good universe" (Foster 1965) is depicted in a joke:

> For years a [fill in type] peasant has been waging an acrimonious microwar with his neighbor in which they fight over inches of land where their fields adjoin and over value in dozens of other forms, including vicious gossip and character assassination. One day God appears to one of them and says he is going to grant him any wish he desires. But a provision of the granting of the wish is that his neighbor will receive the same boon twofold. God says he will give the man a day to consider his wish. All night the man is sleepless, wrestling with the contradiction whereby his good fortune will doubly benefit his neighbor. But at last he comes to his decision and sits down to wait. God soon reappears and asks the man if he has decided on his wish, and the man says, "Yes I have. Please, God, make me blind in one eye."[4]

In conventional political struggle in which opposed parties face off, the act of struggle doubly reinforces already essentialized identities, first in the self-definition of each of the contending subject types and second in the definition ascribed to each such subject by his or her adversary. The patron-client relationship, as a basic dyad of certain "traditional" class relations, exemplifies this structuring of difference.[5] Under normal conditions the client, for example, a manorial peasant, negotiates with his lord within the narrow range of identities defined by the relationship within which their identities are defined. He does so by displaying various forms of deferential and possibly ingratiating behaviors that even as they may move the lord to grant some favor or largesse also reinforce the cultural construction of the structural asymmetry between them two parties. The peasant may also resort to surreptitious tactics to gain economic value, such as poaching, pilfering, or holding back harvested product due the lord. These acts of resistance, according to Scott (1985), also reinforce the functional asymmetry of lord and peasant, as well as the more general 'moral economy' in which they are embedded.

But resistance theory sees no cleavage planes, no lines of fissure along which large-scale oppositions might form. Resistance theory has thus realistically explored the micropolitics of class and in doing so has come to conclusions similar to those of Cook and Binford (1990) regarding the lack of disposition of supposed peasants and proletarians toward mass mobilization (see Chapter 4). But resistance theory stops here and does not point to possible paths beyond this impasse. It provides no analysis of a social basis for progressive social action, and therein is revealed its basically conservative disposition. The structure of the field it describes is dualist, epitomized by the peasant and the patron, but the configuration of inequality is inherently stable.

Like resistance theory, conventional two-class theories of revolutionary political contestation are also dualist, but here the dualism is dialectic in that the goal of the challenging team is not only to win the game (seize power, smash the state, and so forth) but also to alter the structure of the game and the identities of the players—that is, to create, perhaps, the socialist person. Marxist dialectical theory of revolution is thus the major first step in the deconstruction of the class antinomies and, by extension, of the epistemological antinomies of modern society. The unfinished theoretical work is therefore to continue to dismantle the structure of dualist oppositional categories so as to better appreciate the complex identities of contemporary persons. A shift to such a multidimensional field of social practice eliminates the dualist categories that structure definitions of univalent social types, such as *the* proletarian, *the* peasant, and *the* farmer. Such a shift to multidimensional external dimensions and forces affecting the dispositions of persons is also consistent with the complex formation of personal identity I refer to as internal differentiation.

In Chapter 3 I discussed peasant essentialism, and I propose later that the categorical ambiguity of the peasant is dependent on and consistent with the conventional binary categorization of value into use and exchange values. Theories of essentialized peasants and proletarians see them as struggling to maximize their respective essential values, which in the case of peasants are both use and exchange values. Thus, the peasant, unlike the two primary classes of capitalist society, which are constituted out of their structurally determined need for their corresponding forms of value, seems to need both.

It is this basically ambiguous nature of the peasant as defined within the two value discourses that causes it to be such a problematic type for anthropologists and political economists. But what is the source of this ambiguity? Does it lie in peasant society or in the structuring of anthropological thinking that defines peasant society? The preceding chapters argue for the latter possibility. We are now in a position to explore critically this bedrock theoretical dualism of conventional political economy—the opposition of use and exchange values as the only forms of value it recognizes. As my argument goes, this modernist construction of value is permuting into a theory of generalized value. This emergent perspective is more consistent than is dualist theory with the multidimensionality of contemporary transnational identities, and this isomorphism of theory and sociocultural reality is the result of their embedment in a common historical ground.

A major step toward dismantling the dualism of value theory was Baudrillard's (1981) introduction of "sign value" as a third term determinant of subject identity. Baudrillard commits another heresy in proposing that signs effect their transformative power by being consumed, and thus he displaces the classical analysis of value and identity from the sphere of production to the sphere of consumption. Furthermore, according to Baudrillard, the consumption of sign value in late capitalist society is more determinant of identity than is the subject's position in the production process. Baudrillard says, in short, that you are not what you produce but what you consume.

This expansion of value from the discourse of economics to include cultural analysis constitute an assault on the categorical disciplinary underpinnings of economics, threatening to obliterate the boundary that separates it as a field distinct from cultural studies.[6] But try as he might to go beyond Marx in a fundamental way, Baudrillard's project is better seen as the addition of a third term that partakes of both use value and exchange value. A sign value is inherent in exchange value—otherwise money could not have value—just as sign values are embodied in the consumed commodities they define and from which they are in practice inseparable.

Whereas classical Marxist analysis of peasant economics has, as in the case of industrial capitalism, attended primarily to the formation of consciousness by the way in which the person is inserted into the production process, we are now better able—because of Baudrillard and especially Bourdieu—to appreciate the power of consumption to shape consciousness. Modernization theory's concept of diffusion as the major modality of development can be seen as a consumption theory but a simplistic one in which the traits of modernity would simply replace those of the traditional culture, thus transforming it in the image of the modern. But now, after a generation of articulation theory, we are able to appreciate the ways in which consumption of the commodities and signs of modernity figure as much in the perpetuation of subaltern communities and in the genesis of the 'traditional' within them as it does in their development.

Value

Left-leaning theories of underdevelopment underscore extraction of economic surplus as one-way flows (i.e., the reciprocal of the modernization theory of diffusion). But migration and transnational agriculture organize multidirectional flows of economic value between capitalist and noncapitalist participants arrayed in complex spatial and social patterns of production and reproduction. However, net flows and accumulation do accrue from subalterns who are concentrated the most in productive activities where value in the form of goods and services is created, whereas 'nonpeasants' tend to consume a disproportionate share of the value so produced.

Each of the three main essentialized social identities of modern social science is predicated on a presumed distinctive form of use and exchange value.[7] For the peasant, access to land as use value constitutes him or her as such.[8] Just as land as use value is the bedrock of peasant essentialism, each of the other two essentialized social categories of modern political economy, 'the proletariat' and 'the bourgeoisie,' is also predicated on a distinct primary value.[9] The primary value that gives proletarians their distinctive social identity and consciousness is their labor power, whereas the primary constituting value of the bourgeoisie, the capitalist, is money. All forms of value are objects of desire to be acquired or otherwise controlled. Each essential type enters into social relationships with a certain quotient of its characteristic value and seeks guard and augment it.

In the case of the latter two types, the proletarian and the capitalist, each can be constituted only by entering into relationships with its counterpart, for both are reciprocally self-constituting. In Marx's language, these two types come together and exchange their respective values in the process of production and thus articulate the primary classes of capitalist society. The capitalists exchange money (M) for labor power (LP), which they arrange to have transformed into commodities, which in turn can be exchanged for more money. This activity plan can be abbreviated as $M \rightarrow LP \rightarrow M$. Labor power is, of course, a commodity (C) in this social context, and thus this sequence is a variation of the pattern of exchange Marx saw as distintive of capitalist exchange in general, namely, $M \rightarrow C \rightarrow M$.

The complement of this equation is the proletarian counterpart. The wage earner enters into the exchange relationship not with money but with labor power, which is sold for money that can then be used to live, that is, to reproduce more labor power for future exchange for more money: $LP \rightarrow M \rightarrow LP$, the general form of which is $C \rightarrow M \rightarrow C$. The two 'essential' classes of modern society thus exist in a mutually constituting symmetry.

The peasantry, aside from being the historical source of the proletariat, is in this conception of modern history an anachronism that is presumably destined to disappear. Its persistence destroys the symmetry of the fundamental class relationships of modern capitalist society, for its pattern of reproduction is potentially autonomous. It can conceivably reproduce itself in direct relationship to its distinctive primary value, land, even though surplus product in the form of taxes and other levies and forms of unequal exchange are extracted from it.[10] If we let S be this lost surplus, L be land, and P be the product that results when labor power is invested into productive activity, that is, "working the land," then the distinctive nature of the peasant mode of existence can be represented as

$$LP + L \rightarrow P - S \rightarrow LP + L$$

Here, in this classical model, labor power and land are combined through work, which yields a product. Part of this product is consumed as use value to reproduce more labor or power; part is converted to exchange value and paid out for purchase of tools, and so forth, so as to maintain access to and control of the land; and part of it is lost as taxes and other forms of surplus extraction. 'The peasant' as a type is thus partially independent of the other social types. The history of peasant and nonpeasant relations has been one of perennial attempts at control and incorporation by the latter and of resistance by the former. And similarly, just as peasants seek autonomy in the sphere of production, 'peasants' as a category resist neat accommodation within nonpeasant categories.

The 'farmer,' by definition, is unlike the 'peasant' in that for him the product is a commodity, and rather than expending primarily his own labor power, he buys the labor power of farmworkers. To the degree that the 'peasant' producer sees his product as a commodity for sale, he is a farmer. But to the degree that he sees himself as embodied labor power producing a commodity, part of his essential nature is comparable to the proletarian.

Classical theories of social types thus defined them in terms of their presumed essential values or the essential values for which they struggle. Thus, peasants are essentialized by their production and consumption of use value and proletarians and bourgeois types by their association with exchange value. The indeterminacy of the largely dead debates between peasantists and proletarianists was derived from the inherent ambiguity of identity defined in such terms of economic essentialism, which gives peasant identity a both-and quality. But predisposed by prevailing assumptions of unitary individual identity, students of peasants have seen them as either one or the other. Proletarianists, who are modernists, have seen development as an inevitable move from an identity based in production and consumption of use value to one based in wage labor that is called into being by the history of capitalism and socialist agriculture—a move peasantists oppose.

But what are we to make of presumed peasants or proletarians who are displaced from "traditional" sites of production and reproduction and enter into more complex fields of production, reproduction, and struggle for value? A feature of these fields is that the lines of political and social differentiation, which is to say the circuits of exchange and accumulation, that structure them and by which they are structured are not binary. Instead, they are complex circuits of equal and unequal exchange within which subalterns are situated and by which they are constituted in correspondingly complex ways that have the total effect, with respect to the classical conception of the subaltern subject, of de-essentializing that subject. Such repositioning of subjects within complex fields of production and reproduction is the most clearly apparent in the ethnography of migration whereby migrants alternate participation in different, spatially separate kinds of production—thus provoking, for example, the designation 'peasant-worker' (see Figure 4.1).

In classical political economy, the social identity and corresponding conscious-ness of the self is shaped by its social location in the mode of production, and it is from this position that it is seen as struggling to retain and acquire use or ex-change value or both. But what about the 'migrant peasant-workers' or the part-time peasants who also participate in the informal economy? What happens to their identity, to their self when they reproduce themselves in these complex fields?

Clearly, there is now a certain liberation, a certain freeing from the more or less unitary subject position as it was experienced by the nonmigrating subject. This loosened subject is both forced and enabled struggle for economic value in these new spheres. And so, classical theory would suggest that there is a corresponding development in the identity and consciousness of this newly constituted subject that would alter the modes whereby it struggles. And as the logical symmetry of such classical dualist thinking necessitates, a corresponding development should also appear in the theory of top-down domination. Thus, it was to have been ex-pected that Gramsci (1971), wrestling with the two-pronged problem given to him by modern Italian history of how to theorize first the complexity of the Ital-ian subaltern masses—composed of a complex array of southern peasants and northern industrial proletarians—and second why they often acted in their own self-disinterest, should elaborate a theory of hegemony.

Although conceived on the dualist structural underpinnings of the classical and modernist worldviews and indeed, as Laclau and Mouffe (1985) discuss, a be-lated attempt to preserve that worldview to the degree that it informed classical Marxism, Gramsci's theoretical advance into the analysis of culture opened the door to the possibility of moving beyond the limitations of binary thinking. Gramsci thus moved theory into the field of cultural politics which later devel-oped into various forms of "Western Marxism" (Anderson 1976), but he did not directly link the struggle for culture with the struggle for economic value. For it was there in the theoretical bedrock of classical Marxism that the essentialzed raw material of economics lay in its two irreducible atomic forms of use and exchange values.[11]

The next major deconstructive move against the dualism of classical Marxism that would attack the binary composition of value itself had to await the work of Baurdrillard and Bourdieu, who in the 1960s began to elaborate nonbinary con-cepts and analyses of value. Of greater importance here is Bourdieu's theory of capitals and their transformations from one form to another and the mapping of the sociopolitical spaces their distribution defines (e.g., 1984, 1986). Bourdieu's work (e.g., 1984) thus integrates the analysis of economic value with cultural val-ues by way of developing a theory of class differentiation, thus preserving the original Marxist project of theorizing class in terms of the production, accumula-tion, transformation, and consumption of value.

It is for this reason that I prefer to speak of *generalized value*, which is compara-ble to Bourdieu's forms of capital. I, however, prefer *value* since it is a more gen-eral term that does not connote any specific mode of production, as does *capital*, which is associated primarily with capitalism. Value is also more polysemous than capital, equally at home in economics and in aesthetics and ethics. Later I explore the economics and aesthetics of the production and consumption of value with respect to social differentiation, which is inseparable from power.

Value-Power and Class

Resistance theory is primarily concerned with the microtactics used by subalterns to prevent loss of and to gain small amounts of economic value, but it also addresses symbolic resistance, the end of which is the same as more direct forms of economic resistance. Resistance theory thus subsumes consideration of material and symbolic value, precisely a distinction the generalized theory of value seeks to transcend. Thus, like articulation theory, resistance theory reifies its opposition while also pointing beyond it. It achieves this by dealing with multiple forms of value that are contested by means of resistance and that in their sum resist being confined to any of the standard conceptions of value (money, labor power, land, and so forth). Similarly, struggle over diverse immaterial forms of value is also waged in the sphere of culture and aesthetic values. That this is so is well demonstrated in Bourdieu's work on the formation of aesthetic taste as integral to the constitution of class identities.

Thus it is that cultural resistance becomes integral to differentiation. The person seeks to become desired (to be valued) according to the ideals that define personal value in his or her community. These ideals are strongly inflected by class-specific tastes such that their embodiment by individuals sums to the replication of class identity, which is the context within which values are inflected in their class-specific forms. This dynamic of the reproduction of difference comes into play, for example, when a 'peasant' buys new 'traditional' clothes and otherwise spends a good sum of money to sponsor a ceremony in his or her community, so that in doing so he or she will be esteemed and revered in the eyes of the members of the community.

As a collective act, this active reproduction of the 'traditional' can easily be seen as a form of resistance against the encroachment of signs of personal identity that would mark these 'peasants' as perhaps 'workers,' bereft of the comforts and security of their community. But as seen by the social enemies of these 'peasants,' such behaviors and signs are but verification that 'those people' are merely 'hicks' or 'bumpkins' deserving of their lowly existence. Their 'traditional culture,' which for them is indeed a form of resistance, is also a source of their oppression.[12]

This dialectic of difference is also at work in gender-based resistance and oppression. In a society in which women are deprived of economic value disproportionately to men, norms of feminine beauty tend to be inscribed on the body in ways that accentuate its sexual attributes and in general eroticize it. And within this calculus of value it makes sense to most women to resist the exploitation they suffer, that is, their powerlessness, by maximizing their value as aesthetic, erotic objects—a form of value that can be bartered, if not sold outright, for economic value as wives, whores, or beauty queens—to achieve some measure of power.

Such strategies of self-defense, within the logic of gendered resistance, not only mark the victims as targets of oppression but actually constitute them as victims.

The point that such forms of resistance are integral to the reproduction of the gendered oppression they oppose, although obvious, is not what is of immediate concern. For we are interested here in how these integrated strategies of resistance are made possible by the convertibility of basic value into various forms. For example, such eroticization as just noted is often effected—apart from the development of 'feminine' speech and other habits—by the investment of economic value (money) into cosmetics, clothing, and jewelry that enhance the erotic, aesthetic value of the person. The body is nearly miraculous in its ability not only to produce and consume economic value but to transform it into aesthetic value-power.

Such transformations of general value-power can only occur in social fields that are structured by and that structure the differential distribution of general value-power in its manifold forms. Positions of persons within these fields are determined by the forms and quanta of general value-power they embody. These embodied forms and quanta of value-power (compare, for example, Bourdieu's forms of capital: social, symbolic, intellectual, economic) sum to the identity of the person, such personal identity being constituted by its position within the field within which general value-power is distributed among identities. The structured, patterned, uneven distribution of value-power within the field is differential, in that personal and collective tactics of discrimination and resistance create difference such that those already rich and poor in value-power tend to remain so as they continue to employ strategies for acquiring and defending value-power, which shapes their identities as positions within the field, as noted earlier.

In standard political economic theory, class membership is determined by position within the field of material production and by the quanta of value and surplus value that are gained and lost in class struggle. The class system is defined as the structuring of relations of production and the knowledge (consciousness) that inheres in individuals positioned within relations of production. The limitation of this model has been its basically binary view of class, which envisioned a watershed distinction between bourgeois and proletarian identities. But like articulation theory, which presented complex subjects who pointed to the transcendence of the theory that introduced them, the modernist theory of class also points to a general theory of class conceived as a field in which value-power is differentially distributed as a result of physical and cultural strategies of domination and resistance that result in the formation of identities positioned within the field of class. These identities assume cultural-specific forms as genders, ethnicities, races, and so forth, as shaped by specific historical configurations of the distribution of value-power. And indeed, one of the de facto functions of such refractions of class is to occult the primacy of class in the structuring of difference, a primacy it is the task of theory and ethnography to recover.

The complexity of the internally differentiated subject is as often as not reflected in external signs inscribed on the body as postures, gestures, clothing, and other articles that may function as fashion. There are, in other words, types of style that express, in the sense that they externalize, that which is internal. Such style embodies, both metaphorically and literally, the contradictions of resistance whereby acts and signs of resistance become insignia marking the subject as an object of repression and discrimination. And of course, as discussed earlier, this external fashioning of the resisting subject is but the outer manifestation of the inner dialectic whereby the resisting subject, by resisting, becomes constituted as a particular type of subaltern that within the reigning system of class is the target of oppression he or she resists. The style adopted by the internally differentiated transnational subject is aptly labeled pastiche.[13]

Subjects with pastiche identities result from complex patterns of cultural resistance, personal accumulation of cultural capital, and economic necessity. Some pastiche subjects, of which punks are a prime example (Hebdige 1979), actively resist by rejecting, by reworking signs of dominant culture as informed by their partial penetrations. Other subjects who are equally internally differentiated elaborate pastiche styles with less conscious intent.[14]

One index of this shift from local tradition to transnational pastiche in highland Mesoamerica is costume. A major sociocultural achievement of Spanish colonial administration was to create hundreds of local closed corporate peasant communities of indigenous people, each of which evolved a distinctive costume (see Cordry and Cordry 1968). These clothing styles can be taken as an index of a more general community cultural distinctiveness. Thus, even as these communities were drawn into global relations of production and consumption, the dynamics of colonialism promoted local cultural differentiation.

But these local costumes, especially in the case of men, have given or are giving way to seemingly modern dress styles. The transnational indigenous person, especially the young, is typically attired in a pastiche of apparel. I think here, for example, of indigenous transnational migrant workers from Oaxaca shopping for clothing at swap meets in California to complement apparel acquired from other sources throughout their networks. They thus dress themselves with a hodgepodge of new and cast-off objects—for example, jerseys from rock concerts, olive-drab camouflage combat fatigues, athletic team jackets, and all sorts of shirts and hats emblazoned with corporate logos and brand names of beers, cigarettes, tractor companies, fertilizers, herbicides, and pesticides. The pastiche body becomes a walking advertisement for the commodities it consumes, thus consuming them twice.[15]

Recalling the discussion of agroindustrialization (Chapter 5), if peasantlike persons are constituted as such by virtue of producing and reproducing in complex and often disparate and dispersed forms of production that combine seemingly modern and traditional elements, then it is to be expected that they should consequently develop, in addition to clothing styles, other corresponding peasantlike forms of aesthetic expression. One such form is the tourist 'folk' art created in ostensibly peasant communities, which in actuality are populated with peasantlike polybians.

A case in point is the recent fluorescence of 'traditional folk arts' in Oaxaca, which has occurred in a markedly transnational context of which tourism is a basic component. The impact of tourism on the constitution and reproduction of peasantlike communities in Oaxaca is comparable to that of transnational agroindustry. Whereas remittances of migrants who work in the latter are remitted to Oaxaca to sustain a 'traditional' lifestyle, tourists bring millions of dollars into the local economy, where this money circulates through peasantlike households and communities, supplementing the income derived from remittances of agroindustrial wages. These two giant transnational industries are two sides of the same coin that finances the reproduction of Oaxacan peasantlike society and culture. And like agroindustry, tourism promotes the differentiation of peasantlike communities even as it integrates them into the global economy.

Tourism differs somewhat from agroindustry in this regard, however, in that it more directly promotes a cultural distinction between the tourist and the touristed, a distinction that is the basis of such ethnic-oriented tourism and that generates the expenditure of tourist capital, which goes for the reproduction of the touristed as distinct from the tourist. And herein lies a major contradiction of modernizing schemes that are based on the promotion of tourism as a motor of development: The furtherance of the modern depends not just on the perpetuation but on the creation of the 'traditional' but now packaged and promoted as a commodity.

Examples of this dynamic abound, such as the weaving town of Teotitlán del Valle where Stephen (1991) documents how the intervention of state development programs and local and international craft and art dealers revived a moribund weaving industry that produced hand-woven blankets for local markets and reoriented it toward local tourists and international markets. The design motifs of these weavings are now shaped by an interaction among the creativity of the weavers, the advice of buyers, and the tastes of consumers—including collectors, interior decorators, and museums. Design motifs are also stimulated by some success at imitating Navajo blankets and penetrating the markets of Navajo weavers.[16]

The value of tourist art is that it is presented as authentic indigenous art. Indeed, it is this otherness that gives it and embodies in it its symbolic capital, for if the same object were produced by a member of the consumer's (modern) community, it would not possess this otherness—which is a primary source and condition of its economic value (quite apart from questions of material and artistic value).

A necessary condition for the successful commercialization of tourist art is overcoming the contradiction that even as such art stimulated by and produced and consumed within transnational contexts, it must be presented as an autochthonous creation of the traditional Other. Thus, although the conditions for the existence of this artistic expression lie in a complex field of interaction between the subaltern community of the artisan and the society of the commercial promoter and the consumer, in which the latter two are as influential on the character of the artifacts as is the former, the success of the venture depends on the occulting of both this sociology of production and the corresponding polybious identity of the producer who must appear as local and autochthonous, as traditional.

Such containment is achieved in large measure by the promotional imagery that advertises these products and that in their total effect exoticizes them. But for such exoticizing to be effective, the artifacts themselves must be exotic and thus must be appropriate icons of their creators. For the economic capital that becomes embodied in the artifacts depends, within the logic of value of tourist art, on the authenticity of the exotic otherness of their creators.

And here at the point of the commercial creation of cultural difference, the aims of the subaltern producer and the impresario coincide, such that the subaltern collaborates in the creation of his or her cultural distinction, and therefore the strategy of containment elaborated from above has a complementary creation of difference actively elaborated from below. Thus, containment is achieved not only by images of the subaltern other produced by and for consumption by elites, but it may also be engendered by the active, creative collaboration of the subaltern others themselves in what amounts to a sort of hegemony from below but that obviates the necessity of hegemony, for in such creative work subalterns create and inscribe their own difference. In so giving the ersatz indigenous artifact a more potent 'authenticity,' the artisans also occult their own complex identity behind a synthetic tapestry of tradition.

Just as the creators of tourist art are a complex polybian type, so are the artifacts they produce. One such style that has recently emerged in Oaxaca is painted wood carvings characterized by a whimsical combination of morphologies and surface designs (Barbash 1993). At first glance, many of the creatures represented in this genre of tourist art appear *ambiguous* in the sense that ambiguous creatures inhabit indefinite places betwixt and between worlds. Leach (1964) gives angels as an example of such types: They are humanlike but with avian wings and as such mediate between earth and heaven, just as the devil—a human with horns, hoofs, and a tail—links earth and the underworlds.[17] But whereas ambiguity mediates dual opposition, the creatures of contemporary Oaxacan wood-carvers, who are situated in complex transnational fields that lack dual polarity, are appropriately polybious. Rather than hybrid monsters formed by combining species from conventional habitats, they are formed from combinations of multiple real and imagined species, as benefits beings that inhabit multiple real and hyperreal habitats.

The tourist artifact that finds its way into the living room of the First World consumer in, say, Los Angeles and contains within it the occulted polybious identity of its creator is structurally comparable to the maid who dusts it. The maid is, let us say, a young indigenous woman from highland Guatemala who now works as a domestic. Like the artifact she dusts, she is present in this First World home because she is exotic, because she is from the Third World and nonwhite. Thus paradoxically, like the artifact, she is permitted into the most intimate inner recesses of the world of which she is not a part—into its bedroom, into its bathroom, and among its dirty underclothes.

But this intimate presence is made possible, is permitted only because of the difference it implies and perpetuates. This "maid"—really only one of her guises—is a complex polybian. But her maidness depends on being exotic, on being a distinct other even as she is intimately associated with her employers, and she collaborates with them in maintaining the difference between herself and them. She is, as it were, 'in' their home but not 'of' their home, and all concerned have short-term vested interests in maintaining and indeed elaborating this distinction. In the fabric of her life, which extends out of the home of her employers, 'the maid' is a complex polybian living within a transnational community that is one of thousands that make up the cultural and economic landscape of Los Angeles, situated as it is in greater Latin America. In this urbanscape she is one of around 350,000 'indigenous' Guatemalans, many of whom are refugees from the war waged against their 'peasant' communities in the highlands by the Guatemalan Army. Because of the spatial twists history has taken, she is also 'of' that community but not 'in' it.[18]

The complex identity of both the artisan and the maid must be contained and reduced in consciousness to that of distinct univocal others, for such cultural containment is integral to the constitution of the sociopolitical difference between First World self and the essentialized subaltern other. The containment specific to these particular cases suggests that similar containment is at work in other areas of cultural differentiation in the service of economic and political difference. The more general case with which we are concerned here is the ethnographic representation of the peasant as a form of containment of the subaltern to this univocal essentialized identity.

Again, central to this theory of containment is the proposition that subalterns themselves participate in the construction of the univocal identity. In the case of the autochthonous construction of 'the peasant,' not only 'peasant' spokespersons participate in this construction but also sympathetic proxies—for example, anthropologists, political activists, art dealers, and employers who reify peasant identities and thus enter these reifications into circulation in intellectual, commercial, and political discourse. And standing behind all of these interlocutors and creating corresponding official categories and projects of and for peasants is the state.

The argument here is that the drift of thinking on ideology has gone from seeing it as a dominant culture acting from above or, what is but a variation on the same imagery, a counterhegemonic culture from below to a view of power as a constructive force that is effective because it constitutes subjects in the depths of their personal identity. The position that is now coming to structure debates on power and difference locates 'it' as coming not 'from above' versus 'from below' but instead from a dialectic of 'from within' versus 'from without.' There has been a progression of theory, then, from ideology as grand ideas that are formed external to dominated persons into whose consciousness they penetrate, so informing their definitions of realty, to a view of ideology as having a dynamic that is immanent within the persons who, in the very process of enlightened self-interest, work not only to construct themselves as subjects marked for oppression but by doing so also ensure the reproduction of the general structuring of difference within which their resistance behavior is made to appear logical.

This immanence is a common feature of the work of the Birmingham group and of Bourdieu, all of whom detail how dominated subjects elaborate their own subaltern identities in the process of defending themselves within the larger sphere of difference and domination. As of yet, however, this immanent theory of the reproduction of difference has not been applied to peasants, a field still dominated by theories of top-down ideology and external differentiation.

Summary

In this chapter I have argued that conventional class analysis as a modeling of subject identity—of self-conscious social types—is severely limited. 'Peasant' and 'proletarian' persist only as reifications of categories whose referents have passed from history. But class as a structuring of subject positions within differentiated fields of value-power is a valid concept. Class so defined is the structure and physiology of social space within which value-power is created and distributed. Class dynamics have to do with the flows—the production, loss, transfer, accumulation, and consumption, that is, the differential distribution—of value-power by persons situated within class spaces. Class so conceived is far too complex and multidimensional for a two-dimensional space—upper-lower—within which class is conventionally defined. And because class is embodied in the subjects who collectively constitute the structuring of classes, these subjects are also defined by the multiple dimensions of class that run through them, with this interpenetration of class identities resulting in the internal differentiation of the subject I spoke of in Chapter 6.

This theory of internal class differentiation recognizes the formative effects on identity of the subjects' position in systems of production. But the 'typical' subjects of which I speak, that is, those who are often referred to as 'peasants,' are most often involved in complex noncontiguous productive arrangements. This scheduling of productive activities, of work and labor, often integrated within what I have referred to as transnational communities—organized largely as social and communication networks—is of a variety and complexity that defies characterization as "articulation of modes of production."

Articulation theory was, as discussed previously, a step toward appreciation of this complexity, but once this fatal step has been taken, the tremendous intellectual investment that has accumulated in the unitary subject—the individual—of classical social science must be abandoned. The theory of internal differentiation also enlarges the analytic focus beyond the sphere of production to that of consumption as effecting the constitution of the internally differentiated subject. But here we are concerned with the consumption not only of economic values but also of value-saturated signs that when consumed, nurture the class-based identity of the consuming subject who so consumes value in accord with strategies of resistance—resistance that is often integral to the reproduction of class differences.

If indeed, as argued earlier, peasant politics as conventionally conceived and practiced is integral to the reproduction of class systems within which peasants and peasantlike communities are formed, what possible alternative strategies might exist? Chapter 8 examines the ongoing displacement of peasant political projects into several new fields within which the dialectic of resistance and differentiation, and its power to construct and constitute politically vulnerable subalterns, is potentially transcended. Integral to such emancipatory displacment is letting go of 'the peasant' as an analytic category that serves more to contain identities than to free them.

Notes

1. See, for example, the chapters in Colburn (1989).

2. Writers on peasant resistance are usually well aware that resistance is characteristic of other classes as well but are at pains to confine their analysis to 'peasants' and in doing so effectively reify the category. Scott's (1990) last book does, however, extend resistance theory to other subaltern types.

3. Gutmann (1993) offers a similar interpretation of Scott's work; see Scott (1993) for a reply.

4. I thank my friend and raconteur James Stuart for this joke.

5. See Foster (1961) on "dyadic contracts" and Rothstein (1986) on the specific case of patron-client relations.

6. This erosion of the boundaries of economics apparent in the work of Baudrillard and especially in that of Bourdieu (discussed later) is comparable to the decay of the disciplinary boundary between linguistics and ethnography that is occurring in the ambiguous zone of ethnosemantics, which partakes of both disciplines (see Kearney 1984:36), and in Bourdieu's (1991) removal of the theoretical walls structural linguistics erected between language and society.

7. It is more consistent with the argument advanced here to speak of 'forms' of value rather than different 'kinds' of value, for whereas 'kinds' implies that there are different essential values that are inconvertible one to the others, 'forms' in this context implies permutations of one general form of value that can undergo such trans*form*ations.

8. Gudeman and Rivera (1990:2), somewhat modifying Ricardo's theory of land as value, speak of the earth instead of land but essentialize peasants in what is basically a Ricardian way.

9. *The primitive* is the fourth essentialized category of modern anthropological thought. Upon what essential value is it predicated in different styles of anthropology? In Marxist discourse, 'primitives,' unlike peasants, appropriate use value not from 'land,' which has value as property or as a commodity, but instead from 'nature,' which is to say land that has

not yet been civilized—that is, cultivated and made to produce. Producing little in the way of exchange value, primitives do not figure in the calculus of modern life except as its antithesis. The ambiguity of the peasant lies in its being constituted from both forms of value.

10. As Marx put it, "Each individual peasant family is almost self-sufficient; it itself directly produces the major part of its consumption and thus acquires its means of life more through exchange with nature than in intercourse with society" (1963:123–124).

11. It is appropriate to speak of use and exchange values as the atomic forms of value, given that Marx, in Volume 1 of *Capital* (1976), speaks of the "commodity," which is the embodiment of value, as the molecular form of capitalism.

12. This synthetic theory of resistance and differential distribution of value-power obviates dualistically structured top-down versus bottom-up debates such as that over the "culture of poverty," which was based on an assumed distinction between "exogenous" versus "endogenous" causes of poverty. This distinction, laden with corresponding political "left" and "right" ideological presuppositions, mapped onto epistemologically deeper assumptions having to do with "materialism" versus "cultural idealism" (Leacock 1971; Lewis 1959).

13. I have borrowed and adapted this term from Jameson (1991:16–19).

14. See, for example, Comaroff and Comaroff (1987) for a discussion of "the Madman."

15. And recently, in the case of Oaxacan migrants, this pastiche pattern of consumption of attire to dress and differentiate the transnational body has folded into production as Zapotec migrants from Oaxaca find work as sewing machine operators in the Los Angeles garment industry. This assembly work, much of which is done on a putting-out basis, is but one of a growing number of interfaces between Oaxacan indigenous transnational networks and other ethnic minorities. In this case, Zapotec garment workers are employed primarily by Korean "ethnic middlemen" (on the latter see Light and Bonacich [1988]).

16. In producing simulated Navajo blankets, Zapotec weavers now enter into competition with Pakistani and other 'oriental' producers who are also penetrating the Navajo markets to profit from the considerable symbolic capital accumulated there. Contemporary 'traditional' Navajo weaving itself has a recent history similar to that of contemporary Zapotec weaving in that it was strongly shaped by the advice of trading-post operators in Arizona and New Mexico. Mitchell (forthcoming) discusses a comparable case in highland Peru.

17. Elsewhere I describe such ambiguous types, which mediate the bipolarity of the U.S.–Mexican border (Kearney 1991:60–64).

18. For discussion of this distinction between being 'in' versus being 'of' with respect to 'alien' workers in the United States, see Kearney (1991).

Chapter 8

'Peasants' and the New Politics of Representation

This chapter explores the interplay between the two senses of representation. As the social field has changed under the influence of transnationalism, the end of development, the realignment of the primary global tension from East-West to North-South, and the decay of rural-urban distinctions (see Chapter 5), so are the internally differentiated selves brought forth in these new political fields, disposed to form political organizations and advance projects that correspond to their identities and positions within these fields. Human rights and ecopolitics are now possible as issues, and increasingly so; by emerging as dimensions of conflict, protest, and resistance they also change the fields and the terms of engagement. A distinctive feature of both human rights (conceived as 'universal') and ecopolitics (conceived as 'global') is that both are transnational in nature and as such are dynamically related to the transnationalism of ethnicity, which is also emerging as a dimension of identity in contrast to the diminishing power of the nation-state to inform and manipulate 'peasant' identities.

Far from being an idle intellectual exercise, reconceptualization of the peasantry has deep practical implications. Throughout the preceding chapters I have argued that labels—constructed identities—are important because of their constituting power. To construct is, in varying degrees, to constitute. There is, in other words, a dialectical interplay between the two senses of *representation,* namely, the nominal and the political. To name, that is, to label persons or an entire community as a certain type and then to elaborate a theory of their essential social identity is to create a symbolic representation of those persons or that community. If this representation then becomes naturalized, that is, accepted as the "obvious" depiction of its referent, it becomes a mold that shapes the second sense of representation—the political. Simply put, for a community to be labeled 'peasant' and to accept that label as valid implies that its members will adopt political goals and strategies that are consistent with those of peasants. Similarly, nonpeasants who also assume that the community is a 'peasant' community will deal with it as such.

By this dialectic the community will be contained. Far from being the result only of conspiracy on the part of the state or other agencies or interests, the theory of containment assumes that containment is most effective when misrepresentations have become hegemonic, such that subalterns represent themselves as 'peasants' in their self-designations and political strategies. Furthermore, this same critique is applicable to communities that in fact are peasant in some real sense. In both cases, the strategy of practical anthropology is to take command of representation in both senses. The cultural work of such anthropology is to innovate symbolic representations of community that inform organizational forms and political objectives that evade the constructive power of older hegemonic ideas. Such efforts effect *displacements* of intellectual and organizational political work to social and cultural fields in which there is greater opportunity to accumulate forms of symbolic value that can be converted into new organizational forms and political power.

Whereas modernist political economic theory assumes that essentialized types (classes) struggle over economic value and in doing so reifies their identities, the non-essentializing theory of political economy I have proposed herein extends analysis of competition between class-differentiated subjects into the terrain where social identities are constructed and constituted. Thus, rather than accepting 'traditional' unitary identities as positions to be defended and attacked and as defined by the gain and loss of economic values, the politics of general value also seeks to alter the systems of signs that define identities and values and, by extension, the class positions of subjects that do and do not possess them. This reconceptualization of the value-identity nexus within a system of class differences is a Copernican revolution of sorts.

Postpeasant Futures: Class Again

Social class is an abstract concept that historically has provided little basis for deeply felt solidarity among subalterns, which has led to concerted, coordinated, long-term collective political action on their part. Nationalism, ethnicity, democracy, regionalism, and religion have proven to be far more potent bases of collective identity.

Some of the most recent critiques of class analysis have come from new social movement theory, which assumes that political subjects have complex identities, facets of which can come together to form organizations and alliances that can advance democratic projects. Typical of such strategies is a rejection of class as a primary dimension of identity that has much potential to shape effective collective political actions of subalterns. Whereas subaltern politics is conventionally conceived as a struggle for primary value (use and exchange), most theoreticians of new social movements (NSMs) reject such a class-based analysis and theorize subaltern politics as the mobilization of diverse, complex subject identities around broad democratic goals.[1] A basic assumption is that it is now possible in this historical moment to imagine such democratic projects that transcend class differences (see, e.g., Laclau 1990; Mouffe 1988).

Basic to this position is a rejection of the binary structuring of a basic mechanistic conflict and contradiction between *the* proletariat and *the* bourgeoisie. And indeed, this position has been taken herein. But most theorists of NSMs go another fatal step. In correctly assessing the inadequacy of binary categorical analysis of class and rejecting it, they fail to appreciate that class differences and differentiation remain the basic theoretical and political issue. The problem of how to mount a genuinely pro-democratic politics cannot be solved by rejecting class analysis but only by deepening it. And no better ground can be found for such a project than the history of theory of the political economy of the peasantry.

In the history of left-wing theories of peasant society, the primary enduring issue has been class differentiation. In tracing this history, we have seen that theoretical progress has taken the form of realizing ever greater complexity of differentiation. In Chapter 6 I pushed this movement to the idea of internal differentiation.

A similar notion of complex subjects runs through the theoretical literature on NSMs but with a notable difference. In their post-Marxist exploration of the complexity of subject identities and the appropriate political forms and objectives of such identities, the theoreticians of NSMs reject class analysis and the politics of class in favor of coalitions of diverse identities that crosscut class positions— for example, the politics of gender, the environment, and urban neighborhoods. In sharp contrast to the muting of class analysis in the NSM literature, the treatment of internal differentiation herein has been to extend and deepen this most fundamental Marxist concept rather than to abandon it.

Throughout this book the working definition of class employed is that it is the lines of difference in the social field within which general value is differentially produced and consumed. Class identities and relations are defined by this differential distribution of value. In the game of class there are winners and losers. Losers are defined as those who produce more value than they consume, whereas winners are those who acquire and consume the value losers lose.

This differential transfer is effected by many mechanisms. It was Marx's genius to discover the creation and extraction of surplus value within capitalist relations of production. But to that can be added forms of rent, taxation, market transfers, and other types of exchange that are unequal in the sense that the values exchanged are unequal when converted to general value. Class relations are patterns of such unequal exchange between members of different classes, so defined. Exploitation can be minimally defined as such unequal exchange of general value.

Class analysis and the politics based on it have been bedeviled by binary thinking, which predisposes one to look for sharp cleavages between classes marked as such in the competition for value. But class relations exist among internally differentiated persons who gain and lose value vis-à-vis others who, like them, are situated within reticula, within which sharp planes of cleavage are rare (see Chapter 5). Indeed, it is the flow of general value, in its various forms (surplus labor, money, information, goods, services, energy, style), through reticula that forms them. Thus, one's class position is defined as his or her location within such reticula. Clear lines of demarcation between winners and losers are also muted by the fact that most persons are winners vis-à-vis some persons and losers vis-à-vis others, all of whom are knit together in reticula within which value is differentially produced and consumed. It is this differential distribution of value that constitutes the class system.

Given the abstractness and diffuseness of class, it is not surprising that it rarely becomes a basis of subaltern collective identity, even though it is the fundamental, bottom-line economic issue in social life. Class becomes a basis of consciously felt subaltern collective identity only in rare cases where there is minimal internal differentiation and where clear economic and cultural diacritics mark distinctions between classes. Historically, such cases are rare in peasant communities.

The Mixtec Case: Fragmentation of Identity and Politics

We began in Chapter 1 by looking at the seemingly peasant community of San Jerónimo Progreso and several of its members. San Jerónimo is in the Mixteca region, which is approximately the western one-third of the state of Oaxaca and small adjoining areas of the states of Puebla and Guerrero. We can now refer to the Mixtec people in Oaxaca and in diaspora to tie together and illustrate issues discussed in the intervening chapters and to assess developments in contemporary postpeasant Mixtec politics.

In terms of conventional anthropological categories, Mixtecs occur in five primary contexts. The first of these is the closed corporate peasant community in which they appear to be classical peasants, whereas the second context is in agribusiness in northwest Mexico and California, where they appear as migrant "peasant-workers" (defined as such by articulation theory). The third context is the shantytowns of Mexican cities, where they appear as "peasants in cities" and organize as such, and the fourth context is the informal sector on both sides of the border, where they appear as small vendors and providers of services. Finally, a lesser number are small merchants, entrepreneurs, professionals, civil servants, or political bosses found mainly in cities and larger towns, mostly in Mexico.

Numerous persons from the Mixteca move in and out of these various contexts repeatedly from year to year or at major transition points in their lives. Also, families typically have members occupying various positions at any given moment in both Mexico and California. Historically, each of these different contexts promoted corresponding political challenges and organizational forms that fragmented identities and political efforts into disparate, disconnected projects. I will briefly sketch the first four of these political contexts, which pertain to the vast majority of Mixtecs, and their influence on identities and politics.[2]

In Oaxaca, for millennia hundreds of Mixtec towns and villages have been the cradles of "traditional" Mixtec identity (Spores 1984). Each community tends to be a bounded social universe mapped onto a bounded territorial unit. Lack of arable land and other resources in the Mixteca promotes perennial conflict between neighboring communities that often erupts into violence. The politics of these communities focuses on 'peasant' agrarian issues such as roads, dams, irrigation, crop insurance, and agricultural extension services. Typically, in these projects and issues representatives of local communities present themselves as campesinos (peasants) to petition and otherwise confront the state so as to exact financial, technical, and political support. In doing so they confront the virtually monolithic block of Mexican bureaucracy in an unequal relationship in which they are severely disadvantaged by their lack of effective political capital.

Another frequent form of petition to the state is for resolution of community boundary disputes, which are endemic in the region. Such cases are rarely resolved definitively, and frequently both of the towns in conflict may attempt to buy the favor of the same officials. Indeed, there is good reason to assume that de facto government practices promote such intercommunity conflicts and thus inhibit regional peasant organizations that might confront the state with more power from forming (Dennis 1987).

Community petitions to government agencies and projects that originate within agencies are typically framed in terms of rural "development." And indeed, the region has been and is the target of innumerable development programs and projects (Collins 1995). However, the history of the Mixteca since the conquest has been one of constant environmental deterioration and economic stagnation. Today the region is, by standard indicators, one of the poorest and ecologically most devastated in Mexico (Collins 1995; Pastor 1987). There is thus a perverse correlation between the presence of development projects and the persistence of de-development. Typically, development projects in the Mixteca are initially minimally effective, but they soon fall apart because of deterioration of their material bases or administration. Indeed, the landscape is littered with abandoned irrigation, agricultural, and community development projects. This situation suggests, as Ferguson (1990) argues for Lesotho, that government and NGO-sponsored development projects actually function to reproduce rather than improve existing social, political, and economic problems.[3] In any event, the great failure of "development" programs targeting communities considered to be "local," "bounded," "rural," and "campesino" is palpable in the Mixteca.

This situation suggests that breaking through this impasse requires abandonment of the hegemonic definitions of "development" and of "rural peasant communities." For if indeed the present dense matrix of government institutions and programs and the identities they define serve more to perpetuate than to transform the status quo, then a breakthrough might be possible through displacements to other organizational contexts in which alternative identities and projects are possible. In the case of the Mixtecs, such political displacements are nurtured by spatial displacement, namely, migration.

In Chapter 1, it will be recalled, I described how large shortfalls in peasant agricultural production in San Jerónimo forced most of the households in the community to migrate out of the town in search of wage labor. This situation is typical of the Mixteca region. The primary destinations of migrants are the commercial agricultural fields in northwestern Mexico and, more recently, those in California. For several decades Mixtec farm-labor leaders have sought to organize Mixtec farmworkers, as agricultural proletarians, into independent unions. Except for a few modest successes, their efforts have been crushed repeatedly by the superior political, economic, and police power of the corporations and state bureaucracies they confront (Kearney 1988, 1994).

The history of farm-labor organizing in California has been little more successful, except for a period of strength of the United Farm Workers of America (UFW) in the 1970s (Majka and Majka 1982). In the late 1970s migrant Mixtec farmworkers began to be recruited into California farmwork in appreciable numbers, a trend that was associated with the decline of the UFW. At present, we estimate that in peak summer seasons there may be around fifty thousand Mixtecs in California, representing over two hundred communities in Oaxaca (Runsten and Kearney 1994). Most likely, over twice that number cycle in and out of California every few years.

Mixtec migrant farmworkers represent the bottom rung of the agriculture labor markets in California, where working and living conditions have been deteriorating in recent years. Desperate for work in overcrowded labor markets and often vulnerable because of their illegal entry into the United States, these workers are subject to considerable exploitation and abuse.[4] Recent attempts to organize farmworkers in California, as in Mexico, have been severely hampered by glutted labor markets, the highly itinerant lifestyle of the farmworkers, and the political clout of the growers. Thus, for the Mixtec on both sides of the border, the proletarian route to political empowerment has proven no more successful than the peasant route.

In the urban shantytowns in cities where Mixtecs have settled—such as Mexico City and the Mexican border cities of Tijuana, Ensenada, Mexicali, and Nogales—they work mostly as day laborers and in the lower rungs of the formal and informal service economy. In these cities they have formed organizations to obtain services such as water, electricity, and paved streets. These organizations have taken the form of urban squatter associations, which are common in Latin America. The urban Mixtec organizations have achieved a number of local successes, but attempts to build more extensive and powerful organizations on such a base have been repeatedly frustrated by the power of government agencies to co-opt and intimidate leaders, thus effectively neutralizing the more progressive and visionary aspects of these urban movements.

Closely associated with the formation of the urban squatter associations has been experimentation in organizing Mixtec women street vendors who sell handicrafts to tourists in the border cities (Clark 1991; Kearney 1994). This has been virtually the only arena in which Mixtec women and the problems confronting them have found grassroots political expression. Beset by hostile police and commercial interests, these women have made valiant efforts to carve out niches in which they might earn some income while they are in the cities. But in general they have been dominated and controlled by the same combination of superior forces that debilitate the urban squatters' associations. In addition to experiencing violent intimidation and harassment, the Mixtec street vendors have also on occasion been co-opted into official street vendors' unions, just as Mixtec farmworkers are forced into white unions and squatters are co-opted into official squatters' organizations. Thus, in addition to categorical containment, at work here is a form of organizational containment, each of which is a side of the same coin.

Although the lines that demarcate them are diffuse and complex, the positions Mixtecs occupy in the four general zones noted previously are positions within a class system that spans the U.S.-Mexican border. And in each of these positions, when Mixtecs enter into exchange relations with non-Mixtecs, they tend to give more value than they receive. The sum total of the productive and exchange relations within the greater Mixtec community thus amounts to a net flow of general value through and out of its reticula. Such exploitation, which occurs at hundreds of thousands of sites and transactions each year, is the bottom-line political issue. This most fundamental class process—namely, unequal exchange—is, however, embedded in the multiplicity of its forms and sites, which is not amenable to an organized, defensive response based on class identity.

Clearly, part of the weakness of the four expressions of Mixtec self-defense outlined earlier is that each represents a fragment of a total experience. For indeed, the participants in these diverse political activities tend to move in and out of the various fields, with some participating in all four. However, the presence of four different political goals diffuses overall intellectual concentration and organizational effort. Just as the peasant is contained by being channeled into peasant politics, the identity of the same communities and the same persons is fragmented by containment in the other organizational forms noted previously. The immediate theoretical and organizational question that presents itself in this complex arena of political fields is, what sort of identity and what organizational forms might well represent (in both senses of the term) the class needs of subaltern Mixtec persons who are so dispersed and differentiated? Since class position has such low saliency as a marker of collective identity, it can only be mobilized indirectly through other expressions of it that are more readily imagined in ways that promote collective mobilization and escape from containment.

In recent years, Mixtec politics in its transnational context has taken several novel forms that respond to this challenge and that resemble the NSMs noted earlier. Three such forms of transformative politics are the so-called new ethnicity, human rights, and ecopolitics. The basic thesis I wish to present here is that movement into these fields is not limited to gaining political goals within existing fields of contestation but also seeks to transform the construction and constitution—the identity—of their members to position them better within political fields that are also affected by such transformations of contestants.

The Reintegration of Mixtec Identity: From Peasant to Postpeasant Politics

California has a long history of Mexican migrant self-help associations, most of which have been formed by migrants from particular home communities in Mexico. Typically, such migrant associations have raised money to bury deceased members and to support community projects in their hometowns. Mixtecs formed a number of such associations beginning in the 1970s, but they soon began to address a much wider range of problems—including those that affected them in their communities in Oaxaca, in the agricultural fields of Mexico and California, and in the shantytowns of Mexico, as well as health and welfare problems in California (Kearney 1994). Then in the mid-1980s, Mixtec leaders began to experiment with broader forms of associations that combined members from various communities into fronts, which are organizations of associations. Another notable dimension of this strategy was to form working relationships with transnational organizations of Zapotecs, another ethnic group from Oaxaca that has a large and organized presence in Los Angeles. Thus was formed the *Frente Mixteco-Zapoteco Binacional*, which subsequently evolved into the *Frente Indígena Oaxaqueña Binacional* as organizations of other indigenous Oaxacans—such as Triques, Mixes, and Chinantecs—joined (see Kearney 1994, 1995a).

The formation of these transnational multiethnic groups was a novel development in the history of Mexican migrant self-help associations in California, for these political projects represent not only a movement away from peasant and proletarian politics—narrowly defined—and entry into new political fields but also the promotion of those fields. Let us examine each of these new fields, of which ethnicity is the primary one in that it is the basis for the formation of the other two—human rights and ecopolitics.

From Tradition to Ethnicity

Significant currents of ethnicity began to emerge among Mixtecs in the late 1970s and early 1980s; this occurred not in the Mixtec heartland in Oaxaca but instead in commercial agriculture enclaves of northwest Mexico, in urban shantytowns of the border area, and in California (Kearney 1988; Nagengast and Kearney 1990). Two conditions promoted this rather new sensibility. One was the experience of people from many different home communities being thrown together in labor camps and shantytowns, where they began to perceive a common dimension of their identity vis-à-vis nonindigenous people. The other was and continues to be racism directed against them by mestizos, Anglos, and Chicanos on both sides of the border in the north. Mixtec leaders subsequently gave form to these experiences by actively speaking of "the problems of *the* Mixtecs," in the sense of the Mixtec people.

In retrospect, this cultural-political move can be seen as an effort to overcome the fragmentation of identity described previously. The four site-specific and single-identity organizations were disconnected from each other. The architects of this strategy mobilized social and especially symbolic capital that was latent in their communities and persons, namely, their identity as Mixtecs. This identity subsumes the other subidentities and combines them into a single identity. Thus, in a creative political move, the leaders developing these organizations decided to play the indigenous card in the ethnicity game within the greater transnational political field in which Mixtecs live and work.

Ethnicity is a problematic form of social and cultural capital in that it crosscuts class. However, the reality of the contemporary Mixtec case is that it serves mainly to agglutinate diverse subalterns into a single social and political category, defined as such primarily vis-à-vis agents and agencies of the Mexican state and employers. Mixtec leaders promote this strategy by converting a largely negative social capital, embodied in them and their communities as denigrated "Indians," into valuable social and cultural resources that can be invested in political action and alliances that reinforce their identification as 'indigenous peoples' in their own eyes and in those of others.[5]

When ethnicity enters the terrain of subaltern issues, a number of transformations occur. First, ethnicity brings with it a wider spatial focus than the usual anthropological concentration on local towns, villages, neighborhoods, and even regions, conceived as the primary social units. Although ethnic groups may occupy many complex spaces, they are most commonly found within more or less well-defined regions. Typically, the members of the ethnic groups within this region think of it as their homeland, as do members of the ethnic group who may be outside it. The usual case is that the ethnic group in question is situated within the boundaries of one or more nation-states dominated by a different group.

When ethnicity in such situations becomes politicized, the fundamental issue becomes a struggle for greater forms of regional autonomy, the most extreme of which is a secessionist movement that is inevitably opposed by the nation-state. When such movements of ethnically informed regional autonomy occur in areas with peasant populations, then the conventional politics of agrarian reform has evolved from a struggle for land per se as a means of production to territory as a space within which not only autonomous production but also the reproduction of an independent sociocultural identity can occur (Diaz Polanco forthcoming). Ethnicity as a dimension of social identity thus contrasts with peasantness in not being based primarily in the productionist assumptions of the latter term. Instead, the main ethnographic and theoretical issue concerning ethnicity is the cultural construction of person and community.

There are also different ways ethnicity and peasantness can be spatially distributed. Unlike peasantness as an identity that, because of its productionist nature, is tied only to certain environmental and political landscapes that permit it, ethnicity has no such direct dependence on means of production. It is thus a dimension of identity suitable for the dispossessed, the exiled, those in diaspora, the marginal, the migrant, the diverse. Indeed, the ascendancy of ethnicity in the late twentieth century seems to correspond with the appearance of massive numbers of migrants, refugees, and otherwise displaced peoples. And because ethnicity is no respecter of nationality, it is also an appropriate form of identity for transnational communities (Kearney 1991). Ethnicity as a dimension of social identity that is independent of space thus opens up possibilities for constructions of community that go well beyond those of the 'peasant community' or even the 'peasant region,' tied as they are to their spatially specific form of production.

This is not to say that ethnicity may not have a spatial dimension to its construction. The point is, however, that even movements of ethnic autonomy, which may seek some kind of territorial autonomy, nevertheless involve not only the struggle for land and other economic value; they involve the struggle for symbolic value as well. For just as control of land as a means of production allows for the creation and possession of economic value, so does the possession of collective symbolic value translate into political potency. Such a shift from struggles of a mainly productionist nature to the struggle for construction of ethnic identities is apparent in some 'peasant' areas.[6] To the large degree that such political issues of cultural invention and reproduction displace the more usual productionist politics of agrarian reform, the social-historical context within which 'peasants' are found disappears.

The conventional definition of peasants in the modern era as politically subordinate to dominant groups is inevitably predicated on the assumption that this asymmetry is present within the political context of the nation-state. But the insertion of ethnicity into peasant politics reconfigures such relationships. It does so first because whereas issues of national structure are not raised in conventional peasant politics, the essence of political opposition based on ethnicity is a struggle for recognition and concessions gained on the basis of some degree of autonomy that is won from the otherwise totalizing power and authority of the state to assign identity, as, for example, in the form of citizenship and nationality.[7] In extreme cases, the politics of ethnicity leads to secessionist movements with the goal of political independence based in an autonomous territory. Such cases represent a shift in the politics of space from the narrow productionist issues of peasant agrarian politics to much broader issues involving not only the struggle over land as economic value but also a struggle for control over symbolic value and its use in the construction of collective identity.

Typically, contemporary movements based on ethnicity also have the effect of eroding the distinction between 'modern' and 'traditional,' a distinction that has been so important in informing notions of the peasant. Nowhere is this more apparent than in the case of movements for the autonomy of indigenous peoples. Indeed, the indigenous person—the *indígena* (in-DI-hena)—is an identity that perhaps most clearly and effectively deconstructs the opposition of modern and traditional.[8] Also, as used in Latin America, *indígena* maps equally onto populations that are conventionally identified as both peasant and nonpeasant.

Why should Mixtec politics be taking this form at this time? Part of the answer is found in several contemporary socioeconomic conditions that are increasingly present in Mixtec communities: (1) an increase of internal differentiation and of reticular types of organization, and (2) the dissolution of bounded communities as they become more transnationalized and increasingly subject to global processes.

Increase in Internal Differentiation and Reticula

A typical feature of NSMs is that they bring together socially diverse persons who share one or several political objectives. In this sense NSMS are unlike, for example, labor unions or peasant organizations, each of which assumes a single basic essential identity of its members, such as proletarians or peasants. Such organizations are one-dimensional in the sense that they assume that their members have one single essential identity.

In contrast, the social forms of NSMs are best thought of as reticula. The organizational and communicative nature of reticula is also suggested by the terms *network* and *circuits*. These terms, which have presented themselves to indicate these new forms, thus resonate semantically with the new electronic media of communication, which are likewise becoming increasingly deterritorialized fields within which the internally differentiated selves of NSMs are formed (see Chapter 5).

Perhaps the most advanced form of such a dynamic between electronic media and internal differentiation is the electronic bulletin board where, through the World Wide Web, participants who never meet face-to-face can leave messages, read information, have romances, and otherwise dialogue in an essentially depersonalized cyberspace. Single-issue, politically oriented electronic bulletin boards are perhaps the purest form of NSMs with respect to how they coordinate facets of internally differentiated, spatially separated, and otherwise disconnected persons. Although most so-called peasants do not (yet) participate in electronic bulletin boards, the point is that the social networks in which they do participate show a historical trend toward such forms of social organization and communication. Such electronic communication and coordination partly overcome the fragmenting effects of the spatial dispersion of bulletin board participants by recondensing them into a solidarity formed in cyberspace. These disembodied communities represent the widest divergence from the small, face-to-face corporate peasant community idealized in classical and modern ethnography and constitute a type of environment and technology that promotes organizational forms typical of the NSMs.

From Bounded to Transnational Community

In the classical ethnographies of Mesoamerica, local bounded communities are taken as the primary social unit of analysis. Today, in the case of Mixtec closed corporate communities such as San Jerónimo, the local bounded community has become a component within a greater transnational community (Kearney and Nagengast 1989). Typically, such transnational communities (TNCs) each have a territorially bounded parent community in Oaxaca that remains the spiritual core of the greater TNC and the primary point of common reference for its members. And scattered throughout the greater TNC are offspring communities that are local concentrations in the diaspora of migrants and immigrants from the corporate parent community.

The creation and integration of Mixtec TNCs are promoted at this time by the growth of ever faster, more efficient, and cheaper means of long-distance communication. Consequently, each TNC is a reticula created by and mediating internal flows of persons, information, and other forms of value. The new Mixtec organizations and the emergent ethnicity they promote are a result of anastomosis of the reticula of different TNCs. These organizations are forming and are a response to life in the local regions and economic, social, and cultural spaces in which Mixtecs are found and that span the Mexico-U.S. border. This transnational space, popularly referred to as *Oaxacalifornia,* can be thought of as a grand transnational reticulum composed of lesser reticula.[9] In its form, Oaxacalifornia is thus comparable to the internet, which has local area networks within it.

The recent history of the Mixteca has been one of constant extension of its reticula into increasingly diverse and distant social and economic niches as people from local bounded communities in the Mixteca region migrate outward, forming TNCs of which the bounded home community is a component. As in biology, where extension of a population into new niches promotes differentiation, extensive transnational migration of Mixtecs promotes diversity, albeit a diversity that is also internal to persons. The immediate political question that arises, then, is what political issues and what form of organization are most appropriate for such diverse persons, most of whom participate in some combination of the five occupational fields discussed previously.

Globalization of Human Rights and Ecopolitics

Peasant politics around the world is currently being transformed as a result of the interjection of issues having to do with human rights and ecological concerns. This is certainly true of the Mixtecs. First, they are susceptible to endemic violation of their human rights throughout the diverse subregions of their diaspora (see Amnesty International 1986; Nagengast, Stavenhagen, and Kearney 1992). The murder, disappearance, torture, intimidation, and so forth, of Mixtecs were rarely noted beyond the local region in which they occurred. Recently, however, the transnational Mixtec associations and international human rights organizations have identified such abuses not as isolated incidents affecting disparate individuals but instead as human rights abuses against the Mixtec people.

This redefinition of crimes against individuals as human rights violations committed against Mixtecs is occurring in tandem with the emergence of concern with and projects directed at "environmental problems" in Mixtec "indigenous" communities. These two discourses are growing and merging throughout greater Oaxacalifornia, such that to a considerable extent the former centrality of the agrarian and proletarian issues has been folded into a new politics of human rights and environmentalism. The appearance of these two issues has altered agrarian politics and rural politics generally in many areas in ways that favor peasantlike peoples.

This political reconfiguration has been made possible by two kinds of displacements brought about by these robust young movements. The first, a discursive displacement, is the redefinition of agrarian issues from a focal concern with land tenure and other aspects of production to the broader fields of the human rights of residents of rural areas and the ecology of the regions in which they live. The second displacement effected by these new issues is geopolitical because of the imminently transnational character of the human rights and environmental movements. In other words, they establish the local politics of human rights and ecology within international contexts in which, with respect to tension between local subaltern groups and the nation-states that encompass them, there is more chance that the balance of forces might occasionally be tipped in favor of the former.[10]

In recent years the agrarian question as a discourse of 'the peasant' has deteriorated within its national space, where it is hegemonic, and has blended with the youthful and robust discourse of human rights, which has considerably diluted its powers of containment of the 'peasant.' This discursive displacement erodes the peasant as a category of social identity and reconfigures such postpeasants as members of the global community, defined as such and protected by the Universal Declaration of Human Rights and other international human rights instruments.

These new fields are made possible by the growth of the international human rights and environmental movements, which organizationally have taken form mainly as nongovernmental organizations, often with substantial grassroots memberships and nongovernment sponsors. Prime examples are Amnesty International, Human Rights Watch, Earth First, Greenpeace, and the Sierra Club. These organizations and others like them are linked by formal agreements, informal networking, and overlapping memberships. In their totality they constitute a vast reticulated sociopolitical field that exists largely outside of the confines of nation-states and has political goals that are in part beyond the economic, political, and cultural hegemony of nation-states.

Although less overarching of all Mixtec locals than are issues of human rights, environmental issues also span the specificity of each type of local site where Mixtecs produce and reproduce. In the home communities the primary issues are deforestation, soil erosion, and loss of irreplaceable germ plasma in indigenous varieties of corn, beans, and other cultigens specific to local communities that have been selecting them for millennia. In the transnational corporate agriculture in which Mixtecs labor, the primary environmental issue is the use and abuse of pesticides, which harm not only Mixtec fieldworkers and the environment but also consumers (Wright 1990).

The growth of environmental politics and human rights and the anastomosis of peasant politics into these transnational fields alter both the definition of issues and the identities of the protagonists. For example, the agrarian question, which centers on land tenure and agricultural production, is the prototypical peasant issue—*Tierra y Libertad.* It is enacted within the context of the nation-state and takes such forms as peasant wars of national liberation, national programs of land reform, and agricultural development. These political projects are informed by and consistent with a peasantry that is constituted primarily in terms of *land* as a primary value.

Land, so envisioned, is seen as a primary value, convertible, when labor and other inputs are added, into food and income (see Chapter 7). Peasant-agrarian issues are thus constructed as contestation over access to and control of land as a means of production. These issues for the most part are conceptualized and contextualized within national spaces in which the state and capital—in the form of agrarian bureaucracies, transnational corporations, legal systems, and police powers—are typically the most powerful actors. Agrarian politics is thus primarily national politics.

Such a construction of agrarian politics is, as I discussed earlier (Chapter 5), coterminous with the containment of 'peasants,' for it is within the sociology and politics of agrarian issues that 'the peasant' as a social, legal category is constructed. However, the expansion of 'peasant' claims from land as an economic asset to land as a component in a total ecosystem amounts to the redefinition of land as a primary economic value to land as but one kind of value within a much larger panoply of generalized value.

The reframing of productionist issues within the space of human rights has similar deep implications for peasant and agrarian issues as usually conceptualized. Normally, the relationship between a state and its citizens is conceived and enacted as an internal affair, but when state authority becomes identified by international human rights agencies as abusive, the relationship between state and citizen becomes transnationalized. Human rights as a social movement is distinctly transnational in the historical sense of having established a moral and political frame of reference that transcends the sovereignty of nations and is able to bring particular nations to account for their actions. In this transnationalization the social definition of person is expanded from that of subject of nation X to that of global citizen.

Therefore, to the degree that human rights become a dimension of persons formerly defined by the restrictive social identity of 'peasant,' their social identity is broadened in formal terms. In other words, to the degree that human rights emerge as a new cultural construction of the person, they are seen as unfulfilled dimensions of personhood that must be protected. It is subsequently, in such struggle to attain and protect human rights for the persons so constructed, that the new personhood becomes constituted. Such persons also have identities appropriate for members of transnational organizations such as those of the Mixtecs, just as these organizations promote such transnational identities.

For San Jerónimo and the Mixteca region at large, as in degraded agrarian areas elsewhere, peasant politics has not led to resolution of the deep economic and political problems that beset them. And this is true in spite of, or perhaps even because of, policies and programs to "develop" such "rural," "backward," 'peasant' places. To use Daniel Nugent's (1993) apt metaphor from Chihuahua, the peasants of the Mixteca are "spent cartridges" in the sense that the peasant route has not led to a solution of their 'peasant' problems.

The same was true, as we have seen, of Mixtec proletarian and urban *colono* politics. It was in this cul-de-sac that Mixtec leaders began to define new political objectives and new organizational forms to obtain them by reconceptualizing their people as not just campesinos, *proletarianos,* or *colonos* but also as variants of the more generic identity "the Mixtec people." This conceptual move makes it possible to integrate each of these local identities and their respective organizational forms (corporate towns, labor unions, popular urban organizations) without necessarily losing their local specificity. Ethnicity is the common fabric of this new inclusive identity, and human rights constitute the common political issue that can mobilize Mixtecs and non-Mixtecs in the defense of Mixtecs throughout their diaspora.

Notes

1. See, for example, Assies, Burgwal, and Salman (1990); Escobar and Alvarez (1992); Foweraker and Craig (1990); Laclau (1990); Slater (1994); Stephen and Dow (1990).

2. For fuller descriptions of these four contexts, see Bade (1994); Kearney (1986a, 1988, 1994, 1995a); Nagengast and Kearney (1990); Nagengast, Stavenhagen, and Kearney (1992); and Zabin et al. (1993).

3. Data on the relations between government administrative policies and practices and programs for economic development in Oaxaca and elsewhere in Mexico that support this hypothesis can be found in Collins (1995) and Fox (1994); see also Cornelius, Craig, and Fox (1994).

4. For Mixtec farmworkers and the conditions in which they live and work in California, see Bade (1993, 1994); *Los Angeles Times* (July 27, 1995), pp. A1, A16; Mines and Kearney (1982); Nagengast, Stavenhagen, and Kearney (1992); and Zabin et al. (1993). Mixtecs in California are also portrayed in two films: Grieshop and Varese (1993) and Ziff (1994).

5. Numerous indigenous movements based on a comparable revalorization of indigenous ethnicity have recently formed throughout Latin America and elsewhere: see Devalle (1989); Kearney (n.d.); and Kearney and Varese (1995). Such movements can indeed be read as indications of the decline in the intellectual hegemony of developmentalism and its vision of a universal modernity into which subaltern forms of cultural difference will be melded.

6. Three other comparable cases of peasantlike peoples from southern Mexico mobilizing as indigenous peoples are the Mayan Zapatistas in Chiapas (Collier 1994a, 1994b); the *Coalición Obrera Campesina Estudiantil del Istmo,* a Zapotec organization in the Isthmus of Tehuantepec of Oaxaca (Campbell et al. 1993); and the Zapotec transnational migrant organizations in Los Angeles, California, that have formed the *Organización Regional Oaxaqueña* (Kearney 1993c).

7. Indicative of current changing balances in the politics of indigenous containment by the state in Mexico is the 1986 amendment to Article IV of the Mexican Constitution granting legal recognition of the cultural rights of indigenous peoples in Mexico.

8. A prime example is found in Jackson's (1995) description of Tukanoan ethnic politics in Colombia.

9. On Oaxacalifornia, see Grieshop and Varese (1993), Kearney (1995a), Kearney and Varese (1995), and Ziff (1994).

10. For a discussion of the emergence of human rights as an issue among indigenous groups in the Americas, see Brysk (1996).

Bibliography

Abrams, Philip. 1988 "Notes on the Difficulty of Studying the State." Journal of Historical Sociology 1(1):58–89.

Althusser, Louis. 1977 [1965] *For Marx*. London: New Left Books.

Althusser, Louis, and Etienne Balibar. 1970 [1968] *Reading Capital*. London: New Left Books.

Altieri, Miguel A. 1995 *Agroecology: The Science of Sustainable Agriculture*, with contributions by John G. Farrell and others. 2d ed. Boulder: Westview Press.

Amnesty International. 1986 *Mexico: Human Rights in Rural Areas: Exchange of Documents with the Mexican Government on Human Rights Violations in Oaxaca and Chiapas*. London: Amnesty International.

Anderson, Benedict R. 1983 *Imagined Communities: Reflections on the Origin and Spread of Nationalism*. London: Verso.

Anderson, Perry. 1976 *Considerations on Western Marxism*. London: New Left Books.

Anzaldúa, Gloria. 1987 *Borderlands/La Frontera: The New Mestiza*. San Francisco: Spinsters/Aunt Lute.

Appandurai, Arjun. 1986 "Theory in Anthropology: Center and Periphery." *Comparative Studies in Society and History* 28(1):356–361.

Assies, Willem, Gerrit Burgwal, and Ton Salman. 1990 *Structures of Power, Movements of Resistance: An Introduction to the Theories of Urban Movements in Latin America*. Amsterdam: Centre for Latin American Research and Documentation.

Bade, Bonnie Lynn. 1993 "Problems Surrounding Health Care Service Utilization for Mixtec Migrant Farmworker Families in Madera, California." Davis: California Institute for Rural Studies.

Bade, Bonnie Lynn. 1994 *Sweatbaths, Sacrifice, and Surgery: The Practice of Transmedical Healthcare by Mixtec Migrant Families in California*. Ph.D. diss., University of California, Riverside.

Balandier, Georges. 1966 "The Colonial Situation: A Theoretical Approach." In *Social Change: The Colonial Situation*, Immanuel Wallerstein, ed. New York: John Wiley.

Baran, Paul. 1957 *The Political Economy of Growth*. New York: Monthly Review Press.

Barbash, Shepard. 1993 *Oaxacan Woodcarving: The Magic in the Trees*. Photography by Vicki Ragan. San Francisco: Chronicle Books.

Barkin, David. 1978 *Desarrollo regional y reorganización campesina: la Chontalpa como reflejo del problema agropecuario mexicano*. Mexico City: Nueva Imagén.

Barkin, David. 1990 *Distorted Development: Mexico in the World Economy*. Boulder: Westview Press.

Barrett, Michèle, and Anne Phillips. 1992 *Destabilizing Theory: Contemporary Feminist Debates*. Stanford: Stanford University Press.

Barton, Roy Franklin. 1919 *Ifugao Law.* Berkeley: University of California Publications in American Archaeology and Ethnology, Vol. 15, No. 1.

Bartra, Armando. 1979 *La explotación del trabajo campesino por el capital.* Mexico City: Editorial Macehual.

Bartra, Armando. 1985 *Los herederos de Zapata: movimientos campesinos posrevolucionarios en México, 1920–1980.* Mexico City: Era.

Bartra, Roger. 1976 "Si los campesinos se extinguen." *Historia y Sociedad* 8(Winter):71–83.

Bartra, Roger. 1992 *The Imaginary Networks of Political Power.* Transl. C. Joysmith. New Brunswick: Rutgers University Press.

Bartra, Roger. 1993 *Agrarian Structure and Political Power in Mexico.* Transl. Stephen K. Ault. Baltimore: Johns Hopkins University Press.

Basch, Linda, Nina Glick Schiller, and Cristina Szanton Blanc. 1994 *Nations Unbound: Transnational Projects, Postcolonial Predicaments, and Deterritorialized Nation States.* New York: Gordon and Breach.

Baudrillard, Jean. 1981 *For a Critique of the Political Economy of the Sign.* Transl. with an Introduction by Charles Levin. St. Louis: Telos Press.

Benedict, Ruth. 1934 *Patterns of Culture.* Boston: Houghton Mifflin.

Berger, John. 1972 *Ways of Seeing.* London: British Broadcasting System and Penguin Books.

Besserer Alatorre, Federico. 1993 "Los Mixtecos en el campo global de producción de vegetales y significado." Paper presented at the International Congress of Anthropological and Ethnological Sciences, Mexico City, August 3.

Blayney, Robert G., and Diane B. Bendahmane. 1988 *The Inter-American Foundation and the Small and Micro-Enterprise Sector.* Rosslyn, Va.: Inter-American Foundation.

Boas, Franz. 1940 *Race, Language, and Culture.* New York: Macmillan.

Bourdieu, Pierre. 1977 *Outline of a Theory of Practice.* Cambridge: Cambridge University Press.

Bourdieu, Pierre. 1984 *Distinction: A Social Critique of the Judgement of Taste.* Transl. Richard Nice. Cambridge: Harvard University Press.

Bourdieu, Pierre. 1986 "The Forms of Capital." In *Handbook of Theory and Research for the Sociology of Education.* J. B. Richardson, ed. New York: Greenwood Press.

Bourdieu, Pierre. 1990 *The Logic of Practice.* Transl. Richard Nice. Stanford: Stanford University Press.

Bourdieu, Pierre. 1991 *Language and Symbolic Power.* Edited with an Introduction by John B. Thompson. Transl. Gino Raymond and Matthew Adamson. Cambridge: Harvard University Press.

Brelich, Angelo. 1966 "The Place of Dreams in the Religious World Concept of the Greeks." In *The Dream and Human Societies,* G. E. Von Grunebaum and Roger Caillois, eds. Berkeley: University of California Press.

Brinton, Crane. 1965 *The Anatomy of Revolution.* New York: Vintage Books.

Brown, E. Richard. 1976 "Public Health in Imperialism: Early Rockefeller Programs at Home and Abroad." *American Journal of Public Health* 66(9):897–903.

Brysk, Alison. 1996 "Turning Weakness into Strength: The Internationalization of Indian Rights." *Latin American Perspectives* 23(2), in press.

Burawoy, M. 1976 "The Functions and Reproduction of Migrant Labor: Comparative Material from Southern Africa and the United States." *American Journal of Sociology* 81:1050–1087.

Bury, John B. 1920 *The Idea of Progress: An Inquiry into Its Origin and Growth*. London: Macmillan.

Cabral, Amilcar. 1969 *Revolution in Guinea: An African People's Struggle*. London: State 1.

Campbell, Howard, Leigh Binford, Miguel Bartolomé, and Alicias Barabas. 1993 *Zapotec Struggles: Histories, Politics, and Representations from Juchitán, Oaxaca*. Washington, D.C.: Smithsonian Institution Press.

Cancian, Frank. 1965 *Economics and Prestige in a Maya Community: The Religious Cargo System in Zinacantan*. Stanford: Stanford University Press.

Cancian, Frank. 1987 "Proletarianization in Zinacantan, 1960–1983." In *Household Economies and Their Transformations*, Morgan D. Maclachlan, ed. Lanham, Md.: University Press of America.

Cancian, Frank. 1992 *The Decline of Community in Zinacantan: Economy, Public Life, and Social Stratification, 1960–1987*. Stanford: Stanford University Press.

Cancian, Frank, and Peter Brown. 1994 "Who Is Rebelling in Chiapas?" *Cultural Survival Quarterly* 18(1):22–25.

Carlos, Manuel. 1993 "International Agroindustry and Mexican Ejidal Communities: A Comparative Ethnographic Case Study." Manuscript. University of California MEXUS grant proposal.

Casti, John. 1994 *Complexification: Explaining a Paradoxical World Through the Science of Surprise*. New York: HarperCollins.

Castillo, Ana. 1986 *The Mixquihuala Letters*. Binghamton, N.Y.: Bilingual Press/Editorial Bilingüe.

Castillo, Ana. 1993 *So Far from God*. New York: W. W. Norton.

Chavez, Leo R. 1992 *Shadowed Lives: Undocumented Immigrants in American Society*. Fort Worth, Texas: Harcourt Brace Jovanovich.

Chilcote, Ronald H. 1974 "A Critical Synthesis of the Dependency Literature." *Latin American Perspectives* 1(1):4–29.

Chilcote, Ronald H. 1981 "Issues of Theory in Dependency and Marxism." *Latin American Perspectives* 8(3–4):3–16.

Chilcote, Ronald H., and Joel Edelstein. 1986 *Latin America: Capitalist and Socialist Perspectives of Development and Underdevelopment*. Boulder: Westview Press.

Chomsky, Noam. 1982 *Towards a New Cold War*. New York: Pantheon.

Chomsky, Noam. 1987 "The Old and the New Cold War." In *The Chomsky Reader*, James Peck, ed. New York: Pantheon Books.

Chomsky, Noam. 1988 *The Culture of Terrorism*. Boston: South End Press.

Clark Alfaro, Víctor. 1991 *Los mixtecos en La Frontera (Tijuana), sus mujeres y el turismo. Cuadernos de Ciencias Sociales*. Tijuana, Baja Calif.: Universidad Autónoma de Baja California.

Clifford, James. 1988 *The Predicament of Culture: Twentieth-Century Ethnography, Literature, and Art*. Cambridge: Harvard University Press.

Clifford, James, and George E. Marcus. 1986 *Writing Culture: The Poetics and Politics of Ethnography*. Berkeley: University of California Press.

Cohn, Bernard S., and Nicholas B. Dirks. 1988 "Beyond the Fringe: The Nation State, Colonialism and the Technologies of Power." *Journal of Historical Sociology* 1(2):224–229.

Colburn, Forrest D., ed. 1989 *Everyday Forms of Peasant Resistance*. Armonk, N.Y.: M. E. Sharpe.

Collier, George A. 1994a "Roots of Rebellion in Chiapas." *Cultural Survival Quarterly* 18(1):14–18.

Collier, George A. 1994b *Basta! Land and the Zapatista Rebellion in Chiapas.* Oakland, Calif.: Institute for Food and Development Policy.

Collins, Joe. 1995 *Communal Work and Rural Development in the State of Oaxaca in Mexico.* Geneva: International Labor Organization.

Comaroff, Jean, and John L. Comaroff. 1991 *Of Revelation and Revolution: Christianity, Colonialism, and Consciousness in South Africa.* Chicago: University of Chicago Press.

Comaroff, Jean, and John L. Comaroff. 1993 *Modernity and Its Malcontents: Ritual and Power in Postcolonial Africa.* Chicago: University of Chicago Press.

Comaroff, John L., and Jean Comaroff. 1987 "The Madman and the Migrant: Work and Labor in the Historical Consciousness of a South African People." *American Ethnologist* 14(2):191–209.

Cook, Scott, and Leigh Binford. 1990 *Obliging Need: Rural Petty Industry in Mexican Capitalism.* Austin: University of Texas Press.

Cordry, Donald, and Dorothy Cordry. 1968 *Mexican Indian Costumes.* Foreword by Miquel Covarrubias. Austin: University of Texas Press.

Cornelius, Wayne A., Ann L. Craig, and Jonathan Fox. 1994 *Transforming State-Society Relations in Mexico: The National Solidarity Strategy.* San Diego: Center for U.S.-Mexican Studies, University of California, San Diego.

Corrigan, Philip, and Derek Sayer. 1985 *The Great Arch: English State Formation as Cultural Revolution.* Oxford: Basil Blackwell.

Davis, Mike. 1990 *City of Quartz: Excavating the Future in Los Angeles.* London: Verso.

de Janvry, Alain. 1981 *The Agrarian Question and Reformism in Latin America.* Baltimore: Johns Hopkins University Press.

Deleuze, Gilles, and Félix Guattari. 1987 *A Thousand Plateaus: Capitalism and Schizophrenia.* Transl. B. Massumi. Minneapolis: University of Minnesota Press.

Dennis, Philip. 1887 *Inter-Village Conflict in Oaxaca.* New Brunswick, N.J.: Rutgers University Press.

Devalle, Susana B.C., ed. 1989 *La diversidad prohibida: resistencia étnica y poder de estado.* Mexico City: El Colegio de México.

Diaz Polanco, Hector. Forthcoming. *Indigenous Peoples in Latin America: The Quest for Self-Determination.* Trans. Lucia Rayas. Boulder: Westview Press.

Dos Santos, Theotonio. 1970 "The Structure of Dependence." *American Economic Review* 40(2):231–236.

Eagleton, Terry. 1991 *Ideology: An Introduction.* London: Verso.

Early, Daniel K. 1993 "Effects of the International Coffee Market and State Intervention in Nahuatl Peasant Communities in Zongolica, Veracruz, Mexico." Paper presented at the International Congress of Anthropological and Ethnological Sciences, Mexico City, August 3.

Escobar, Arturo. 1991 "Anthropology and the Development Encounter: The Making and Marketing of Development Anthropology." *American Ethnologist* 18(4):658–682.

Escobar, Arturo. 1992 "Planning." In *The Development Dictionary: A Guide to Knowledge and Power,* Wolfgang Sachs, ed. London: Zed Books.

Escobar, Arturo, and Sonia E. Alvarez, eds. 1992 *The Making of Social Movements in Latin America: Identity, Strategy, and Democracy.* Boulder: Westview Press.

Esteva, Gustavo. 1978 "¿Y si los campesinos existen?" *Comercio Exterior* (Mexico City) 28 (June):699–732.

Esteva, Gustavo. 1983 *The Struggle for Rural Mexico*. South Hardy, Mass.: Bergin and Garvey.

Esteva, Gustavo. 1992 "Development." In *The Development Dictionary: A Guide to Knowledge and Power*, Wolfgang Sachs, ed. London: Zed Books.

Evans-Pritchard, E. E. 1940 *The Nuer: A Description of the Modes of Livelihood and Political Institutions of a Nilotic People*. Oxford: Clarendon Press.

Fabian, Johannes. 1983 *Time and the Other: How Anthropology Makes Its Object*. New York: Columbia University Press.

Feder, Ernest. 1977 *Strawberry Imperialism: An Inquiry into the Mechanisms of Dependency in Mexican Agriculture*. The Hague: Institute of Social Studies.

Ferguson, James. 1990 *The Anti-Politics Machine: "Development," Depoliticization, and Bureaucratic Power in Lesotho*. Cambridge: Cambridge University Press.

Fernández de Lizardi, José Joaquín. 1949 (1816) *El periquillo sarniento*. Mexico City: Editorial Porrua.

Foster, George M. 1961 "The Dyadic Contract in Tzintzuntzan, II: Patron-Client Relationship." *American Anthropologist* 63:1173–1192.

Foster, George M. 1965 "Peasant Society and the Image of Limited Good." *American Anthropologist* 67:293–315.

Foster, George M. 1979 *Tzintzuntzan: Mexican Peasants in a Changing World*. Rev. ed. New York: Elsevier.

Foster-Carter, Aiden. 1978 "Can We Articulate 'Articulation'?" In *The New Economic Anthropology*, John Clammer, ed. New York: St. Martin's Press.

Foweraker, Joe, and Ann L. Craig. 1990 *Popular Movements and Political Change in Mexico*. Boulder: Lynne Rienner Publishers.

Fox, Jonathan. 1994 "Targeting the Poorest: The Role of the National Indigenous Institute in Mexico's Solidarity Program." In *Transforming State-Society Relations in Mexico*, Wayne A. Cornelius, Ann L. Craig, and Jonathan Fox, eds. San Diego: Center for U.S.-Mexican Studies, University of California, San Diego.

Frank, Andre Gunder. 1967 *Capitalism and Underdevelopment in Latin America*. New York: Monthly Review Press.

Frank, Andre Gunder. 1969 *Latin America: Underdevelopment or Revolution*. New York: Monthly Review Press.

Frank, Andre Gunder. 1979 *Dependent Accumulation and Underdevelopment*. New York: Monthly Review Press.

Gates, Marilyn. 1993 *In Default: Peasants, the Debt Crisis, and the Agricultural Challenge in Mexico*. Boulder: Westview Press.

Geertz, Clifford. 1963 *Agricultural Involution: The Process of Ecological Change in Indonesia*. Berkeley: University of California Press.

Geertz, Clifford. 1973a "Person, Time, and Conduct in Bali." In *The Interpretation of Cultures: Selected Essays*. New York: Basic Books.

Geertz, Clifford. 1973b "Thick Description: Toward an Interpretive Theory of Culture." In *The Interpretation of Cultures: Selected Essays*. New York: Basic Books.

Geertz, Clifford. 1983 *Local Knowledge: Further Essays in Interpretive Anthropology*. New York: Basic Books.

Geertz, Clifford. 1988 *Works and Lives: The Anthropologist as Author.* Stanford: Stanford University Press.

Ghani, Ashraf. 1987 "A Conversation with Eric Wolf." *American Ethnologist* 14(2):346–366.

Gibson, William. 1984 *Neuromancer.* New York: Ace Books.

Gibson, William. 1988 *Monalisa Overdrive.* New York: Bantam Books.

Gleick, James. 1987 *Chaos: Making a New Science.* New York: Viking.

Glick Schiller, Nina, Linda Basch, and Cristina Blanc-Szanton. 1992 "Transnationalism: A New Analytic Framework for Understanding Migration." In *Towards a Transnational Perspective on Migration: Race, Class, Ethnicity, and Nationalism Reconsidered,* Nina Glick Schiller, Linda Basch, and Cristina Blanc-Szanton, eds. New York: New York Academy of Sciences.

Gliessman, Stephen R., ed. 1990 *Agroecology: Researching the Ecological Basis for Sustainable Agriculture.* New York: Springer-Verlag.

Goody, Jack. 1987 *The Interface Between the Written and the Oral.* Cambridge: Cambridge University Press.

Gorak, Jan. 1988 *The Alien Mind of Raymond Williams.* Columbia: University of Missouri Press.

Gordon, Robert J. 1992 *The Bushman Myth.* Boulder: Westview Press.

Gottdeiner, Mark. Forthcoming *Post-Suburban California.* Berkeley: University of California Press.

Gouldner, Alvin W. 1970 *The Coming Crisis of Western Sociology.* New York: Basic Books.

Gramsci, Antonio. 1971 *Selections from the Prison Notebooks of Antonio Gramsci.* Edited and translated by Quintin Hoare and Geoffrey Nowell Smith. New York: International Publishers.

Griault, Marcel. 1938 *Masques Dogons.* Paris: Institut d'Ethnolgie.

Grieshop, James, and Stefano Varese. 1993 *Invisible Indians: Mixtec Farmworkers in California.* A film. Applied Behavioral Sciences, University of California at Davis.

Gudeman, Stephen. 1978 *The Demise of a Rural Economy: From Subsistence to Capitalism in a Latin American Village.* London: Routledge and Kegan Paul.

Gudeman, Stephen, and Alberto Rivera. 1990 *Conversations in Colombia: The Domestic Economy in Life and Text.* Cambridge: Cambridge University Press.

Guha, Ranajit. 1988 "The Prose of Counter-Insurgency." In *Selected Subaltern Studies,* Ranajit Guha and Gayatri C. Spivak, eds. Oxford: Oxford University Press.

Guha, Ranajit, and Gayatri C. Spivak, eds. 1988 *Selected Subaltern Studies.* Oxford: Oxford University Press.

Gupta, Akhil. 1992 "The Song of the Nonaligned World: Transnational Identities and the Reinscription of Space in Late Capitalism." *Cultural Anthropology* 7(1):63–79.

Gupta, Akhil, and James Ferguson. 1992 "Beyond 'Culture': Space, Identity, and the Politics of Difference." *Cultural Anthropology* 7(1):6–23.

Gutmann, Matthew C. 1993 "Rituals of Resistance: A Critique of the Theory of Everyday Forms of Resistance." *Latin American Perspectives* 20(2):74–92.

Hakim, Catherine. 1980 "Census Reports as Documentary Evidence." *Sociology Review* 28(3):551–580.

Haraway, Donna. 1985 "Manifesto for Cyborgs: Science, Technology, and Socialist Feminism in the. 1980s." *Socialist Review* 15(80):65–108.

Hardin, Garrett. 1968 "The Tragedy of the Commons." *Science* 162:1243–1248.

Hardin, Garrett. 1993 *Living Within Limits: Ecology, Economics, and Population Taboos.* New York: Oxford University Press.

Harding, Neil. 1983 "Russian Commune." In *A Dictionary of Marxist Thought,* Tom Bottomore, ed. Cambridge: Harvard University Press.

Harding, Timothy F. 1976 "Dependency, Nationalism and the State in Latin America." *Latin American Perspectives* 3(4):3–11.

Hebdige, Dick. 1979 *Subculture: The Meaning of Style. London:* Methuen.

Herman, Edward S. 1982 *The Real Terror Network: Terrorism in Fact and Propaganda.* Boston: South End Press.

Hewitt de Alcántara, Cynthia. 1984 *Anthropological Perspectives on Rural Mexico.* London: Routledge and Kegan Paul.

Hobsbawm, Eric, and Terrance Ranger, eds. 1983 *The Invention of Tradition.* New York: Cambridge University Press.

Hogbin, H. Ian. 1958 *Social Change.* London: Watts.

Holston, James. 1989 *The Modernist City: An Anthropological Critique of Brasilia.* Chicago: University of Chicago Press.

Horne, Haynes. 1989 "Jameson's Strategies of Containment." In *Postmodernism/Jameson/Critique,* Douglas Kellner, ed. Washington, D.C.: Maisonneuve Press.

Horton, Robin. 1993 *Patterns of Thought in Africa and the West: Essays on Magic, Religion, and Science.* Cambridge: Cambridge University Press.

Hunt, David. 1983 "Theda Skocpol and the Peasant Route." *Socialist Review* 13(4):122–144.

Hunt, E. K. 1992 *History of Economic Thought: A Critical Perspective.* 2d ed. New York: HarperCollins.

Jackobson, Cardell K. 1984 "Internal Colonialism and Native Americans: Indian Labor in the United States from 1871 to World War II." *Social Science Quarterly* 65:158–171.

Jackson, Jean. 1995 "Preserving Indian Culture: Shaman Schools and Ethno-Education in the Vaupés, Colombia." *Cultural Anthropology* 10(3):302–329.

Jameson, Frederic. 1981 *The Political Unconscious: Narrative as a Socially Symbolic Act.* Ithaca, N.Y.: Cornell University Press.

Jameson, Frederic. 1984 "Postmodernism, or the Cultural Logic of Late Capitalism." *New Left Review* 146:53–92.

Jameson, Frederic. 1991 *Postmodernism and the Logic of Late Capitalism.* Durham: Duke University Press.

JanMohamed, Abdul R. 1983 *Manichean Aesthetics.* Amherst: University of Massachusetts Press.

Janowitz, Tama. 1987 *A Cannibal in Manhattan.* New York: Washington Square Press.

Jarvie, I. C. 1964 *The Revolution in Anthropology.* New York: Humanities Press.

Kautsky, Karl. 1988 (1899) *The Agrarian Question: In Two Volumes.* Transl. Pete Burgess. Introduction by Hamza Alavi and Teodor Shanin. London: Zwan Publications.

Kearney, Michael. 1972 *The Winds of Ixtepeji: World View and Society in a Zapotec Town.* New York: Holt, Rinehart and Winston.

Kearney, Michael. 1980 "Agribusiness and the Rise or the Demise of the Peasantry." *Latin American Perspectives* 7(4):115–124.

Kearney, Michael. 1984 *World View.* Novato, Calif.: Chandler and Sharp.

Kearney, Michael. 1986a "Integration of the Mixteca and the Western U.S.-Mexican Border Region via Migratory Wage Labor." In *Regional Impacts of U.S.-Mexican Relations,* Ina

Rosenthal Urey, ed. San Diego: Center for U.S.-Mexican Studies, Monograph Series, No. 16, University of California, San Diego.

Kearney, Michael. 1986b "From the Invisible Hand to Visible Feet: Anthropological Studies of Migration and Development." *Annual Review of Anthropology* 15:331–361. Stanford: Stanford University Press.

Kearney, Michael. 1988 "Mixtec Political Consciousness: From Passive to Active Resistance." In *Rural Revolt in Mexico and U.S. Intervention,* Daniel Nugent, ed. San Diego: Center for U.S.-Mexican Studies, Monograph Series, No. 27, University of California, San Diego.

Kearney, Michael. 1991 "Borders and Boundaries of State and Self at the End of Empire." *Journal of Historical Sociology* 4(1):52–74.

Kearney, Michael. 1992 "A Very Bad Disease of the Arms." In *The Naked Anthropologist: Tales from Around the World,* P. DeVita, ed. Belmont, Calif.: Wadsworth Publishing.

Kearney, Michael. 1993a Review of *China's Peasants: The Anthropology of a Revolution,* by Sulamith Heins Potter and Jack M. Potter, Cambridge: Cambridge University Press, 1990. *Journal of Anthropological Research* 49(2):177–179.

Kearney, Michael. 1993b Review of *The Imaginary Networks of Political Power,* by Roger Bartra. *American Anthropologist* 95:738–739.

Kearney, Michael. 1993c "From Corn Fields to Force Fields: Cultural-Political Strategies of Indigenous Oaxacan Transnationals." Paper presented at the annual meeting of the American Anthropological Association, San Francisco, November.

Kearney, Michael. 1994 "Desde el indigenismo a los derechos humanos: etnicidad y política más allá de la mixtec." *Nueva Antropología* 14(46):49–67.

Kearney, Michael. 1995a "The Effects of Transnational Culture, Economy, and Migration on Mixtec Identity in Oaxacalifornia." In *The Bubbling Cauldron: Race, Ethnicity, and the Urban Crisis,* Michael Peter Smith and Joe R. Feagin, eds. Minneapolis: University of Minnesota Press.

Kearney, Michael. 1995b "The Local and the Global: The Anthropology of Globalization and Transnationalism." *Annual Review of Anthropology* 24:547–565.

Kearney, Michael. 1996 "Introduction." *Latin American Perspectives* 23:4–15.

Kearney, Michael, and Carole Nagengast. 1989 "Anthropological Perspectives on Transnational Communities in Rural California." Working Group on Farm Labor and Rural Poverty, Working Paper No. 3. Davis, Calif.: Institute for Rural Studies.

Kearney, Michael, and Stefano Varese. 1995 "Latin America's Indigenous Peoples Today: Changing Identities and Forms of Resistance in Global Context." In *Capital, Power and Inequality in Latin America,* Richard Harris and S. Halebsky, eds. Boulder: Westview Press.

Kennan, George F. 1947 "The Sources of Soviet Conduct." *Foreign Affairs* 25:566–582.

Klein, Martin A. 1980a "Introduction." In *Peasants in Africa: Historical and Contemporary Perspectives,* Martin A. Klein, ed. Beverly Hills: Sage.

Klein, Martin A., ed. 1980b *Peasants in Africa: Historical and Contemporary Perspectives.* Beverly Hills: Sage.

Kroeber, Alfred. 1948 *Anthropology.* New York: Harcourt Brace.

Kuhn, Thomas S. 1957 *The Copernican Revolution: Planetary Astronomy in the Development of Western Thought.* Cambridge: Harvard University Press.

Kuhn, Thomas S. 1970 *The Structure of Scientific Revolutions.* 2d ed., Chicago: University of Chicago Press.

Kuhn, Thomas S. 1977 *The Essential Tension*. Chicago: University of Chicago Press.

Kureishi, Hanif. 1990 *The Buddha of Suburbia*. New York: Penguin Books.

Laclau, Ernesto. 1971 "Feudalism and Capitalism in Latin America." *New Left Review* No. 67 (May–June):19–38.

Laclau, Ernesto. 1990 *New Reflections on the Revolution of Our Time*. London: Verso.

Laclau, Ernesto, and Chantel Mouffe. 1985 *Hegemony and Socialist Strategy: Towards a Radical Democratic Politics*. London: Verso.

Lauria Perricelli, Antonio. 1989 *A Study in Historical and Critical Anthropology: The Making of "The People of Puerto Rico."* Ph.D. diss. Political and Social Science Department, New School, New York.

Lave, Jean, and Etienne Wenger. 1991 *Situated Learning: Legitimate Peripheral Participation*. Cambridge: Cambridge University Press.

Leach, Edmund R. 1964 "Anthropological Aspects of Language: Animal Categories and Verbal Abuse." In *New Directions in the Study of Language*, E. H. Lenneberg, ed. Cambridge: MIT Press.

Leacock, Eleanor Burke, ed. 1971 *The Culture of Poverty: A Critique*. New York: Simon and Schuster.

Leitch, Vincent B. 1983 *Deconstructive Criticism: An Advanced Introduction*. New York: Columbia University Press.

Lenin, V. I. 1956 [1899] *The Development of Capitalism in Russia: The Process of the Formation of a Home Market for Large-Scale Industry*. Moscow: Progress Publishers.

Lenin, V. I. 1975 (1898) *Marxism and Revisionism: The Heritage We Renounce*. In *V. I. Lenin, Selected Works*. Moscow: Progress Publishers.

Levinson, Jerome, and Juan de Onis. 1970 *The Alliance That Lost Its Way: A Critical Report on the Alliance for Progress*. Chicago: Quadrangle Books.

Lewis, Oscar. 1951 *Life in a Mexican Village: Tepoztlán Restudied*. Chicago: University of Chicago Press.

Lewis, Oscar. 1959 *Five Families: Mexican Case Studies in the Culture of Poverty*. New York: Basic Books.

Light, Ivan Hubert, and Edna Bonacich. 1988 *Immigrant Entrepreneurs: Koreans in Los Angeles, 1965–1982*. Berkeley: University of California Press.

Lomnitz-Adler, Claudio. 1982 *Evolución de una sociedad rural*. Mexico City: Fondo de Cultura Económica.

Maine, Henry James Sumner, Sir. 1877 *Ancient Law, Its Connection with the Early History of Society, and Its Relation to Modern Ideas*. New York: H. Holt and Company.

Majka, Linda C., and Theo J. Majka. 1982 *Farm Workers, Agribusiness, and the State*. Philadelphia: Temple University Press.

Malinowski, Bronislaw. 1922 *Argonauts of the Western Pacific: An Account of Native Enterprise and Adventure in the Archipelagoes of Melanesian New Guinea*. Preface by Sir James Frazer. New York: Dutton.

Manganaro, Marc. 1990 "Textual Play, Power, and Cultural Critique: An Orientation to Modernist Anthropology." In *Modernist Anthropology: From Fieldwork to Text*, Marc Manganaro, ed. Princeton: Princeton University Press.

Mangin, William. 1970 *Peasants in Cities: Readings in the Anthropology of Urbanization*. Boston: Houghton Mifflin.

Marcus, George E., and Michael M.J. Fischer. 1986 *Anthropology as Cultural Critique: An Experimental Moment in the Human Sciences*. Chicago: University of Chicago Press.

Martínez, Ruben. 1982–1983 "Internal Colonialism: A Reconceptualization of Race Relations in the United States." *Humboldt Journal of Social Relations* 10(1):163–176.

Marx, Karl. 1963 [1852] *The Eighteenth Brumaire of Louis Bonaparte.* New York: International Publishers.

Marx, Karl. 1976 [1867] *Capital: A Critique of Political Economy.* Vol. I. Transl. Ben Fowkes. Introduction by Ernest Mandel. New York: Random House.

McCay, Bonnie, and James M. Acheson, eds. 1987 *The Question of the Commons.* Tucson: University of Arizona Press.

McClelland, David. 1961 *The Achieving Society.* Princeton, N.J.: Van Nostrand.

Mead, Margaret. 1928 *Coming of Age in Samoa: A Psychological Study of Primitive Youth for Western Civilization.* Foreword by Franz Boas. New York: Morrow.

Meillassoux, Claude. 1981 *Maidens, Meal and Money: Capitalism and the Domestic Economy.* Cambridge: Cambridge University Press.

Memmi, Albert. 1965 *The Colonizer and the Colonized.* Boston: Beacon Press.

Miner, Horace. 1952 "The Folk-Urban Continuum." *American Sociological Review* 17:529–537.

Mines, Richard, and Michael Kearney. 1982. *The Health of Tulare County Farmworkers: A Report of 1981 Survey and Ethnographic Research for the Tulare County Department of Public Health.* Sacramento: State of California Department of Health Services, Rural Health Division, and Tulare County Department of Health.

Mitchell, William P. 1991 *Peasants on the Edge: Crop, Cult, and Crisis in the Andes.* Austin: University of Texas Press.

Mitchell, William P. Forthcoming "Pressures on Peasant Production and the Formation of Regional Culture." In *Migrants and Regional Cultures in Latin American Cities,* T. Altamirano and L. Hirabayashi, eds. Publication Series of the Society for Latin American Anthropological Association, 20.

Mitrany, David. 1951 *Marx Against the Peasant: A Study in Social Dogmatism.* Chapel Hill: University of North Carolina Press.

Morgan, Lewis Henry. 1877 [1963] *Ancient Society.* New York: World Publishing Company.

Mouffe, Chantal. 1988 "Hegemony and New Political Subjects: Toward a New Concept of Democracy." In *Marxism and the Interpretation of Culture,* Cary Nelson and Lawrence Grossber, eds. Urbana: University of Illinois Press.

Nagengast, Carole. 1991 *Reluctant Socialists, Rural Entrepreneurs: Class, Culture, and the Polish State.* Boulder: Westview Press.

Nagengast, Carole, and Michael Kearney. 1990 "Mixtec Ethnicity: Social Identity, Political Consciousness, and Political Activism." *Latin American Research Review* 25(2):61–91.

Nagengast, Carole, Rodolfo Stavenhagen, and Michael Kearney. 1992 "Human Rights and Indigenous Workers: The Mixtecs in Mexico and the United States." San Diego: Center for U.S.-Mexican Studies, Current Issue Brief 4, University of California, San Diego.

Nelson, Cynthia. 1971 *The Waiting Village: Social Change in Rural Mexico.* Boston: Little, Brown.

Netting, Robert McC. 1993 *Smallholders, Householders: Farm Families and the Ecology of Intensive, Sustainable Agriculture.* Stanford: Stanford University Press.

Nugent, Daniel. 1993 *Spent Cartridges of Revolution: An Anthropological History of Namiquipa, Chihuahua.* Chicago: University of Chicago Press.

Nugent, Stephen. 1988 "The 'Peripheral Situation.'" *Annual Review of Anthropology* 17:79–98.

Ong, Walter J. 1982 *Orality and Literacy: The Technologizing of the World.* London: Methuen.

Palerm, Angel. 1980 *Antropológia y marxismo.* Mexico City: Editorial Nueva Imagen.

Palerm, Juan Vicente. 1989 "Latino Settlements in California." In *The Challenge: Latinos in a Changing California.* Riverside: University of California Consortium on Mexico and the United States.

Palerm, Juan Vicente. 1991 "Farm Labor Needs and Farm Workers in California, 1970–1989." Sacramento: Employment Development Department, State of California.

Palerm, Juan Vicente, and José Ignacio Urquiola. 1993 "A Binational System of Agricultural Production: The Case of the Mexican Bajío and California." In *Mexico and the United States: Neighbors in Crisis,* Daniel G. Aldrich and Lorenzo Meyer, eds. San Bernardino, Calif.: Borgo Press.

Park, Robert. 1915 "The City: Suggestions for the Investigation of Human Behavior in the Urban Environment." *American Journal of Sociology* 20(5):577–612.

Pastor, Rodolfo. 1987 *Campesinos y reformas: la mixteca, 1700–1856.* Mexico City: El Colegio de México.

Polyani, Karl. 1944 *The Great Transformation.* New York: Farrar and Rinehart.

Potter, Sulamith Heins, and Jack M. Potter. 1990 *China's Peasants: The Anthropology of a Revolution.* Cambridge: Cambridge University Press.

Radcliffe-Brown, A. R. 1922 *The Andaman Islanders: A Study in Social Anthropology.* Cambridge: Cambridge University Press.

Ravenstein, Ernest George. 1976 [1885, 1889] *The Laws of Migration.* New York: Arno Press.

Redclift, Michael. 1987 *Sustainable Agriculture: Exploring the Contradictions.* London: Routledge.

Redfield, Robert. 1930 *Tepoztlán: A Mexican Village.* Chicago: University of Chicago Press.

Redfield, Robert. 1941 *The Folk Culture of Yucatan.* Chicago: University of Chicago Press.

Redfield, Robert. 1947 "The Folk Society." *American Journal of Sociology* 52:293–308.

Redfield, Robert. 1950 *A Village That Chose Progress: Chan Kom Revisited.* Chicago: University of Chicago Press.

Redfield, Robert. 1956 *The Little Community, and Peasant Society and Culture.* Chicago: University of Chicago Press.

Redfield, Robert, and Alfonso Villa Rojas. 1934 *Chan Kom: A Maya Village.* Washington, D.C.: Carnegie Institution of Washington. Publication 448.

Reyes Osorio, Sergio, Rodolfo Stavenhagen, Salomón Eckstein, and Juan Ballesteros. 1974 *Estructura agraria y desarrollo agrícola en México.* Mexico City: Fondo de Cultura.

Roberts, Bryan. 1978 *Cities of Peasants: The Political Economy of Urbanization in the Third World.* London: E. Arnold.

Roseberry, William. 1989a *Anthropologies and Histories: Essays in Culture, History, and Political Economy.* New Brunswick: Rutgers University Press.

Roseberry, William. 1989b "Peasants and the World." In *Economic Anthropology,* Stuart Plattner, ed. Stanford: Stanford University Press.

Rostow, W. W. 1960 *The Stages of Growth: A Non-Communist Manifesto.* Cambridge: Cambridge University Press.

Rothstein, Frances. 1986 "The Class Basis of Patron-Client Relations." In *Modern Mexico: State, Economy, and Social Conflict,* Nora Hamilton and Timothy F. Harding, eds. Beverly Hills: Sage.

Rouse, Roger. 1988 *Mexican Migration to the United States: Family Relations in the Development of a Transnational Migrant Circuit.* Ph.D. diss., Department of Anthropology, Stanford University, Stanford, Calif.

Rouse, Roger. 1991 "Mexican Migration and the Social Space of Postmodernism." *Diaspora* 1(1):8–23.

Rouse, Roger. 1992a "Making Sense of Settlement: Class Transformation Among Mexican Migrants in the United States." In *Towards a Transnational Perspective on Migration: Race, Class, Ethnicity, and Nationalism Reconsidered,* N. Glick Schiller, L. Basch, and C. Blanc-Szanton, eds. New York: New York Academy of Sciences.

Rouse, Roger. 1992b "Moving Stories: Anthropological Knowledge and the Politics of Translation." Paper delivered at the meeting of the American Anthropological Association, San Francisco.

Runsten, David, and Michael Kearney. 1994 *A Survey of Oaxacan Village Networks in California Agriculture.* Davis: California Institute for Rural Studies.

Sachs, Wolfgang. 1990 "The Obsolete Race: Development After East-West Rivalry." *New Perspective Quarterly* 7(2):52–55.

Sagan, Eli. 1985 *At the Dawn of Tyranny: The Origins of Individualism, Political Oppression and the State.* New York: Vintage Books.

Sangren, Steven P. 1988 "Rhetoric and the Authority of Ethnography." *Current Anthropology* 29:405–435.

Sassen, Saskia. 1991. *The Global City: New York, London, Tokyo.* Princeton, N.J.: Princeton University Press.

Scott, James C. 1985 *Weapons of the Weak: Everyday Forms of Peasant Resistance.* New Haven: Yale University Press.

Scott, James C. 1989 "Everyday Forms of Resistance." In *Everyday Forms of Peasant Resistance,* Forrest D. Colburn, ed. Armonk, N.Y.: M. E. Sharpe.

Scott, James C. 1990 *Domination and the Arts of Resistance: Hidden Transcripts.* New Haven: Yale University Press.

Scott, James C. 1993 "Reply" [to Gutmann 1993]. *Latin American Perspectives* 20(2):93–94.

Shanin, Teodor, ed. 1987 *Peasants and Peasant Societies.* 2d ed. Oxford: Basil Blackwell.

Silverman, Sydel. 1979 "The Peasant Concept in Anthropology." *Journal of Peasant Studies* 7(1):49–69.

Simic, Andrei. 1973 *The Peasant Urbanites: A Study of Rural-Urban Mobility in Serbia.* New York: Seminar Press.

Slater, David. 1994 "Power and Social Movements in the Other Occident: Latin America in an International Context." *Latin American Perspectives* 21(2):11–37.

Solway, Jacqueline, and Richard Lee. 1990 "Foragers, Genuine or Spurious? Situating the Kalahari San in History." *Current Anthropology* 31(2):109–146.

Spores, Ronald. 1984 *The Mixtecs in Ancient and Colonial Times.* Norman: University of Oklahoma Press.

Stavenhagen, Rodolfo. 1978 "Capitalism and the Peasantry in Mexico." *Latin American Perspectives* 5(3):27–37.

Stephen, Lynn. 1991 *Zapotec Women.* Austin: University of Texas Press.

Stephen, Lynn, and James Dow, eds. 1990 *Class, Politics, and Popular Religion in Mexico and Central America.* Washington, D.C.: Society for Latin American Studies, American Anthropological Association.

Steward, Julian H. 1949 "The Native Populations of South America." In *Handbook of the South American Indians,* J. Steward, ed. Washington, D.C.: Bureau of American Ethnology. Bulletin 143, Vol. 5:655–688.

Stocking, George W., Jr. 1989 "The Ethnographic Sensibility of the 1920s and the Dualism of the Anthropological Tradition." In *Romantic Motives: Essays on Anthropological Sensibility,* George W. Stocking Jr., ed. Madison: University of Wisconsin Press.

Ströbele-Gregor, Juliana. 1994 "Social Movements and Political Change in Latin America." *Latin American Perspectives* 21(2):106–123.

Stuart, James, and Michael Kearney. 1981 "Causes and Effects of Agricultural Labor Migration from the Mixteca of Oaxaca to California." *Working Papers in U.S.-Mexican Studies,* No. 28. San Diego: Program in U.S.-Mexican Studies, University of California, San Diego.

Sullivan, Robert. 1990 "Marxism and the 'Subject' of Anthropology." In *Modernist Anthropology: From Fieldwork to Text,* M. Manganaro, ed. Princeton: Princeton University Press.

Sutton, Constance R. 1987 "The Caribbeanization of New York City and the Emergence of a Transnational Sociocultural System." In *Caribbean Life in New York City: Sociocultural Dimensions,* C. R. Sutton and E. M. Chaney, eds. Staten Island, N.Y.: Center for Migration Studies.

Taussig, Michael. 1980 *The Devil and Commodity Fetishism in South America.* Chapel Hill: University of North Carolina Press.

Tax, Sol. 1937 "The Municipios of the Midwestern Highlands of Guatemala." *American Anthropologist* 39:423–433.

Taylor, John G. 1979 *From Modernization to Modes of Production: A Critique of the Sociologies of Development and Underdevelopment.* London: Macmillan.

Thompson, Edward P. 1978 *The Poverty of Theory and Other Essays.* London: Merlin Press.

Tokman, Victor, ed. 1992 *Beyond Regulation: The Informal Economy in Latin America.* Boulder: Lynne Rienner Publishers.

Tönnies, Ferdinand. 1912 *Gemeinschaft und Gesellschaft: Grundbegriffe der reinen Soziologie.* Leipzig: K. Curtius.

Torgovnick, Marianna. 1990 *Gone Primitive: Savage Intellects, Modern Lives.* Chicago: University of Chicago Press.

Vogt, Evon A. 1970 *The Zinacantecos of Mexico: A Modern Maya Life Way.* New York: Holt, Rinehart and Winston.

Vogt, Evon A. 1978 *Bibliography of the Harvard Chiapas Project: The First Twenty Years, 1957–1977.* Cambridge, Mass.: Peabody Museum of Archaeology and Ethnology, Harvard University.

Wakin, Eric. 1992 *Anthropology Goes to War: Professional Ethics and Counterinsurgency in Thailand.* Madison: University of Wisconsin Center.

Wallerstein, Immanuel. 1976 *The Modern World-System.* New York: Academic Press.

Walton, John. 1975 "Internal Colonialism: Problems of Definition and Measurement." In *Latin American Urban Research,* Vol. 5, W. A. Cornelius and F. Trueblood, eds. Beverly Hills: Sage.

Williams, Raymond. 1973 *The Country and the City.* New York: Oxford University Press.

Williams, Raymond. 1977 *Marxism and Literature.* Oxford: Oxford University Press.

Williams, Raymond. 1984 *Keywords: A Vocabulary of Culture and Society.* 2d ed. New York: Oxford University Press.

Willis, Paul. 1977 *Learning to Labour: How Working Class Kids Get Working Class Jobs.* Farnborough, England: Saxon House.

Wilmsen, Edwin N. 1989 *Land Filled with Flies: A Political Economy of the Kalahari.* Chicago: University of Chicago Press.

Wilmsen, E. N., and J. R. Denbow. 1990 "Paradigmatic History of San-Speaking Peoples and Current Attempts at Revision." *Current Anthropology* 31(5):489–524.

Wirth, Louis. 1964 *On Cities and Social Life.* Albert J. Reiss Jr., ed. Chicago: University of Chicago Press.

Wissler, Clark. 1923 *Men and Culture.* New York: Thomas Y. Crowell.

Wolf, Eric R. 1955 "Types of Latin American Peasantry: A Preliminary Discussion." *American Anthropologist* 57(3):452–471.

Wolf, Eric R. 1956a "San José: Subcultures of a 'Traditional' Coffee Municipality." In *The People of Puerto Rico,* Julian Steward, Robert Manners, Eric Wolf, Elena Padilla, Sidney Mintz, and Raymond Scheele, eds. Urbana: University of Illinois Press.

Wolf, Eric R. 1956b "Aspects of Group Relations in a Complex Society: Mexico." *American Anthropologist* 58:1065–1078.

Wolf, Eric R. 1957 "Closed Corporate Communities in Mesoamerica and Central Java." *Southwestern Journal of Anthropology* 13:1–18.

Wolf, Eric R. 1959 *Sons of the Shaking Earth.* Chicago: University of Chicago Press.

Wolf, Eric R. 1966 *Peasants.* Englewood Cliffs, N.J.: Prentice-Hall.

Wolf, Eric R. 1969 *Peasant Wars of the Twentieth Century.* New York: Harper and Row.

Wolf, Eric R. 1982 *Europe and the People Without History.* Berkeley: University of California Press.

Wolf, Eric R. 1986 "The Vicissitudes of the Closed Corporate Peasant Community." *American Ethnologist* 13(2)325–329.

Wolf, Eric R., and Sidney Mintz. 1957 "Haciendas and Plantations in Middle America and the Antilles," *Social and Economic Studies* 6:386–412.

Wolpe, H. 1972 "Capitalism and Cheap Labour-Power in South Africa: From Segregation to Apartheid." *Economy and Society* 1:425–456.

Worsely, Peter. 1990 "Models of the Modern World-System," In *Global Culture: Nationalism, Globalization and Modernity,* Mike Featherstone, ed. Newbury Park, Calif.: Sage.

Wright, Angus. 1990 *The Death of Ramon Gonzales: The Modern Agricultural Dilemma.* Austin: University of Texas Press.

Zabin, Carol, Michael Kearney, Anna Garcia, David Runsten, and Carole Nagengast. 1993 *Mixtec Migrants in California Agriculture.* Davis: California Institute for Rural Studies.

Zea, Leopoldo. 1978 *El positivismo en México: nacimiento, apogeo y decadencia.* Mexico City: Fondo de Cultura Económica.

Ziff, Trisha. 1994 *Oaxacalifornia.* A film. Los Angeles: Citron Nueve Productions.

About the Book and Author

The concept of "peasant" has been constructed from residual images of pre-industrial European and colonial rural society. Spurred by Romantic sensibilities and modern nationalist imaginations, the images the word *peasant* brings to mind are anachronisms that do not reflect the ways in which rural people live today. In this path-breaking book, Michael Kearney shows how the concept has been outdistanced by contemporary history. He situates the peasantry within the current social context of the transnational and post–Cold War nation-state and clears the way for alternative theoretical views.

Reconceptualizing the Peasantry looks at rural society in general and considers the problematic distinction between rural and urban. Most definitions of and debates about peasants have focused on their presumed social, economic, cultural, and political characteristics, but Kearney articulates the way in which peasants define *themselves* in a rapidly changing world. In the process, he develops ethnographic and political forms of representation that correspond to contemporary postpeasant identities. Moving beyond a reconsideration of peasantry, the book situates anthropology in global context, showing how the discipline reconstructs itself and its subjects according to changing circumstances.

Michael Kearney is professor of anthropology at the University of California at Riverside.

Index

Printed in the United States
80978LV00003B/208-249